SOCIAL WORK RESEARCH USING ARTS-BASED METHODS

Research in Social Work series

Series Editors: **Anna Gupta**, Royal Holloway, University of London, UK and **John Gal**, Hebrew University of Jerusalem, Israel

Published together with the European Social Work Research Association (ESWRA), this series examines current, progressive and innovative research applications of familiar ideas and models in international social work research.

Also available in the series:

Critical Gerontology for Social Workers
Edited by **Sandra Torres** and **Sarah Donnelly**

Involving Service Users in Social Work Education, Research and Policy
Edited by **Kristel Driessens** and **Vicky Lyssens-Danneboom**

Adoption from Care
Edited by **Tarja Pösö, Marit Skivenes** and **June Thoburn**

Interprofessional Collaboration and Service User Participation
Edited by **Kirsi Juhila, Tanja Dall, Christopher Hall** and **Juliet Koprowska**

The Settlement House Movement Revisited
Edited by **John Gal, Stefan Köngeter** and **Sarah Vicary**

Social Work and the Making of Social Policy
Edited by **Ute Klammer, Simone Leiber** and **Sigrid Leitner**

Research and the Social Work Picture
By **Ian Shaw**

Find out more at:

policy.bristoluniversitypress.co.uk/
research-in-social-work

Research in Social Work series

Series Editors: **Anna Gupta**, Royal Holloway, University of London, UK and **John Gal**, Hebrew University of Jerusalem, Israel

---

Forthcoming in the series:

The Origins of Social Care and Social Work
By **Mark Henrickson**

Find out more at:

policy.bristoluniversitypress.co.uk/
research-in-social-work

Research in Social Work series

Series Editors: **Anna Gupta**, Royal Holloway, University of London, UK and **John Gal**, Hebrew University of Jerusalem, Israel

International Editorial Board:

Find out more at:

policy.bristoluniversitypress.co.uk/
research-in-social-work

SOCIAL WORK RESEARCH USING ARTS-BASED METHODS

Edited by
Ephrat Huss and Eltje Bos

First published in Great Britain in 2023 by

Policy Press, an imprint of
Bristol University Press
University of Bristol
1-9 Old Park Hill
Bristol
BS2 8BB
UK
t: +44 (0)117 374 6645
e: bup-info@bristol.ac.uk

Details of international sales and distribution partners are available at
policy.bristoluniversitypress.co.uk

British Library Cataloguing in Publication Data
A catalogue record for this book is available from the British Library

ISBN 978-1-4473-5788-9 hardcover
ISBN 978-1-4473-5789-6 paperback
ISBN 978-1-4473-5790-2 ePub
ISBN 978-1-4473-5791-9 ePdf

Cover design: David Worth
Front cover image: iStock-1189731479

Bristol University Press and Policy Press use environmentally responsible
print partners.

Printed in Great Britain by CPI Group (UK) Ltd, Croydon, CR0 4YY

We would like to thank Tessa van Ham for managing this book, and Sharón Benheim for editing it,

Without your amazing professional and dedicated work – this book would not have happened!

Contents

List of figures and tables

Figures

Table

Notes on contributors

Maria Regina A. Alfonso, PhD, MSEd, ATR-BC, LCPAT, is an educator, mental health clinician and published author with a combined 30 years of experience in teaching and therapy. She earned her masters in education from Fordham University, a masters in art therapy Lesley University, and her doctorate in expressive arts at the European Graduate School. The focus of her research has been on psychosocial support, neuroaesthetics, and the use of the arts to create healing classrooms around the world. She is the founder and Director of Magis Creative Spaces. Email: ginaalfonso@gmail.com

Andrés Arias Astray is Full Professor of Social Work at the Complutense University of Madrid and a member of GrupoLab, a research laboratory on Social Work with Groups where he combines his teaching and research on social group work and his interest in the development of a critical epistemology that allows to make a radical commitment to fostering diversity and plurality of methods and perspectives in the promotion of personal and social well-being.

Joey A. Atayde is a registered dance/movement therapist with the American Dance Therapy Association and Assistant Clinical Director at MAGIS Creative Spaces. Prior to pursuing her graduate studies at Pratt Institute in New York, where she finished her Master of Science in dance/movement therapy, she danced professionally with Philippine Ballet Theater.

Elizabeth Barton, PhD, is a psychologist and adjunct associate research professor at Wayne State University, where she teaches child and adolescent psychology and human developmental psychology. Elizabeth's expertise includes youth violence, conflict resolution and bullying and victimization. She was a co-investigator in the study ArtsCorpsDetroit, the research component of a service-learning initiative.

Kathleen Bautista is a master's student in expressive arts therapy at Lesley University, and a freelance creative with diverse experience in visual arts and voicework. Kathleen supports a variety of work at MAGIS, including research documentation, programme facilitation, and content creation.

Eltje Bos, PhD, heads the research group entitled Cultural and Social Dynamics of the University of Applied Sciences in Amsterdam. Also trained as a drama teacher, she mainly works on the use of arts and creativity in social work, and strategies of collaboration to increase livability in the city, often using creative interventions. In her research and practice, she addresses the role of implicit (and explicit) power structures and diversity in these dynamics, and she intends to unfold unseen cultural dynamics. Eltje works in field labs in neighbourhoods in Amsterdam, Rotterdam and the Hague, using arts-based interventions funded by the Dutch Scientific Council (RAAK, 2016–2018 and 2019–2021). She has been involved in various local projects that have been co-financed by the municipality of Amsterdam, such as the future perspective – youngsters using storytelling. She conducts research on social entrepreneurship and refugees. She has been a participant in running Erasmus+ project PiCs on the use of storytelling, and pictures to connect groups of youngsters. Her PhD thesis focused on cultural policies and immigrants (2011 in Dutch). Email: e.bos@hva.nl

Emma Buzzard, MA, LPC, ATR, has a master's degree in counselling and art therapy from Wayne State University and was a research assistant for the study ArtsCorpsDetroit. She is currently employed by the Rochester Center for Behavioral Health.

Paola de Bruijn, artist educator, works for the Academy of Social Studies at the HAN University of Applied Sciences. She is conducting her doctoral study at Maynooth University in Ireland, in cooperation with the Research Center for Social Support and Community Care at HAN University, on the pedagogical utility of art with respect to existential questions. Paola's overall ambition is to explore how students in social work can be sufficiently prepared to utilise visual arts in working with older people. Email: Paola. deBruijn@han.nl

Mike de Kreek, PhD, works as a lecturer in the Master Social Work programme and as a researcher in the Cultural and Social Dynamics research programme in the Amsterdam Research Institute for Societal Innovation at the Amsterdam University of Applied Sciences. His research focuses on the relation between cultural interventions and collaborative learning processes in contexts where various stakeholders face the challenge of taking up roles in new collaborations. One of his favourite topics is: How arts-based interventions can unleash other human intelligences than reason. Email: m.de.kreek@hva.nl

Mark Doel is Professor Emeritus at Sheffield Hallam University, and a registered social worker. He has many years of practice experience in community settings, as well as student supervision, academic management, post-qualifying education and research. Mark's main areas of research are practice education, groupwork, and international social work. He is widely published, including 21 books, eight in foreign translations. He was co-editor of *Groupwork Journal*, Vice President of the International Association of Social Work with Groups, and is an Honorary Professor at Tbilisi State University, Georgia. Email: markdoel@icloud.com

Julie Drolet is Professor in the Faculty of Social Work at the University of Calgary in Edmonton. Her research in the field of international social work focuses on disaster social work, immigrant settlement and integration, social protection, social development, and social work field education. She is a registered social worker with the Alberta College of Social Workers.

Linda Ducca Cisneros is a social worker and has a master's degree in social work research methods. She works as a pre-doctoral Research Assistant at Complutense University of Madrid. Her research is mainly about Social Work with Groups with Adolescents and how to improve the quality of practice. She has experience leading groups of adolescents in different countries and hopes to continue facilitating groups, in order to get research linked to the actual practice.

Holly Feen-Calligan, PhD, ATR-BC, ATCS, is Associate Professor and Coordinator of the Art Therapy programme at Wayne State University. At Wayne State, she blends teaching, service, and scholarship to nurture an art therapy programme strong in service-learning and community partnerships. She is founding member of ArtsCorpsDetroit, a service-learning research and community engagement programme for students, alumni, and members of the surrounding community. Email: hfeen@wayne.edu

Arielle Friedman conducts research about visual texts made by children and teens via new and old media. Her research interests include visual literacy, visual culture, and the connection between music, lyrics, and visual images in music videos. Dr Friedman chairs the Department of Communication at Oranim College of Education, and heads the Film and Media committee, Art Department, Ministry of Education, Israel. She is also the head of Colleagues Encounters Channel and head of the Department of Conferences and Seminars, the MOFET Institute. Email: arielle_f@oranim.ac.il

Carlota García Román is a licensed social worker and has a master's degree in health social work. She works as a health social worker in a rehabilitation brain injury hospital. Currently, she is doing a PhD in social work at the Complutense University of Madrid. Her line of research is about overprotection and self-determination in young people with intellectual disabilities. She has experience in groups with parents and young people with intellectual disabilities, as well as in groups with relatives of people with acquired brain injury.

David González Casas is Doctor in Social Work. He currently works as a postdoctoral researcher at the Complutense University of Madrid. He is a specialist in research with people with disabilities and has developed working groups with the collective and their families. Currently, he carries out work related to quality of life and social support for people with disabilities in Spain and Portugal.

Genevieve Guetemme, PhD, is Senior Lecturer at the Faculty of Education of the University of Orléans (INSPE-CVL). A specialist in visual arts with a focus on the artistic representations of contemporary migration (poetry, photography, film, and performance), she is project leader of an educational programme aimed at young migrants and situated the intersection of arts, language, and social sciences. It focuses on the contexts and actors of migration in relation with gender, culture, and identity issues. Email: genevieve.guetemme@univ-orleans.fr

Lucía Hervás Hermida is an artist, art therapist, gestalt therapist, and Associate Professor of Art Therapy and Art Education at the Autonoma University of Madrid, where she developed her PhD on art therapy with mothers and families as a way to support positive parenting and women empowerment. She is part of the board of the Iberoamerican Forum of Art Therapy and the Spanish Federation of Art Therapist Associations, committed to the use of art-based methods for human and social development. Email: luciahervashermida@gmail.com

Ephrat Huss, PhD, Full Professor, Ben-Gurion University. Ephrat Huss is Professor of Social Work and Art Therapy at Ben-Gurion University of the Negev. She heads an innovative MA social work specialisation that integrates arts in social practice and so has 40 students doing social arts projects per year. She has a background in fine arts. Her overall areas of research are the interface between arts and social practice and arts-based research: using arts as a way for accessing the voices of marginalised populations, specifically she has received competitive grants and published much on arts-based research with indigenous Bedouin women and youth in unrecognised villages in the south of Israel. She has published four books and over 80 articles on these subjects, and has extensive collaborations with social arts projects in Israel and abroad. She is currently researching use of arts with refugees in Greece: She has set up and researched an Arab–Jewish youth group using the arts as communication, and is active in the Women for Peace movement where she also introduced quilt-making as a method to gain media attention. Email: ehuss@bgu.ac.il

Marion (Mame) Jackson, PhD, is a renowned art historian and co-director of Con-Vida: Popular Arts of the Americas. She is a Wayne State University Distinguished Professor Emerita, and founder of ArtsCorpsDetroit.

Erik Jansen is Associate Professor of Capabilities in Care and Wellbeing at HAN University of Applied Sciences. He is associated with the Research Center for Social Support and Community Care at the Academy for Social Studies. His primary research interest regards issues on the contextual and situational influences on wellbeing and quality of life. This concerns material aspects of the world, in particular focusing on art, culture, and technologies. He is further interested in developing methods for social and wellbeing professionals to apply these aspects to benefit individuals, communities, and a more just and equal world. To this purpose he builds on narrative and art-based methods. Email: erik.Jansen@han.nl

Brian L. Kelly, PhD, MSW, CADC, is Associate Professor at Loyola University Chicago in the School of Social Work. His research explores current and historical uses of recreational, art, and music-based activities in social work and related fields as sites and opportunities for strengths-based social work practice. He holds an associate degree in audio engineering and incorporates audio documentary and other audio-based ethnographic methodologies in his work as means to increase strengths-based, participatory research practices. Findings from his work have been presented at national and international conferences and published in peer-reviewed journals and edited texts. Dr Kelly has several years of clinical experience working with individuals with substance use issues as a certified alcohol and drug abuse counsellor. In addition, he has several years of practice experience working with the homeless, including adults living with HIV/AIDS and other chronic medical conditions as well as young people. Dr Kelly is an advocate for the advancement of social work practice with groups and incorporates group work in his teaching, research, and scholarship. Email: bkelly6@luc.edu

Nasreen Lalani is Assistant Professor in the School of Nursing at the Purdue University in West Lafayette. She is an experienced researcher, clinician, and educator with diverse background in nursing and health disciplines. Her experience spans three continents – working in Pakistan, Australia, and North America.

Ronald P.M.H. Lay, MA, AThR, ATR-BC, is Programme Leader of the MA Art Therapy programme at LASALLE College of the Arts. This is the first postgraduate training of its kind in southeast Asia, asserting its strategic positioning in progressing the discipline in ways that are culturally relevant in Asian and global contexts. Ronald has an extensive practice-based career in forensic mental health, and has varied research interests that has led to national, regional, and international consultation, development, training, collaborative arts projects, and leadership. He has designed, facilitated, and supervised multiple arts, culture, and mental health collaborative overseas experiential trips for his students. He is co-editor of *Found Objects in Art Therapy: Materials and Process*. Rounding off his professional pursuits is his passion for creating artwork that tends to be constructive and conceptual. He is currently engaged in research on postgraduate art therapy training, experiential learning, and culturally informed practice. Email: ronald.lay@lasalle.edu.sg

M. Imelda Lukban has worked in the fields of education, customer service, human resources, and medical services. This experience has supported research at MAGIS with a fresh perspective.

Caroline McDonald-Harker is Associate Professor in the Department of Sociology and Anthropology, as well as Director of the Centre for Community Disaster Research at Mount Royal University in Calgary. Her areas of expertise include the sociology of disaster, families, children and youth, trauma and mental health, resilience, and mixed methods research.

Rogério Meireles Pinto, PhD, is Professor and Associate Dean for Research at the University of Michigan School of Social Work. Pinto focuses on finding academic, socio-political, and cultural venues for broadcasting voices of oppressed individuals and groups. Funded by the National Institute of Mental Health, his community-engaged research focuses on the impact of interprofessional collaboration on the delivery of evidence-based services (HIV and drug-use prevention and care) to marginalised racial/ethnic and sexual minorities in the US and Brazil. Pinto conducts arts-based scholarly research. He has performed *Marília*, a one-person play, on New York City's Theatre Row in 2015 and at the University of the Free State in Bloemfontein, Vrystaat, in 2016. *Marília* won the United Solo Festival Best Documentary Script. In *Marília* Pinto explores the tragic death of his barely three-year-old sister, and how such loss haunts and inspires the family members she left behind. Funded by the University of Michigan Office of Research and several other sources, he is building *The Realm of the Dead*, an art installation to investigate his own marginalisation as a gender non-confirming, mixed-race, and Latinx immigrant. *Marília/Realm of the Dead* will be performed in 2021 at the University of Michigan as part of the centennial celebration of the School of Social Work. Email: ropinto@umich.edu

Julie Moreno, PhD, is an art therapist at Michigan Medicine at the University of Michigan's Milestones Pediatric NeuroRehabilitation Program, and STEPS Autism Treatment Program, and she is an adjunct professor of art therapy at Wayne State University. As a graduate student, Julie was a research assistant for the study, ArtsCorpsDetroit.

Adrienne M. Santos Lagmay is an artist, designer, and researcher trained in Design and Craft at the University of Brighton. She is MAGIS Creative Space's Creative Director and leads the design of communications and services to engage communities through the expressive arts.

Eitan Shahar, PhD, serves as Deputy Director of the Social Services Department in Ofakim and as Lecturer in the Department of Social Work at Ben-Gurion University of the Negev. He is a member of the Board of Directors of *Gvanim*, an organisation that provides an array of solutions for people with disabilities. His areas of expertise include: international social work, community social work, social work in rural communities and with ethnic and migrant groups, qualitative research methods, trauma and resilience in community work. Email: eitansh@sapir.ac.il

Orna Shemer, PhD, is a faculty member at the School of Social Work and Social Welfare at the Hebrew University of Jerusalem, and a social worker. Her research focuses on the fields: community work, participative relationships between service providers and service users, context-informed perspective, intentional communities. She conducts research and develops learning processes in participative and critical approaches. Email: orna. shemer@mail.huji.ac.il

Peter Szto is Professor of Social Work at the Grace Abbott School of Social Work, University of Nebraska at Omaha. His research foci are social welfare development in China, mental health care, spirituality, and photography as a tool of social research. He is currently working on a visual study of stigma, spirituality and mental health. Peter has earned degrees from Calvin University, Michigan State University, Westminster Theological Seminary, and the University of Pennsylvania. He lives happily with his wife and dog in Omaha. Email: szto@unomaha.edu

Sofie Vindevogel, Phd, is affiliated with the EQUALITY// ResearchCollective and Department of Social Educational Carework at HoGent. Her research is situated at the nexus of strengths-oriented, community-based, and transcultural approaches. She particularly studies community resilience in contexts of collective violence and social injustice and has been working with populations affected by armed conflict and political violence. Email: sofie.vindevogel@hogent.be

Margareta von Salisch is originally a theatre maker and drama teacher. She works for different universities of applied science as coach/supervisor, lecturer, and facilitator in the area of the social domain, health care and education. With the help of drama techniques, she researches the mechanisms in interaction on a personal, organisational, and systemic level. The last years she provided and developed training courses in the context of professionalisation of social professionals in the SamenDoen teams of the Municipality of Amsterdam. In the project interactive casuistry training, she is researching action alternatives for social professionals, making use of Theaterforum. Her interest is finding ways for profound learning, formal and informal. Sources of inspiration: B. Brecht, A. Boal, Theory U (Otto Scharmer & team) and the Presencing Institute.

Hila Zaguri Duvdevani is an experienced educator trained in social and community education and holds certification in teaching communication. She is the head of the program for gifted children in the periphery. Hila is affiliated with the Oranim Academic College for Education.

Introduction

Ephrat Huss and Eltje Bos

The connection between arts and social work is a rapidly developing area. However, the specific advantages of arts-based research for social work have yet to be articulated.

In research in general, arts are defined as less important than words, or numbers – a leitmotif, or illustration (Martinez-Brawley et al., 1997). Often 'art' is experienced as the opposite of 'science' and thus the opposite of 'evidence'. In social work specifically, arts are experienced as a luxury, an illustration rather than content, peripheral rather than the 'on the ground' problems that social work deals with. Often social workers feel that they have not been trained in the arts and so cannot use it. This is based on a misunderstanding of what social art is. Indeed, arts-based research is most traditionally connected to education, where the use of images is a natural language for children (Eisner, 1997).

Of late, however, we see a 'visual turn' in social sciences in general, and also in social work practice and research. This includes the use of community art, Photovoice, outsider art, arts for social change, arts and health, arts to humanise institutions, de-stigmatise minorities, and to give voice to silenced groups (Chamberlayne & Smith, 2008; Huss, 2012, Huss & Bos, 2019). This has extended the use of arts-based research in social work.

This book aims to capture this promising process. It will show how arts-based research is in fact an especially effective methodology to embody, and will articulate many of the epistemological aims of, social work research. It will attempt to help break down the challenges for social workers when using arts-based methods through multiple methods and examples.

The aim of this introduction is to provide a conceptual rationale for using arts-based research in social work, as a theoretical lens through which to approach the chapters in this book, that then expand on this connection. This introduction also hopes to provide a general understanding of social arts that will help to demystify what is meant by arts in arts-based research. (Walton, 2012). This is an outline of the basic concepts of arts-based research, such as social art and art placement in research, that are illustrated in much more detail in the following chapters in this book.

Firstly, to understand what we mean by arts in this book it is important to define what is 'social arts' or the type of arts used in arts-based research.

Art is not a single unity but has multiple roles and discourses in different cultures and social contexts. Common art discourses in Western culture within the art world include fine art that often focuses on aesthetic innovations that are in dialogue with past fine art innovations. The art product leaves its creator to enter a museum, album, or stage, and becomes judged by and encapsulated within the discourses and paradigms of the fine art world. Another use of art is in political and media where art is often didactic, aiming to change stands, or to evoke a specific reaction in the viewer. The evaluation is dependent on the impact of the art on the viewer (Shank, 2005).

From social theories in psychology, art is often a projective medium, a representation of the de-contextualised unconscious self. The psychological expert is thus the judge of the meaning of the art. Another social discourse about art is phenomenological and humanistic concepts of art as self-expression, such as in education and in humanistic therapies. These focus on arts as an important facet of emotional and cognitive development and as a way to express and to reach the authentic self (Betinsky, 1995). This corresponds to both arts therapy and arts-based research. The arts gain meaning in light of the process that the artist undergoes rather than in the aesthetic quality of the product.

Anthropological theories will understand art as an expression of and thus as a way to understand a specific cultural and socio-geographical reality. Arts is a culturally constructed concept that can include multiple and evolving forms and social roles, such as crafts, ritual, didactic art, high and low art expressions, creative placemaking, and others (Rose, 1988; Emmison & Smith, 2000; Harrington, 2004; Huss, 2015; Huss & Maor, 2015; Huss & Bos, 2019).

Arts-based research can include all these understandings of art. It can be projective, expressive, didactic, political, or culturally situated, and it can be all of these things at the same time. From this, then, the arts in arts-based research can focus on arts process, arts product, or reactions to the arts product. It can be the method for gathering data, the subject of the research, or the end product of the research (Huss, 2012). It can be some of these things together. For example, in Photovoice the photo taking becomes a reflective and critical process, but the end exhibition becomes a way to change hegemonic stands. A researcher can also explore the exhibition as a subject of research.

Having discussed what we mean by 'arts' in arts-based research, the next concern of this book is how arts-based research is relevant for social work research. In other words, why use arts in the first place (Huss, 2012; Huss & Sela-Amit, 2018) ?. This book hopes to show, through its multiple case studies, how the arts can be an especially relevant methodology to help social work reach central research aims based on the epistemology of social work.

This introduction hopes to provide a basic outline of rationales for using arts-based research in social work that is further developed in the following chapters.

Firstly, the arts can help to excavate and make heard silent facets of experience, due to traumatic content, culturally taboo content, or due to marginalisation. This can be explained through the fact that arts are aesthetically constructed by the dynamic relationship or aesthetic tension between form and content. That is, by deciding what to depict – a heart to express love for example. Secondly, the creator of the art has to decide how to depict the heart: what size, colour, texture, and placement on the page the heart will have, or what type of tune, or stage, or movement in space, will depict this specific experience of love. Thus, through the compositional elements chosen, the experience is further defined, first to self, and second, to others. This process includes emotions, cognitions, and embodiment. It enables the deep exploration of research participants in an embodied expressive but also reflective process.

When the above heart or art depiction is explained to someone else (group or researcher) then a further hermeneutic level of the research participants' experience is provided. These are dual levels of excavating and creatively depicting the experience, which then acts as a trigger to the expertise on their own experience. Often research participants do not have professional words, or may not be from the same culture or might not be overly verbal or used to expressing their experience in abstract terms. As Lippard (1990) states, 'Educated Westerners use language as control, while poorer, less educated people, especially those from rural backgrounds, control language through expressive formulations.' Thus, the art work itself serves as a trigger for additional narratives and interpretations by the participants, on the level of content as well as on the level of the process.

This process of aesthetic exploration and explanation correlates to the aim of social work research to excavate and to amplify experiences that may be silenced due to trauma (a broken heart) or cultural taboo (loving the wrong person). It connects to Indigenous and feminist methodologies that situate research participants as experts, while emphasising the need for multilingual texts. (Tuhiwai-Smith, 1993; Wang & Burris, 1994; Pink & Kurti, 2004; Segel-Engelchin et al., 2019).

Secondly, social work aims to intensify the connection between micro and macro experience, that is to enable a socially critical understanding of personal experience. Arts embody this connection through the aesthetic tension between elements and are inherent to all types of art making, as in the relationship between actor and stage, dancer and space, tune and background music, and figure and background. This interrelationship between figure and background automatically situates the 'subject', or personal phenomenological experience, within a social context. This spatiality of arts also helps to shift research from professional and verbal abstractions. The arts thus help maintain a broad 'picture' of both personal experience and social context as interactive elements that construct each other (Freire & Macedo, 1987; Mernissi, 2003; Foster, 2007; Huss, 2015, 2018).

Thirdly, social work research aims to understand both stress and coping from within a specific cultural construct. The arts are both metonymic and metaphorical, revealing cultural values and ways of seeing and understanding the world. As such they are an ethnographic tool, showing the cultural realities and perspectives of research participants. (Mason, 2002; Amthor, 2017; Huss et al., 2018). For example, when a Bedouin woman speaks of her 'house', a cultural difference may not be apparent until she draws a tent to represent her house, at which point the cultural difference becomes obvious (Huss, 2012).

These three points, the excavation of silenced experience, the situation of this experience within a specific physical context, and the cultural context, help to intensify the research participants' ability to convey their experience of the world.

Fourthly, social work research searches for strategies through which to co-produce knowledge with service users. In a continuation of the empowerment perspective, participants in social work research are often members of marginalised or disempowered cultural groups or classes who have complex power relationships with the social workers in research positions. Arts enable both researchers and social practitioners to enter spaces that are less power infused and within which to actualise the aim to co-create knowledge with service users. Rather than being defined by experts, or social workers, arts enables a space in which both participants and researchers (as non–artists) can bridge differences in language cultures (Narhi, 2002; Huss, 2012, 2018; Walton, 2012; Segel-Englechin et al., 2019).

Arts, as a broader hermeneutic space enables multiple interpretations and negotiations of meanings (Arnheim, 1996; Huss, 2018). hooks (1992) describes the difference between being objectified through others' gaze as compared with 'seeing' and thereby self-defining issues for oneself (Abu Gazaleh, & Bos, 2019).

Spivak & Guha state:

> The place where female and marginalized 'speech acts' can be heard is not in historical, academic and political writings that are male dominated, but in the areas of symbolic self-expression where resistance is removed from reality, and thus does not threaten the central male discourse.
>
> (Spivak & Guha, 1988, p. 207)

Fifthly, and in continuation, social work research often addresses vulnerable groups of children, who are not protected and privileged by their childhood status (Aubrey, & Dahl, 2006). As such, it is important to understand the experience of these youth and children as the experts on how they cope and as well as participants in setting policies meant to protect them. Children have ideas, attitudes, and interests that may be perceived successfully through interacting with them via the arts, which are a central developmentally appropriate language for children, who can distance painful experience onto arts, and who may not have abstract thinking skills yet (Bowler, 1997; Clark, 2011; Amthor, 2017; de Kreek & Bos, 2017; Huss et al., 2020).

Sixthly, social work aims to focus on strengths, that is, to capture self-defined recourses of participants, shifting the focus from victimhood, to a focus on how people cope (Antonovsky, 1987; Simon, 2005; Eriksson, 2017). Culturally contextualised arts are a space where people naturally make meaning of their lives, thus enhancing resilience, and gaining strength from personal and cultural symbols. Images are a deep construct though which people process and organise their experiences, to integrate past and present, and create new perceptions of the future. Embodied relational aesthetic experience enables us to interact positively with the world, making spaces special, creating meaning, manageability, and comprehension of the world, Creative thinking helps enhance problem solving and resilience (Conway & Pleydell-Pearce, 2000; Huss & Sarid, 2014). This is an important point, because it means that arts can be used to describe stress and coping, but also to enhance coping through engaging in meaning-making activities (Huss & Samson, 2018; Huss et al., 2018).

Seventhly, social change oriented social work research aims to disrupt existing power systems through amplifying marginalised voices. Arts are intensely communicative through turning to the senses, and thus enable to change positions, as we see in advertising. Arts also help to maintain the safety of those without power through using metaphors and symbols rather than direct confrontation. Thus, the artist can regulate the degree of direct or symbolic confrontation with him or herself, and with his social environment, through the use of metaphors that do not directly challenge power holders (Eisner, 1997; Gauntlett & Holzwarth, 2006; Foster, 2007; Huss, 2012; Segel Engelchin et al., 2019).

Continuing this, then, the eighth point is that social work research aims to have maximum impact not only on other researchers, but also on the communities, service users, and policy makers: Arts are used as the end product of a research process, such as in community theatre, documentary films, and exhibitions. These all help to effectively disseminate and broaden the impact of research knowledge, making it more accessible and relevant to audiences outside of academic discourses. (Huss, 2012, 2018).

All these methodological rationales and additional ones are explained in the chapters here, which will demonstrate benefits of arts-based research through specific case studies. One of the aims of this book is to demystify the use of arts in social work research through showing how to overcome potential pitfalls, giving examples of how social workers though untrained in arts utilised arts-based research, and through providing a rationale and a focus on the method including nuts and bolts, and how it worked with a specific population. The examples will show how arts were used as method, subject, or end product of research, as process, product, trigger, or end point (Huss, 2012). Analyses of arts will be varied, including multiple theoretical lenses, and both qualitative and quantitative methods.

This book is divided into three sections. The first section of our book shows how arts-based research was used with different populations to access the voices of marginalised groups. This includes examples of different art forms, such as fine art, image analyses using Visual Thinking Strategies (VTS), poetry, photography, music recording, directive group art activities, and theatre. These are used to excavate, reflect upon, and capture the phenomenological experience of research participants. These phenomenological experiences include the ways that people experience, make meaning of, evaluate, and cope with marginalising social contexts or positions within society and within social work care contexts.

Paola de Bruijn (PhD candidate) and Professor Erik Jansen, from the Netherlands, focus on VTS – used observation of fine art by groups of elderly – as a phenomenological and projective tool through which to explore meanings they attribute to old age. The projective quality of the images enabled them to articulate difficult feelings of loss from a safe distance. Dr Orna Shemer and Dr Eitan Shahar focus on poetry writing and sharing as a participatory research method with cognitively challenged youth in a care home. The aim was to understand how they experience their lives in preparatory programmes for independent living. The freedom of poetry formats for populations not used to expressing their ideas in formalised abstract ways was used as a way to access internal experiences of their day-to-day life in the youth centre. Professor Lucía Hervás Hermida and colleagues utilised arts-based methods to evaluate needs of young single mothers. Using an intersectional feminist perspective, they aimed to create new 'pictures' of the experience of motherhood that could challenge existing patriarchal and institutional definitions of the mothering role. Art was also used to evaluate the intervention, using a shared fruit basket image, to reflect visually on which aspects of the group had been 'fruitful' for them.

Professor Brian Kelly describe how recording in a music studio with homeless youth was artful, actional, and analogical forms of solution-seeking. This helped stimulate group members' engagement and problem solving that provided knowledge about how the youth cope. Dr Sofie Vindevogel shows how digital stories can be used to open spaces for the voices of marginalised women, dealing with addictions and with migrant status. Professor Rogério M. Pinto describes how autoethnographic playwriting and performance can help to access and tell coherent stories about major life transitions, such as immigration, shifts in gender identity, and loss of loved ones. Conversely, Professor Peter Szto presents the use of Photovoice to research the 'other'. He describes how a group of American social work students used Photovoice to understand experiences of deep poverty of the floating population in China.

The second part of this book utilises arts-based methods as a way to access the voices and knowledge of marginalised children who often have to be their own experts on how to cope with their environments. The arts-based research helps to include their voices on issues to do with children.

Dr Arielle Friedman and her colleague utilised Photovoice with at-risk children to understand how they experience their residential framework. This enables them to situate their phenomenological experience within the specific institution where they are cared for. Dr Genevieve Guetemme used artists' images of migration as stimuli to develop a discussion and focus group around the heuristic experience of migration of refugee children. Professor Julie Drolet and colleagues used a 'paint nite' joint community arts evening activity as a resilience-enhancing method to assess the coping of children after a natural disaster. In these examples, the arts were used with children not as a projective diagnostic tool, but as a phenomenological, interactive, and socially situated way of accessing children's experience.

The third and final section of the book shows how arts-based research is a tool that can be used with communities. This section demonstrates arts-based methods to create a space of dialogue within the community (as described above in terms of a broad hermeneutic space). Arts are also used to unify a coherent narrative of how the community self-defines both stressors and strengths. It shows methods of using arts as a participatory evaluative and reflective tool with the community. The methods used include community murals and photography, mapping techniques, play back theatre, 'rhizomatic storytelling', 'ripple effects' art work, and creative placemaking.

Firstly, Professor Holly Feen-Calligan and colleagues describe the use of community murals and photography as a tool through which to evaluate the impact on the community of an urban research university's community engagement programme. A mural painted on a corner food store was used as a catalyst for dialogue and needs evaluation around food security issues.

Dr Mike de Kreek, Professor Eltje Bos, and Margareta von Salisch explain the use of playback theatre by social workers as a way to 're-search' disrupted cases. This enabled contributions to practise theory and practice development in a bottom-up model of addressing difficult cases. Maria Regina A. Alfonso and colleagues outline the methods of 'rhizomatic storytelling', and also 'ripple effects mapping' as a mapping methodology to evaluate the impact of frontline support on communities during their experience of the COVID-19 crises. Professor Mark Doel considers the use of objects found on social workers desks to trigger reflective research about their professional identity. Ronald P.M.H. Lay describes the use of crafts to help social practitioners 'weave together' their practiced-based and theory-based knowledge, which emerge from their experience of working with service users. Finally, García Román, Ducca Cisneros, González Casas, & Arias Astray explore how to improve participatory action research using art.

We hope that the examples in this book will help illustrate the deep potential connections that social work specifically can have with arts-based research. We also show that it will demystify this area through suggesting a range of possible theoretical rationales, methods, pitfalls, and the great advantages of using arts-based research in social work research.

References

Abu Gazaleh, N., & Bos, E. (2019). *Social Initiatives Around Refugees.* HvA.

Amthor, R.F. (2017). "If only I did not have that label attached to me": foregrounding self-positioning and intersectionality in the experiences of immigrant and refugee youth. *Multicultural Perspectives, 19*(4), 193–206. https://doi.org/10.1080/15210 960.2017.1366862

Antonovsky, A. (1987). *Unraveling the Mystery Of health: How People Manage Stress and Stay Well.* Jossey-Bass.

Arnheim, R. (1996). *The Split and the Structure: Twenty-Eight Essays.* University of California Press.

Aubrey, C., & Dahl, S. (2006). Children's voices: the views of vulnerable children on their service providers and the relevance of services they receive. *British Journal of Social Work, 36*(1), 21–39. https://doi.org/10.1093/bjsw/bch249

Betinsky, M. (1995) *What Do You See? Phenomenology of Therapeutic Art Experience.* Jessica Kingsley Publishers.

Bowler, M. (1997). Problems with interviewing: experiences with service providers and clients, In G. Miller & R. Dingwall (Eds.), *Context and Method in Qualitative Research* (pp. 66–77). Basic Books.

Chamberlayne, P., & Smith, M. (2008). *Art Creativity and Imagination in Social Work Practice.* Routledge

Clark, A. (2011). Breaking methodological boundaries? Exploring visual, participatory methods with adults and young children. *European Early Childhood Education Research Journal, 19*(3), 321–330.

Conway, M.A., & Pleydell-Pearce, C.W. (2000). The construction of autobiographical memories in the self-memory system. *Psychological Review, 107*(2), 261–288.

de Kreek, M., & Bos, E. (2017). Playfully towards new relations. In S. Majoor, M. Morel, A. Straathof, F. Suurenbroek, & W. van Winden (Eds.), *Lab Amsterdam: Working, Learning, Reflections.* (pp. 78–88). Thoth.

Eisner, E. (1997). The promises and perils of alternative forms of data representation. *Educational Researcher, 26*(6), 4–20.

Emmison, M., & Smith, P. D. (2000). *Researching the Visual: Images, Objects, Contexts and Interactions in Social and Cultural Inquiry.* Sage.

Eriksson, M. (2017). The sense of coherence in the salutogenic model of health. In M.B. Mittelmark, S. Sagy, M. Eriksson, G.F. Bauer, J.M. Pelikan, B. Lindström, & G.A. Espnes (Eds.), *The Handbook of Salutogenesis* (pp. 91–96). Springer International. https://doi.org/10.1007/978-3-319-04600-6_11

Foster, V. (2007). Ways of knowing and showing: imagination and representation in feminist participatory social research. *Journal of Social Work Practice, 21*(3), 361–376.

Freire, P., & Macedo, D. (1987). *Literacy, Reading the Word and the World.* Routledge.

Gauntlett, D., & Holzwarth, P. (2006). Creative and visual methods for exploring identities. *Visual Studies, 21*(1), 82–91.

Harrington, A. (2004). *Art and Social Theory: Sociological Arguments in Aesthetics.* Polity Press.

hooks, b. (1992). *Black Looks: Race and Representation.* South End Press.

Huss, E. (2012). *What We See and What We Say: Using Images in Research, Therapy, Empowerment, and Social Change.* Routledge.

Huss, E. (2015). *A Theory-Based Approach to Art Therapy: Implications for Teaching, Research, and Practice.* Routledge.

Huss, E. (2018). Arts as a methodology for connecting between micro and macro knowledge in social work: examples of impoverished Bedouin women's images in Israel. *British Journal of Social Work, 48*(1), 73–87.

Huss, E., & Bos, E. (Eds.). (2019). *Art is Social Work Practice: Theory and Practice: International Perspectives.* Routledge.

Huss, E., & Maor, H. (2015). Towards an integrative theory for understanding art discourses. *Visual Art Research, 40*(2), 44–56.

Huss, E., & Samson, T. (2018). Drawing on the arts to enhance salutogenic coping with health-related stress and loss. *Frontiers in Psychology, 9*, 1–9.

Huss, E., & Sarid, O. (2014). Visually transforming artwork and guided imagery as a way to reduce work related stress:a quantitative pilot study. *Arts Psychotherapy, 41*, 409–412.

Huss, E., & Sela-Amit, M. (2018). Art in social work, do we really need it? *Research on Social Work Practice, 29*(6), 721–726.

Huss, E., Braun-Lewensohn, O., & Ganayiem, H. (2018). Using arts-based research to access sense of coherence in marginalized indigenous Bedouin youth. International Journal of Psychology, *53*(S2), 64–71. https://doi.org/10.1002/ijop.12547

Huss, E., Ben Asher, S., Shahar, E., Walden, T., & Sagy, S. (2020). Creating places, relationships and education for refugee children in camps: lessons learnt from the 'The School of Peace' educational model *Children & Society* DOI: 10.1111/chso.12412

Lippard L. (1990). Mixed Blessings: Art in a Multicultural America. Pantheon.

Martinez-Brawley, E., Paz, M., & Endz, M. (1997). At the edge of the frame: beyond science and art in social work. *British Journal of Social Work, 28*(2), 197–212.

Mason, J. (2002). *Qualitative Use of Visual Method*. Sage.

Mernissi, F. (2003). The meaning of spatial boundaries. In R. Lewis & S. Mills (Eds.). *Feminist Postcolonial Theory: A Reader*, (pp. 489–502). Edinburgh University Press.

Narhi, K. (2002). Transferable and negotiated knowledge: constructing knowledge for the future. *Journal of Social Work, 2*(3), 317–336.

Pink, S., & Kurti, L. (2004). *Working Images: Visual Research and Representation in Ethnography*. Routledge.

Rose, G. (1988). *Visual Methodologies*. Sage.

Segal-Engelchin, D., Huss, E., & Massry, N. (2019). Arts-based methodology for knowledge co-production in social work. *The British Journal of Social Work, 50*(4), 1277–1294. https://doi.org/10.1093/bjsw/bcz098

Shank, M. (2005). Transforming social justice: redefining the movement: art activism. *Seattle Journal for Social Justice, 3*, 531–559.

Simon, R.M. (2005). *Self-Healing Through Visual and Verbal Art Therapy*. (S.A. Graham, Ed.). Jessica Kingsley Publishers.

Spivak, G.C., & Guha, R. (Eds.). (1988). *Selected Subaltern Studies*. Oxford University Press.

Tuhiwai-Smith, L. (1993). Getting out from under: Maori women, education, and the struggles of Mana Wahine. In M. Arnot & K. Weiler (Eds.). *Feminism and Social Justice in Education. International Perspectives* (pp. 58–78). Falmer Press.

Walton, P. (2012). Beyond talk and text: an expressive visual arts method for social work education. *Social Work Education, 31*(6), 724–741.

Wang, C., & Burris, M. (1994). Empowerment through Photo-Novella. *Health Education Quarterly, 21*, 172–185.

SECTION I

Arts-based research as a method to understand and give voice to marginalised groups

1

Using arts-based methods to explore existential issues around ageing

Paola de Bruijn and Erik Jansen

Introducing the research setting

This chapter presents an arts-based research method enabling the study of existential dilemmas regarding ageing by using the visual artwork as a medium to evoke a profound dialogue between researcher and respondent. The application of the method will be shown in an arts-educational setting – focusing on the existential dimensions of life. The method is based on Visual Thinking Strategies (VTS: Housen, 1997; Yenawine, 2013), an art education method for conducting conversations on attentive and conscious perceptions of visual artworks. To further enhance the focused engagement with artworks, VTS has been expanded with a set of eXisTential Reflective Additional questions (XTRA: Bruijn & Jansen, 2019). This allows the VTS XTRA method to be applied in social work settings for use by workers and

Figure 1.1: Photo by Menno Bausch

researchers to gain insight into older people's existential questions making use of visual artworks.

The research setting for our case example is the application of VTS XTRA with ageing visitors of the 'Special Award' exhibition in the Dutch Nicolaïkerk in Utrecht. The Special Award is a national competition for visual artists with a disability, organised by the Special Arts foundation. In its peripheral programme, ageing visitors were invited to participate in conversations by looking at the artworks during a VTS XTRA session. These discussions generate data for an ongoing doctoral study of the first author (PB) on the pedagogical utility of art with respect to existential questions.

Rationale for using arts-based methods to study existential questions: care for ageing people and the value of dignity

Contemporary health care for older people is focalised on sustaining or fostering physical vitality. This is particularly relevant with the societal trend in Western European countries to stimulate ageing citizens to live independently for as long as possible. It is mainly motivated by economic arguments on the one hand, that is, slimming down the costs of care and cure, and substantive person-driven arguments on the other, that is, many older adults have a strong preference to remain in their familiar habitat over moving to an institutional environment.

Although physical resilience is definitely important for living a meaningful life, for older adults it should also be accompanied by mental resilience. In fact, when asked to tell stories about everyday life, independently living older adults tend to underemphasise medical problems and physical discomfort and stress what they deem meaningful in terms of values as autonomy and reciprocal relations (Jansen et al., 2017). Moreover, the notion of health as one's capacity to adapt resiliently to changes in life is gaining ground as an alternative to viewing health as the mere absence of disease (Huber et al., 2011). Thus, for good care it is essential to not only focus on physical resilience, but to bring it into balance with mental resilience and sense-making.

Working with images of visual art in social work can provide entry to these themes. Works of fine art, such as paintings or spatial objects, often affect people emotionally, touch upon deeper issues and thereby stimulate them to seek new understandings of the objects in relation to themselves and the world (NEA, 2012). Fine arts therefore create 'beautiful risks' for the personal, subjective experiences in which we are exposed to ourselves and encounter life (Biesta, 2017). Artworks provide broadening imaginaries for alternative opportunities to live a life one values and desires to come to terms with. Therefore, important for mental wellbeing is whether one is able

Figure 1.2: *Still life with fish* by Bob van Buuren, 2018

to see what realistic opportunities a person has to substantiate a dignified life (Jansen, 2018b).

Utilising arts-based experiences in social work research thus opens up new avenues to study existential issues and disentangle the restrictive effects of social norms. This may lead to insights and understandings otherwise difficult to achieve. By gaining access to new imaginaries, participants' critical consciousness may grow and this may enable them to reflect on how social change on their behalf can be made possible. This route to emancipation via critical reflection, resonates Paolo Freire's critical pedagogy (Freire, 1996), and connects to more recent proposals on how to discern socially-induced distortions of personal preferences from the life one really values (Terlazzo, 2016). Whereas all wellbeing and health professionals may find the VTS XTRA method useful, social work in particular can benefit from the broad integral and personal perspectives opening up while discussing the various layers of visual artworks (Bruijn & Jansen, 2019).

Method

Below we will introduce the VTS XTRA method and show how we applied it in the Special Awards research project, exploring how art can be helpful in enhancing people's capacities to endure changes in their life circumstances. The working hypothesis was that visual art can help people to conceptualise, understand, organise and reflect on their lives while interacting with others and the artwork.

Procedure of VTS XTRA

Visual Thinking Strategies (VTS, Yenawine, 2013) is a procedural tool for discussing images and social identity facilitated by collaboratively looking at visual art and art objects. The method induces a safe environment in which a facilitator invites a group of participants to silently look at a work of art, and then answer three key questions. With these questions participants extend their first impressions and explore new meaningful layers in the visual presentation.

The facilitator's task is to address and stimulate reflection on the observations. Furthermore, she ensures that all participants feel free to contribute and are engaged with respect and attention.

The underlying VTS theory of aesthetic development (Housen, 1997) surmises that viewers understand works of art in predictable patterns, described as five stages of aesthetic development characterising five viewer types:

- Stage 1: *Accountive* viewers are storytellers. Using their senses, memories, and personal associations, they make concrete narrative observations about the work. Judgments are based on what is known and what is liked. Emotions colour the commenting, as viewers enter the artwork and unfold their narratives.
- Stage 2: *Constructive* viewers attempt to build a framework for looking at works of art, using logical and accessible tools: perceptions, knowledge of the natural world, and moral, social and conventional values. If the work is not as it is 'supposed to be' – craft, skill, technique, hard work, utility, and function are not evident, or the topic is deemed inappropriate – this viewer judges the work as 'weird,' lacking, and valueless. The viewer's sense of what is realistic is a standard often applied to determine value. Emotional reactions submerge, while objective distance from the work increases.
- Stage 3: *Classifying* viewers adopt an analytical arts–historical stance. They want to identify the work for its place, school, style, time, and provenance by decoding it with their knowledge of facts and figures. Such viewers believe that if properly categorised, the work of art's meaning and message can be fully understood.
- Stage 4: *Interpretive* viewers seek personal encounters with works of art. Exploring the canvas, a work's meaning slowly unfolds, while they appreciate the subtleties of line, shape and colour. Critical skills are used to express feelings and intuitions while underlying meanings or symbols in the work emerge. Repeated encounters with works induce new

comparisons, insights, and experiences. Aware of these reinterpretations, these viewers regard their own viewing as dynamic.

- Stage 5: *Re-creative* viewers have established a viewing and reflecting history about works of art and 'willingly suspend disbelief.' To them familiar paintings are like old friends with whom they can uphold social relations. As in all friendships, development over time endures, allowing Stage 5 viewers to experience intimate understanding of the work. Re-creative viewers combine personal contemplation with universal concerns approaching the sublime: an experience of being elevated between the personal and the universal.

In our project VTS and Housen's stages of viewing (1997; 1999) are used to inform the intended direction of development for the existential dialogue. To induce this development with participants, we extended the three VTS questions with additional ones based on Housen's five stages: eXisTential Reflective Additional questions (XTRA questions):

- What in this image do you like or dislike?
- What is an important part in this image to you?
- What in this image do you find appealing or causing resistance?
- What in this image is valuable to you?
- Through art, what existential needs do you encounter?

Figure 1.3: *The flat with the interior* by Lenneke Zoeteman, 2019

- In a complex society, how may art help us to contemplate?
- How can art humanise the individual?

VTS XTRA procedure

- Step 1. Create an interview guide in which you document your introduction, aim(s), main research topics, the VTS XTRA questions and closure.
- Step 2. Select suitable works of art. Prepare the collection of the responses, for example, by making answer sheets or setting up recording equipment and ask participants for permission.
- Step 3. Invite your audience to gather around the first artwork you want to discuss and ask them to take a silent look at the 'image' or 'object' (do not define it as a painting, photo or drawing for staying neutral about what it is you are all looking at).
- Step 4. Open up the conversation with Q1 (only once) "What's going on in this picture?" for sharing perceptions and associations.
- Step 5. Listen carefully to each moment and acknowledge every answer by *paraphrasing* each discussed feature (in qualifying language) and point out what the participants discovered and expressed their opinions about. Interpretations are exchanged as group conversation develops.
- Step 6. Facilitate the discussion as it progresses by asking Q2 and repeat Step 5 and *link* related opinions to bring the viewpoints together. *Frame* ideas to identify themes to discover 'the big idea'. *Label* thoughts about how the participant is making meaning. This step details the observations recognising features of the artwork.
- Step 7. Bring in Q3 for encouraging further inquiry of new details and interpretations and echo Step 6, remaining open, accepting, and neutral.
- Step 8. After about ten minutes, set the stage for making the conversation more engaging and profound for the next 20 minutes by bringing in Q4 and echoing Steps 6 and 7.
- Step 9. To facilitate the discussion thoughtfully bring in Q5–Q10 while echoing Step 6s and 7 between each question.
- Step 10. To close the session, compliment your audience on how they participated and thank them for taking part at the VTS XTRA discussion. You can also ask questions such as: What about this discussion did you enjoy, was anyone surprised by anything that happened and/or does anyone have any question they would like to ask?

VTS (standard questions)

Q1. What's going on in this picture?
Q2. What do you see that makes you say that?
Q3. What more can you/we find?

VTS XTRA (additional reflective questions)

Q4. What in this image do you like or dislike?

Q5. What is an important part in this image to you?

Q6. What in this image do you find appealing or is causing resistance?

Q7. What in this image is valuable to you?

Q8. Through art, what existential needs do you encounter?

Q9. In a complex society, how may art help us to contemplate?

Q10. How can art humanise the individual?

Application of VTS XTRA in this study

In the Special Arts exhibition, the researcher (author PB) walked around with 12 groups of 75 visitors and followed the procedure as indicated above,

Figure 1.4: *The Paradise* by Johan van der Wal, 2018

thereby fulfilling a role of tour guide and enabling her to ask the VTS XTRA questions and engage in conversation with the participants.

Each tour consisted of two selected artworks by artists from the exhibition. Besides considered interesting for people visiting an exhibition, the viewed artworks were selected by their accessibility in giving meaning, contained a possible narrative and were ambiguous by intention.

The three standard questions (VTS) were mainly used for opening up the conversation, introducing personal observations and values (Stages 1 and 2) and identifying classifying viewers (Stage 3). The additional reflective questions (XTRA) Q4, Q5, Q6 and Q7 led to further discussing for engaging deeper with viewers' feelings and intuitions (Stage 4). The XTRA questions were used to generate insight in how underlying meaning and symbolisation emerge in participants' encounters of the image. Finally, Q8 and Q9 invited viewers to suspend their preconceptions (Stage 5) and connect their personal life themes to the existential themes discovered.

Thoughtful selection of the artworks is essential in setting the substantive dialogue topics. The artwork functions in a similar way as a generative question with narrative interviewing (Wengraf, 2001). Similar to narrative interviewing is also that the researcher–facilitator needs to ensure that conversation touches on deeper levels of substantive reflection instead of remaining superficial or merely on form or technique aspects of the work of art. The Special Award's artworks were selected based on their narrative evocativeness for people aged 55 or over and consisted of iconic or figurative works.

Immediately after the VTS XTRA tour, all statements made by the participants were recorded on sheets, which were prepared for these sessions. These notes (data) were interpreted as narratives intended to be analysed according to the Illuminative Evaluation method.

Summary of findings

Participants in the VTS-sessions reported having gained topical insights and that words and concepts related to old age had received new and deeper meanings. They also indicated that while contemplating their own and others' perspectives on life, they felt strengthened by opening up to the artworks and to each other. This emphasises the experiential qualities of this approach to art education (see Dewey, 2005) that in combination with day-to-day life narratives generates alternative interpretations of everyday lived experience.

Participants reactions during the Special Award session were categorised using Housen's five classification stages. Within the limited time and space during the walks, participants expressed rich and nuanced views of how to relate to ageing-related themes.

The VTS XTRA questions led to surprises and reactions such as: "Discussing a work of art with each other in this way is so much more beautiful", "Art is like a vehicle for yourself to find out what your questions about how you relate to life are", "This story takes me back to the past", and "That dark part, I experience the same... first, I have to go inside to encounter myself". Also, the conversations raised specific existential questions: "Can you call yourself a dead person if you don't think about the future?" or "How is it possible that a work of art can tell you something about your own life?" One participant thanked us for having a lovely afternoon, commenting that the conversations had made his day brighter and more pleasant adding that he had wanted to use the words 'more bearable'. His remark "I am so surprised by the fact that by looking at a work of art in this way I can have a conversation with people I don't know at all" turned out to be a widely-shared experience among participants.

In sum, working with VTS XTRA stimulates a structured but profound dialogue on ageing themes moderated by the visual artworks. It stimulates participants to engage and relate to the works of art, but also to each other. The evocative strength of the images enhanced the power of the dialogue. Our findings at least suggest that the VTS XTRA questions nuanced participants' thinking about the ageing process.

Figure 1.5: *Without title* by Kyi Myint Mik Mik, 2019

Conclusion: using VTS XTRA as arts-based method

A number of lessons on the use of VTS XTRA as arts-based method for social work research can be drawn from the current project. First, the VTS XTRA questions supported participants to discuss themes that are sometimes hard to articulate, but that are evocatively and non-discursively represented in visual works of art. In doing so the procedure expands the subjective space of opportunities of older adults on what they deem feasible and therefore their horizon of possible ways to grow older (Jansen, 2017a). This enhances their effective freedom to live the lives they have reason to value, or in other words their capabilities (see Sen, 1999; Nussbaum, 2011). Working with art in this way also enhances inclusion (Bruijn, 2016).

Second, by engaging with works of art, participants learned a lot about themselves and their pre-existing social notions. The VTS XTRA questions and artworks on ageing challenged participants' notions on what it means to be an older person and stimulated their empathic imagination and critical reflection on social norms about ageing. As a result, it enabled them to take a critical position towards the status quo of these social norms. Such reflection is a first step towards demarginalisation and empowerment in older adulthood.

Thirds, the artworks have great potential in mediating a substantive and challenging meeting between generations, for instance allowing young people to engage older adults and discuss what it means to grow older. This may enhance mutual understanding and increased opportunities for intergenerational exchange and assist in destigmatising (care for) older people.

Challenging for the application of VTS XTRA is that facilitators cautiously select the artworks, while being aware that not all evocations can be anticipated. Thus, some expertise in art and skilled dialogue facilitation is recommended. Further, for practical reasons group size, time, and space for viewing and discussion will not always be optimal but will influence the quality and depth of dialogue.

In closing, when applying arts-based methods in social work research, it is essential to have insight into the conditions for addressing existential questions, in order to gain full benefit of the power of the arts. As such a method, VTS XTRA is a promising addition to the social work researchers' toolkit for gaining insight into insiders' perspectives while simultaneously supporting clients and society in dealing with existential themes and support empowerment.

References

Biesta, G. (2017). *Letting Art Teach: Art Education 'after' Joseph Beuys.* ArtEZ Press.

Bruijn, P. de. (2016). Sociale inclusie door beeldende narratieven. *Cultuur+ Educatie, 45,* 106–124.

Bruijn, P. de, & Jansen, E. (2019). Enhancing capabilities for social change with the arts. In E. Huss & E. Bos (Eds.), *Art in Social Work Practice. Theory and Practice: International Perspectives.* Routledge.

Dewey, J. (2005). *Art as Experience.* Penguin.

Freire, P. (1996). *Pedagogy of the Oppressed (revised edition).* Penguin.

Housen, A. (1997). Theory of aesthetic development: Aesthetic stage descriptions. https://vtshome.org/aesthetic-development/

Housen, A. (1999). Eye of the beholder: Research, theory and practice. https://vtshome.org/aesthetic-development/

Huber, M., Knotterus, J.A., Green, L., van der Horst, H., Jadad, A.R., Kromhout, D., et al. (2011). How should we define health? *British Medical Journal, 343,* d4163.

Jansen, E. (2018a). Art and creativity as a capability: utilizing art in social work education. *Social Dialogue, 19,* 34–38.

Jansen, E. (2018b). Art and wellbeing: towards a capability account of the arts. Paper presented at the *Annual Conference of the Human Development and Capability Association,* August 30-September 1, Buenos Aires.

Jansen, E., Pijpers, R. & de Kam, G. (2017). Expanding capabilities in integrated service areas (ISAs) as communities of care: a study of Dutch older adults' narratives on the life they have reason to value. *Journal of Human Development and Capabilities.* http://dx.doi.org/10.1080/ 19452829.2017.1411895

Nussbaum, M. (2011). *Creating Capabilities: The Human Development Approach.* Belknap Press.

Sen, A. (1999). *Development as Freedom.* Oxford University Press.

Terlazzo, R. (2016). Conceptualizing adaptive preferences respectfully: an indirectly substantive account. *Journal of Political Philosophy, 24*(2), 206–226.

Wengraf, T. (2001). *Qualitative Research Interviewing: Biographic Narrative and semi-Structured Methods.* Sage.

Yenawine, P. (2013). *Visual Thinking Strategies: Using Art to Deepen Learning Across School Disciplines.* Harvard Education Press.

2

Arts- and music-based activities and nondeliberative participatory research methods: building connection and community

Brian L. Kelly

Arts exposure and engagement have been used throughout the history of the social work profession, particularly in community-oriented forms of social work and social group work. As one of the leading voices of the settlement house movement, Jane Addams, along with cofounder Ellen Gates Starr, championed the use of the arts at the Chicago-based settlement, Hull House (Glowacki, 2004). This practice lives on today as practitioners, researchers, and scholars argue for the inclusion of arts- and music-based activities in social work practice, education, and research (Huss & Sela-Amit, 2019; Nissen, 2019). While several expressive therapies have grown into substantial fields of practice with bodies of literature to support their efficacy and effectiveness (Malchiodi, 2013), including art, dance, music, and play therapies, these areas of practice tend to focus on micro-level interventions to address behavioural and medical health problems.

There is a small but growing body of literature exploring the use of music-based activities to create opportunities for empowerment (Travis et al., 2019a, 2019b, 2020) and to engage participants' talents, strengths, and interests (Kelly, 2017, Kelly, 2019). While these studies show that music-based activities have the power and potential to engage, harness, and foster participants' strengths, less is known about how these types of activities might be used as nondeliberative participatory research methods to build connection and community, particularly within groups. This chapter will explore this idea, beginning with brief reviews of Norma Lang's (2016) theory of nondeliberative practice and participatory research methods, followed by a case study of a research project I conducted that used audio documentary as a nondeliberative participatory research method. The chapter closes with a reflection and summary of the project and related processes, including lessons learned and implications for future work.

Nondeliberative group work practice

Nondeliberative group work practice considers and incorporates 'artful, actional and analogic forms of solution-seeking' (Lang, 2016, p. 103) in order to stimulate group members conative styles of engagement and problem solving. A key distinction of nondeliberative practice, is to 'do, *then think*' (p. 101), with activity serving as a catalyst for the unfolding group process. In previous archival work, a coauthor and I reviewed the use of arts- and music-based activities during the recreation movement, the settlement house movement, mid-20th century social group work, and contemporary social work practice (Kelly & Doherty, 2016, 2017). We found strong connections among historical and contemporary uses of arts- and music-based activities, community-oriented forms of social work and social group work, and nondeliberative group work practice. From our reviews, it is clear that arts- and music-based activities offer actional and conative means of engaging group members.

By prioritising the activity, followed by group process and reflection, members are able to foster connection and community through the doing and then deepen their connections and sense of community through reflective processes. The 'do, *then think*' model creates a universal experience for the group and subsequent space for members to process the experience, including similarities and differences, which further serves to build connection and community among the membership. While the literature is rich with examples of practitioners using arts- and music-based activities as forms of nondeliberative practice with promising outcomes, there is little that speaks to how researchers might use these activities and a nondeliberative approach as participatory research methods.

Participatory research methods

Participatory research methods represent a set of collaborative and inclusive approaches to conducting research with community members. Rather than positioning research participants as the subjects of a study, participatory research approaches engage participants as fully equal collaborators in the research process. From identifying a problem or phenomenon, to developing research questions or aims, to collecting and analysing data, to dissemination of findings and ongoing evaluation, participatory research methods operate under the assumption that all those whose lives are impacted by the problem or phenomenon should be engaged in the entire research process.

Stringer (2014) identifies several key characteristics of participatory research methods, including:

- It is *democratic*, enabling the participation of all people.
- It is *equitable*, acknowledging people's equality of worth.

- It is *liberating*, providing freedom from oppressive, debilitating conditions.
- It is *life enhancing,* enabling the expression of people's full human potential.

(p. 10)

These characteristics align well with several guiding principles of social work practice, including strengths and empowerment-based approaches. In addition, they reflect many of the benefits identified in the literature around the use of arts- and music-based activities in social work practice and related fields, including creating opportunities for empowerment (Travis et al., 2020) and engaging participants' talents, strengths, and interests (Kelly, 2017). Participatory research methods and the above characteristics also align with the actional and engaging properties of nondeliberative practice. The following section will further explore the connections among arts- and music-based activities in social work practice, nondeliberative practice, and participatory research approaches through the analysis of the co-production of an audio documentary with emerging adults experiencing homelessness.

Audio documentary co-production as nondeliberative participatory research

Research site and setting

In an effort to better understand how service providers use art and music-based activities, I conducted a study that explored a music studio in a transitional living programme for emerging adults experiencing homelessness (Kelly, 2017, 2019). Grounded in the strengths perspective (Saleebey, 2012) and using qualitative methods, such as participant observation and semi-structured interviews, the study focused on (1) the processes involved in developing and sustaining the studio, (2) participants' experiences while engaged in the studio, and (3) the meaning they attached to their experiences. Given the nature of the research site (that is, a music studio) and the phenomena under exploration (that is, music production, education, and general recreation), I also invited a small group of participants to co-produce an audio documentary that sonically explored their experiences in the music studio and the meanings they attached to their experiences (Kelly, 2015).

Co-producing an audio documentary with these emerging adults complemented the larger study in several important ways. Given the sound-based nature of the studio, it made good empirical sense to capture sonic representations of their experiences in the studio and their attached meaning. The documentary also provided an avenue to include participants' studio work in the study, which included original music productions and spoken word performances. We could literally bring their work off the page and into action. I was also interested in creating an opportunity to engage participants' talents, strengths, and interests in the research process. While the emerging adults were accommodating in allowing me to observe them and engaged and conversational in our interviews, the study felt like it was mine and I wanted a way to make it ours; to invite the participants to take a more active role in the study and create a more participatory process.

Data collection and analysis

While conducting interviews with the participants for the larger study, I invited those who used the studio most to join the audio documentary co-production group. Four emerging adults agreed to participate in the group. True to the essence of nondeliberative practice (that is, 'do, *then think*'), I prioritised the activity of co-producing the audio documentary and reserved reflection of our process for the latter stages of the project. We agreed on a purpose for the documentary (that is, a sonic exploration of their experiences in the studio and their attached meaning) and left the rest of the project fairly open as we developed our production plan over the course of 12 weekly sessions.

During our first session, I provided each participant with a Zoom H1 recording device. Participants used the Zoom H1 to capture field recordings of their work in the studio and other spaces they felt reflected their connections to the studio and their experiences within it. While participants needed some training with the equipment, they were quite adept at picking up the basics due to their prior exposure to recording equipment in the studio. Sessions 2–4 involved some additional troubleshooting with the equipment, listening to and analysing other audio documentary work to contextualise and critique various approaches to recording and producing, developing additional questions for exploration, and listening to and analysing participants' initial field recordings with an eye toward offering each other feedback and sound quality tips.

Sessions 5–8 involved increased attention to capturing and selecting quality field recordings that reflected the purpose of the documentary and participants evolving interests. This is where we began to analyse our data (that is, field recordings, music productions, and spoken word performances). Our focus was to identify recordings that best reflected our purpose: to capture participants' experiences in the studio and their attached meaning. We also considered the sonic quality of recordings, something often referred to as capturing 'good tape' in the industry (that is, capturing a recording with minimal background noise). This proved to be challenging as the participants were residing in a communal transitional living programme for emerging adults experiencing homelessness. They rarely had privacy and, when they did, it was often outdoors in a bustling and hectic urban environment. Therefore, a good portion of our middle sessions were spent re-recording ideas they had initiated on their own.

Once we had 'good tape', we turned our attention to sequencing the recordings and producing the documentary during sessions 9–12. Throughout this process, we sought to ensure equitable representation of participants' voices as we critically considered recordings. At times, these discussions were tense as they navigated over and under representation of themselves and each other in the documentary. For example, one participant experienced multiple absences during the sessions where we captured 'good tape' of participants reflecting on what the studio meant to them. When it came time to sequence these verbal reflections, it became clear that this participant's physical voice was missing from the documentary. To address this under representation, the group decided to feature more of this participant's music productions in the documentary to create a more equitable representation of their experiences in the studio and their attached meaning. In these moments, it was important for me to lean into facilitating the process and not lead it by making decisions for the group. In doing so, I believe we were able to develop a process and construct a space where the participants felt empowered and grounded in their strengths and talents as co-producers.

Once we selected field recordings, we loaded the files into a digital audio workstation and began to sequence the documentary. This was an exciting time for the group as we began to hear the narrative come to life with participants' reflections, music productions, and spoken word performances. It was also challenging as co-producing an audio documentary involves meticulously listening to content, often dozens of times, as we played with a variety of sequences for the final mix and adjusted audio equalisers, compressors, and recoding fade-ins and outs. Once we had a final version of the documentary, we reflected on our work, our process, and hosted a premiere party for family, friends, and residents and staff of the transitional living program. A full recording of the audio documentary may be heard here: https://soundcloud.com/brianlkelly/tlp-audio-doc-mastered-1.

Reflection and summary

The nondeliberative participatory nature of the co-produced audio documentary group

While the co-produced audio documentary group was informed by research questions from a lager study (Kelly, 2017, 2019), our work together was very much informed by Lang's (2016) theory of nondeliberative practice to 'do, *then think*'. Our work evolved organically from those initial questions and developed in rhythm with the interests of the participants and the demands of the project timeline. In doing so, we were able to engage in a holistic, intuitive, spontaneous, creative, and inventive process. Our approach was inherently holistic in that we sought to create a sonic representation of participants' experiences in the studio and their attached meaning. While the larger study did this with more traditional qualitative methods (that is, participant observation and interviews), the audio documentary created avenues for additional authentic and holistic representations of participants' experiences and opportunities to include their studio productions. Much of our work together was intuitive and spontaneous. As we worked across the 12 sessions, we reflexively engaged with field recordings and mapped out a course, often pivoting as necessitated by the interests of the participants and the needs of the project. We demonstrated creativity and inventiveness is these processes, which is perhaps best exemplified in the final product where one can hear the personality of each participant come through the audio. By engaging in this nondeliberative process, we co-produced something that was well beyond what we anticipated, something we could not have planned for had we tried.

This nondeliberative approach was informed and enhanced by the participatory nature of the project. The emerging adult participants were involved in almost every aspect of the project, from the development of additional research questions (for example, How do you feel when you're in studio? Do you experience challenges in the studio?), to collecting and analysing field recordings and their studio productions, to disseminating their work at the documentary premiere party and sharing it with their larger social networks. While I do not want to overstate the value of participatory research projects with emerging adults experiencing homelessness, it is imperative not to undervalue the importance of collaborating with members of this historically oppressed and stigmatised population. The majority of youth homelessness research is done with little if any input from participants on research questions, design, or dissemination. It often focuses on the risks that lead to homelessness for youth and consequences they experience while homeless. Incorporating participatory approaches in research with emerging adults experiencing homelessness creates opportunities for engagement and empowerment, which is a much-needed shift in the field (Kidd, 2012). Findings from this project support the democratic, equitable, liberating, and life-enhancing characteristics of participatory research methods (Stringer, 2014).

In bringing nondeliberative group work practice and participatory research approaches together, we successfully co-produced an audio documentary that sonically explores participants' experiences in the studio and the meaning they attach to their experiences. The nondeliberative approach allowed for higher levels of adaptability and creativity, and the participatory approach created opportunities for the emerging adults to have a greater voice in the research process and to truly collaborate as co-producers. The synergy of these two complimentary, yet understudied and underutilised approaches facilitated connection and community among the participants.

This is perhaps best reflected in examining the process and the product of the documentary project.

The co-produced audio documentary as process and product

Activity-based groups serve a dual purpose by offering participants opportunities to collaboratively work toward common goals and, in doing so, experience interpersonal group dynamics (Kinnevy et al., 1999; Dutton, 2001). As I and a co-author have explored in greater detail elsewhere (Kelly & Hunter, 2016), the co-produced audio documentary group experienced a very similar phenomenon, whereby coming together to collaborate on a nondeliberative participatory project, we experienced a deepening of interpersonal connection and community throughout the process. Communication and interaction patterns deepened as we engaged in our work, shifting from leader-centered patterns in the initial sessions to participant-centered patterns in the latter sessions as participants took greater ownership of the documentary. As participants took more ownership of the product (that is, the documentary), our process and connections deepened. Bonds tightened as we spent more time together and brought the vision of the project to life, creating a greater sense of cohesion among us. These deeper connections and cohesion created opportunities for rich conversations that extended beyond the scope of our work together, but greatly shaped the day-to-day experiences of the emerging adults, including stories of resilience and determination in the face of prejudice and discrimination.

As this analysis makes clear, the process and product of the co-produced audio documentary group were equally important. In follow-up sessions after the documentary premiere party, participants reflected on the importance of completing the project, having an artefact, and being able to share it with others. They took great pride in having completed the audio documentary and were eager to share it with folks in their circles. In addition, they spoke about the importance of the process that informed the co-production of the audio documentary – taking ownership of the project, deepening our connections, and at times becoming vulnerable with each other during the production process. Listening to them it was clear that the process of co-producing the documentary and the product itself were deeply connected and interwoven. One could not exist without the other; both product and process created connections and a sense of community among the group members.

Challenges and implications

While there were gains in connection and community building for the participants in this project, it was not without challenges. It would be difficult to facilitate a project like this without some prior training or knowledge in audio documentary and production. Thankfully there are several useful free online resources for training, including docsociety.org. Co-producing an audio documentary required a significant time commitment from the group members. We met for two to three hours a week for 12 weeks. This was a big commitment for emerging adults residing in a transitional living programme. With many demands on their time (for example, educational and vocational commitments), it was often difficult for them to manage all their responsibilities. The project also required funding for Zoom H1 recorders, stipends for the participants, and some existing knowledge of how to operate recording equipment and audio production software. There are several alternatives to the equipment that we used, including voice memo recorders on most current mobile phones to capture field recordings and entry level audio production options, such as Garage Band.

Challenges aside, this nondeliberative participatory audio documentary work embodies the central tenets of strengths and empowerment-based social work epistemologies. It builds on the work of settlement house workers, social group work practitioners, and others who promote the use of arts- and music-based activities in their practice. Further, it prioritises the experiences and the expertise of participants to shape the process and product of their work, creating opportunities for deeper connections and a sense of community. Additional research on the use of nondeliberative practice and participatory research methods with arts- and music-based activities is needed to continue to demonstrate the synergistic potentials of intentionally combining these approaches. As this chapter has demonstrated, doing so can be of real tangible and relational benefit to participants, as well as those of us who are lucky enough to facilitate these projects.

References

Dutton, S.E. (2001). Urban youth development-Broadway style: using theatre and group work as vehicles for positive youth development. *Social Work with Groups, 23*(4), 39–58. doi: 10.1300/J009v23n04_04

Glowacki, P. (2004). Bringing art to life: the practice of art at Hull House. In C.R. Ganz & M. Strobel (Eds.), *Pots of Promise: Mexicans and Pottery at Hull House, 1920–40* (pp. 5–29). University of Illinois Press.

Huss, E. & Sela-Amit, M. (2019). Art in social work: do we really need it? *Research on social work practice, 29*(6), 721–726. doi: 10.1177/1049731517745995

Kelly, B.L. (2015). Using audio documentary to engage young people experiencing homelessness in strengths-based group work. *Social Work with Groups, 38*(1), 68–86. doi:10.1080/01609513.2014.931665

Kelly, B.L. (2017). Music-based services for young people experiencing homelessness: engaging strengths and creating opportunities. *Families in Society, 98*(1), 57–68. doi:10.1606/1044-3894.2017.9

Kelly, B.L. (2019). Positive youth development: developing and sustaining music-based services for young people experiencing homelessness. *Emerging Adulthood, 7*(5), 331–341. doi:10.1177/2167696818777347

Kelly, B.L., & Doherty, L. (2016). Exploring nondeliberative practice through recreational, art, and music-based activities in social work with groups. *Social Work with Groups, 39*(2/3), 221–233. doi:10.1080/01609513.2015.1057681

Kelly, B.L., & Doherty, L. (2017). A historical overview of art and music-based activities in social work with groups: nondeliberative practice and engaging young people's strengths. *Social Work with Groups, 40*(3), 187–201. doi:10.1080/01609513.2015.1091700

Kelly, B.L., & Hunter M.J. (2016). Exploring group dynamics in activity-based group work with young people experiencing homelessness. *Social Work with Groups, 39*(4), 307–325. doi:10.1080/01609513.2015.1061962

Kidd, S. (2012). Invited commentary: seeking a coherent strategy in our response to homeless and street-involved youth: A historical review and suggested future directions. *Journal of Youth and Adolescence, 41*, 533–543. doi:10.1007/s10964-012-9743-1

Kinnevy, S.C., Healey, B.P., Pollio, D.E., & North, C.S. (1999). BicycleWORKS: task-centered group work with high-risk youth. *Social Work with Groups, 22*(1), 33–48. doi:10.1300/J009v22n01_03

Lang, N.C. (2016). Nondeliberative forms of practice in social work: artful, actional, analogic. *Social Work with Groups, 39*(2–3), 97–117. doi: 10.1080/01609513.2015.1047701

Malchiodi, C.A. (Ed.). (2013). *Expressive Therapies*. Guilford Publications.

Nissen, L.B. (2019). Art and social work: history and collaborative possibilities for interdisciplinary synergy. *Research on Social Work Practice, 29*(6), 698–707. doi.org/10.1177/1049731517733804

Saleebey, D. (Ed.). (2012). *The Strengths Perspective in Social Work Practice* (6th ed.). Pearson Education.

Stringer, E.T. (2014). *Action Research* (4th ed.). Sage.

Travis, R., Jr., Rodwin, A.H., & Allcorn, A. (2019a). Hip Hop, empowerment, and clinical practice for homeless adults with severe mental illness. *Social Work with Groups, 42*(2), 83–100. doi:10.1080/01609513.2018.1486776

Travis, R., Jr., Gann, E., Crooke, A.H., & Jenkins, S.M. (2019b). Hip Hop, empowerment, and therapeutic beat-making: Potential solutions for summer learning loss, depression, and anxiety in youth. *Journal of Human Behavior in the Social Environment, 29*(6), 744–765. doi:10.1080/10911359.2019.1607646

Travis, R., Jr., Gann, E., Crooke, A.H., & Jenkins, S.M. (2020). Using therapeutic beat making and lyrics for empowerment. *Journal of Social Work*. Online first. doi:1468017320911346

3

Arts-based methods to co-create knowledge and reconstruct power relations with marginalised women in and through research

Fien Van Wolvelaer, Tijs Van Steenberghe,
Jessica De Maeyer and Sofie Vindevogel

Academic and professional knowledge have dominated the history of social work research and practice. As a result, new knowledge has been grafted predominantly onto an existing base of professional authority and expertise. Arts-based research is emerging as an alternative approach to knowledge production, broadening the understanding of how scientific evidence is created and who is in the position to create it (Boydell et al., 2012). It is intended to open space for deliberately engaging with voices from the margin, hence rendering it a meaningful approach to advance social inclusion and social justice in and through social work research. In this chapter, we draw on our experience with arts-based research projects to contemplate this potential and to contribute to a critical dialogue regarding the impact of arts-based research on power relations and structures in social work academia and practice. We start by briefly introducing our research collective, explaining our rationale for working with arts-based methods, and describing two projects in which visual arts were used. We continue this chapter by elaborating on the merits and challenges of this methodology in relation to co-creating knowledge and altering power relations, derived from our own experiences in relation to the strand of literature on arts-based research.

Introduction

Background of the research collective and arts-based research projects

EQUALITY//ResearchCollective, embedded in Artevelde University of Applied Sciences, member of the Ghent University Association (AU GENT) seeks to respond to social inequality and exclusion by initiating research from within a human rights and quality of life framework. Specific attention is directed towards involving people in socially vulnerable situations and their perspectives, as well as to establishing participatory approaches whereby co-creation with participants is key to addressing power relations in society. In several projects we employ arts-based methodology to pursue this objective.

This choice is grounded in the understanding that research plays a crucial part in knowledge production and dissemination, but also risks being an elitist structure in which social inequalities and (mis)representations are (re)produced by voices from the centre. The experiences and stories of citizens living in socially vulnerable situations are rarely sought in research, hence excluding their perspectives from knowledge frameworks (Mizock et al., 2014). This is troubling for social work because it is inevitably connected to the goals and values of the social domain, like striving for social justice, human rights, and quality of life for all.

Furthermore, social work is increasingly situated in a superdiverse society and interconnected with global dynamics (Schrooten, 2020). This challenges us to explore alternative ways in which diversity can enter the realm of research and while we are confronted with established research structures that may create or reinforce structural inequalities.

It is precisely because of this awareness that we employ at our centre arts-based research methods in projects with underrepresented and misrepresented communities, wherein we seek to create more space for counter-stories in which diverse citizenship practices can become visible and recognised. We believe that, by doing so, social work research and knowledge construction can better realise its ambition to contribute to inclusive citizenship. We illustrate this through two of our research projects wherein arts-based methods and, more specifically, visual arts were employed, to further reflect on how the 'social' potential of this approach can be maximally realised. (Wang et al., 2017)

Photovoicing recovery pathways

Photovoice is a participatory action-based research method that uses photography as a way to gain insight into individuals' living situations and to make these accessible to others. Participants receive cameras to record and reflect on their daily experiences, including personal and community strengths and concerns (Wang, 1999). Photovoice captures the 'point of view' of the person holding the camera (Booth & Booth, 2011). The aim of this project was to gain insight and to visualise how women experience recovery from addiction in their daily lives, with attention to the complex interplay of personal, social, and structural factors shaping their recovery pathways. By using photovoice, this project aimed to engage in a collaborative dialogue, to create a photo exposition, a website, and an academic article. Eight women in recovery and two researchers engaged in this research. The women varied in age (between 25 and 54), time in recovery, substance use, and the care and support they received. The two researchers (one male and one female) had (academic) experience in the topic of addiction and with photovoice and/or photography. The project, which lasted one and a half years, was built as six group sessions with the possibility for additional individual meetings.

At the start, participants were provided with a manual, containing the content of the project, ways to photograph and exercises, and the work of other photographers and photovoice projects as inspiration. The first group meeting was focused on getting to know each other, the project, and photography. After dialogue about the central topics, a specific focus was chosen together with the participants. The group decided that the first topic to photograph was what brings quality of life in day-to-day life, with a focus on what constitutes 'me-time'. This entry point led to discussions of important topics that determined their recovery process and how this was influenced by personal, institutional, and societal factors. The following group meetings were each based on a specific structure. The first part of the meeting focused on photo selection and dialogue about the graphical or creative elements that shaped the photos. After a shared lunch, the focus of the meeting shifted towards the content of the photos. Participants had the space to talk about their photos and connect them with the content of other participants' photos and stories. After each session, the focus for the coming month was determined together. The overall focus on what constituted quality of life and how this influenced recovery processes remained.

The data collection revolved around the process of making and discussing of the photos. The photos were collected by the researchers and printed out for each session. All the group sessions were recorded and transcribed verbatim. After each group session and during additional individual meeting, notes were made by the researchers on the content and the process of the project. The data analysis was built on several steps. Firstly, participants were involved in data analysis by introducing them to the central framework and inviting them to analyse the photos together with the researchers. In this way, the idiosyncratic meaning of photos became connected both with other photos and with lived experiences. This was an important step towards a collective content analysis. The second analytic step was a thematic analysis of all qualitative data (group sessions, individual interviews, photos), with participants and researchers. This produced a first structure of themes and selection of photos. In the third analytic step, the researchers presented their preliminary analysis to the participants. Each participant received a document with a proposed structure, explanation, and corresponding photos, as well as the invitation to make corrections or suggestions. The goal was to ensure that the proposed content matched how participants saw their own photos. They could also make suggestions about titles and quotes for their photos in relation to each theme.

Digital storytelling on gender and changing surroundings in the context of migration

Digital storytelling (DST) is a method for storytelling using digital media. It enables creative arts-based processes to capture lived experiences, in which people make short personal narratives combining audio, images, and a voice-over (Lambert, 2013). The application of DST in research is still in its infancy, yet its value is apparent for both researchers and participants (de Jager et al., 2017). DST was employed in a project that sought to understand how changing surroundings in the context of migration intersect with gender. The project entailed a co-creative trajectory with community co-researchers and newcomers, aimed at gaining insight into newcomers' lived experiences with gender and how they can be supported in a gender-sensitive way during this transition.

We deliberately sought to engage in a co-creating and co-learning process with co-researchers who are newcomers themselves in our centre, to create the emic perspective in the research design. Other advantages of working with community co-researchers were their experiential knowledge, familiarity with the 'target group' (without generalising this group), access to prospective participants, and potential to bridge cultural and language barriers (Israel et al., 2010). A preparatory process was organised to train co-researchers in qualitative research, DST, and research ethics but also to facilitate the co-creative process. The academic researchers clarified their objectives and described their ideas that had led them to initiation of this project, alongside the expectations of the external funder regarding the process and outcomes of the project. They also actively prompted and made time for the community researchers to contribute their views on this topic, share their ideas on the DST sessions, express themselves on expected do's and don'ts, and delineate their role in this project. Throughout the DST project, regular meetings were held between all the researchers to prepare the sessions and reflect upon them afterwards.

Three gender-homogeneous groups made up of participants, one community researcher, and one academic researcher were created. The co-creative trajectory consisted of six consecutive group sessions about gendered experiences in the context of migration, including two DST workshops in which the participants actively transformed their narratives into digital stories. Data were collected during the thematic group sessions and individual in-depth exchanges with participants in between group sessions. Data included their sharing of (parts of) narratives, their search for constituents for their digital stories, and their contextualisation and joint reflection on the screening of the stories. For various reasons, some newcomers interested in the project could not (continue to) commit themselves to a longer research trajectory. Therefore, additional individual interviews were carried out. All data were audio recorded and transcribed verbatim. Deductive data analysis was based on our theoretical framework on gendered experiences in migration. This part of the research was led by the academic researchers; however, the process and findings were discussed with the community co-researchers to incorporate their impressions and interpretations of the digital storytelling process. The findings were presented as part of a collaborative discussion with all participants during a gathering in which they all screened their digital stories. Further, all involved parties jointly designed the valorisation strategy of the project, based on the question how the stories could lead to more gender-sensitive and -supportive reception and integration supports for newcomers.

(How) do arts-based methods facilitate co-creation of knowledge?

Perspectives from the margin

In the two research projects presented here, arts-based methods were employed to broaden the means of eliciting the participants' perspective, with the aim of co-creating knowledge on lifeworld phenomena. To articulate this potential of arts-based methods, we draw on the theoretical perspectives of standpoint theory and vernacular creativity.

According to standpoint theory (e.g. Collins, 1990; Smith, 1990; Harding, 1992), marginalised lives are considered better places from which to start asking causal and critical questions about the social order than the (often unquestioned) centre. Eisner (in Wang et al., 2017) has described this potential of arts-based approaches as contributing to the understanding of the 'whole' by making the particular vivid.

'Vernacular creativity serves as another useful concept to consider knowledge production from the margins, as it describes "creative practices that emerge from highly particular and non-elite social contexts and communicative conventions"' (Burgess, 2006 p. 206). Vernacular creativity can disrupt and revitalise commodified existence and build new, relational knowledge that is intertwined with emotions and everyday arts.

Both photovoice and DST have great potential to give space to vernacular creativity and to transform social structures in research. However, this potential cannot be taken for granted and requires researchers to carefully reflect upon what is needed to actually reach co-creation of knowledge and achieve empowerment of participants in and through research. By sharing our centre's experiences in these projects in relation to insights from the literature on arts-based research methods, we aim to stimulate such reflections.

Lived experiences and self-representation

The social phenomena of interest in arts-based research are often situated in the life worlds of disempowered communities. Arts-based research engages with the everyday life, and arts stimulate deeper reflection and richer expression of these lived experiences (Liebenberg, 2018). Centralising people's lived experiences strengthens and broadens the recognition of diverse citizenship practices (McGuigan, 2005). Burgess (2006) and Livingstone (2004) describe DST as a practice of content creation that is crucial for the democratic agenda and different notions of citizenship. By doing so, arts-based research may contribute to belonging, legitimacy, and membership within the context of the research setting and the broader society, by acknowledging the embodiment of personal experiences (Chen & Schweitzer, 2019). Furthermore, arts-based methods create spaces where citizens can negotiate hybrid identities and construct new notions of the self (Darvin & Norton, 2014; Botfield et al., 2018). These spaces can counteract experiences of being unheard or having one's identity reduced to being 'an addict' or 'a migrant'.

Therefore, arts-based methods may leverage self-representation, agency, and claiming voice. Arts offer a broader language for self-representation, by going beyond the narrative and including the body, affect, and emotions in the research process. Arts also appeals to alternative literacies, thus differentiating knowledge mobilisation. Arts-based methods like DST have potential to foster the participants' agency in constructing and sharing their stories according to what is important to them (Alexandra, 2008; Lenette et al., 2015; Johnson & Kendrick, 2016), especially when they can control their representations by using a broad array of artistically inspired methods. They are author and director of their own stories, and eventually co-constructors of knowledge (Alexandra, 2008; Darvin & Norton, 2014). Centralising people's lived experiences through the use of arts while simultaneously sharing power on how they can represent themselves is crucial for the democratic agenda. In other words, finding ways to share responsibility in all phases of the arts-based research process is shaping an inclusive practice of citizenship.

Social impact

Liebenberg (2018) recommends embedding arts-based methods in participatory-action research to orient efforts towards anticipating social impact. This draws attention to mobilising audiences around the created pictures and digital stories. Arts-based methods encompass creative possibilities to make the content public and to engage with different audiences (Boydell et al., 2012). Van Wolvelaer, Longman, and Vindevogel (under review) argue that story*listening* is as crucial as story*telling* and that the responsibility for democratic participation is as much directed towards the audience as it is to the storytellers. Verschelden et al. (2019) call for connecting with a diverse audience and creating ways to hear, learn, and discuss different perspectives. They show how being integrated in the regular art circuit has destigmatising effects since the creators of art are addressed as artists and not as socially vulnerable citizens who make art.

However, simply using arts is insufficient to alter power relations in research and broader knowledge construction processes. It requires a critical reflection of their positionality from researchers and an awareness of the dynamics within and beyond the research project that impact on the position of participants. In that sense, arts-based research acknowledging complexity may raise questions and uncertainties rather than only give answers (Barone & Eisner, 2011). Moreover, we experienced that arts-based methods can evoke challenges in all research phases, some of which we share here.

Challenges and questions in arts-based research projects

An important concern in our projects revolved around our own positioning. We questioned whether our participation during the group sessions could influence the data collection. We noticed that sharing personal experiences with participants exposed constructions of privilege and subordination and stimulated the connectedness within the group. At the same time, the differences in knowledge and perspectives often led to important discussions, evoking a richer understanding. Being transparent about our position, while at the same time expressing personal experiences and uncertainties, helped us to acknowledge different socio-economic positions and to respond to the challenge of building participatory practices in which unequal positions are being recognised rather than concealed. It further helped us to employ our ability to listen deeply to the multi-layered ways in which participants represented their experiences and to use visual arts to understand them in lived and embodied ways. In the project on gender and migration, DST's focus on 'deep listening' (de Jager et al., 2017) enabled the researchers to engage deliberately with the perspectives of newcomers whose life worlds and experiences were very diverse and different from those of the researchers.

Another concern resulted from the participatory nature of arts-based methods. While intense engagement and close involvement from the participants is key to co-creating knowledge, we also experienced that it is a time-consuming practice that may clash with socially vulnerable situations. Time is not equally available for participants and spaces of time are often inhabited in different ways (Rice et al., 2018). Also, these research projects may become very intense for participants and precisely because of their situation they may not be able to fully submerge themselves in these projects. In the photovoice project, a participant dropped out because she experienced the research as too confrontational and absorbing too much of her time and energy. To deal with this, we often adjusted our pace and twisted our plans creatively to make most of it while being consciously concerned with the wellbeing of the participants. We stretched the research space, for example by creating a WhatsApp group or planning gatherings over weekends, to maximally interact with participants. This partly addressed the issue of time constraint for planning meetings. Moreover, this facilitated connectedness and trusting relationships. It also gave participants more control to claim voice. Another major concern pertained to the responsibility for the analysis and interpretation of the data. We found it challenging to involve the participants extensively in this time-consuming process. We tried to figure out how different responsibilities could still be equally connected and meaningful collaboration continued throughout the project. Notwithstanding, we acknowledged that participants do not get paid (equally) for their investment in the research and their time is used as a commodity. We therefore need to carefully consider and ensure that as researchers we do not consume participants to achieve our goals.

Furthermore, we were challenged by the question how to cope with constrained access to participants, when inclusion goes hand in hand with exclusion. Since reaching and engaging with participants throughout the projects can be challenging, we must be aware of people's motivations for (not) participating and especially be thoughtful of those we did not reach at all. In the DST project, we only reached newcomers who spoke Dutch, French, or English. We also realised that the participants already had a critical opinion on gender topics and that we probably did not reach those who consider gender in a sphere of taboo and silence. Another source of exclusion may be found precisely in the 'creative nature' of arts-based methods. In the search for participants, some stated that they did not have creative skills or even that they did not wish to be approached as toddlers in a crafting-class. These experiences call for awareness of your 'blind spots' as a researcher. It is inherent that because arts-based methods have great participatory potential, they are all inclusive.

Another challenge relates to discussions about ethics and who benefits from the research. We approached the ethics in arts-based research as an 'ongoing, iterative, and complex process' (Gubrium et al., 2014, p. 1613). More than obtaining an informed consent at the onset of projects, we opted for a continuous ethical negotiation grounded in the everyday situations throughout the research project (Clark et al., 2010). The academic researchers regularly checked with participants if they still felt comfortable with their participation and the outcomes of the project, and under which conditions.

To protect the participants' privacy, the visual output is often anonymised. However, by again rendering the participants invisible, hegemonic centres may be reinforced instead of disrupted, as it is the professional researcher who typically receives credit for the outputs and whose name is on highly elitist academic articles that are seen as the most valid forms of knowledge dissemination in academia (Jung, 2016; Warr et al., 2016). In both projects, we attempted to use the potential of arts-based research to stretch these boundaries and complement academic output with artistically inspired actions such as exhibitions, performances, or websites in which participants could take credit as co-producers of knowledge. We jointly determined these disseminations and constructed some 'rules of use' and contextualisation for the pictures and digital stories we shared publicly.

We also struggled with the aesthetic output of voices: what if participants create 'bad' stories or pictures that risk the disempowerment and further marginalisation of them in the understandings of the audience? What if their outputs confirm rather than counter harmful meta-narratives? Who decides what is good enough to share? What if some participants excel in using visual arts, rendering others insecure? We attempted to respond to these struggles by building liminal safe spaces in which all people involved in the research process took responsibility to both speak and listen deeply to each other (Van Wolvelaer et al., under review) and by creating a platform to listen, see, and connect different perspectives (Verschelden et al., 2019).

This also connects to considerations on how art works are made public. The spaces in which interconnected voices are speaking and are being listened to should go beyond the safe environment of the research group and extend to the interaction with 'the audience'. Impactfully sharing research outputs is 'both politically and contextually shaped' (Mitchell et al., 2017 in Liebenberg, 2018, p. 6). Depending on the forum where these outputs are shown, different social and cultural norms come into play. Several practices that explicitly combine the arts and the social led to the experience of how the participants' identities become reaffirmed when their artwork does not fit in or challenges the dominant canon. In our projects, we also struggled with how to engage with the audience and its interpretation of the visual output, and how these influence images of the participants. We dealt with this by carefully determining those dissemination strategies that offered space for contextualisation and exchange with the audience.

Furthermore, we need to consider both the possible short- and long-term impact of our projects and the artistic outputs. Too often it remains unclear what happens with these and who reaps the benefits over time. We need to think about who is in the audience and how we can continuously engage in constructive dialogue even after the project is finished.

Concluding reflections

In both photovoice and DST, people are encouraged to share and visualise their lived experiences and, as such, these methods expose what is often unseen by the wider society. By doing so, these methods hold the potential to question and challenge hegemonic discourses and meta-narratives (Alexandra, 2008; Lenette et al., 2015), to transform researcher–participant boundaries, and to acknowledge people's everyday realities as a way of practicing citizenship, embedded in specific contexts of power (Pessar & Mahler, 2003). Arts-based methods thus enable those involved to construct alternative representations that may promote dialogue and shared knowledge construction, eventually contributing to social change (Chilton & Leavy, 2014). However, this potential of arts-based methods can only be realised through relentless consideration of the (unequal) dynamics between researchers, participants, and audience, and as part of a wider research process that critically engages with established authorities and positionalities in search of social justice. It therefore remains crucial to acknowledge that arts-based methods are not all inclusive but do open up essential spaces for voices from the margins that can contest and transform hegemonic understandings and representations. The knowledge we produce with arts-based methods will inevitably be biased because of the absence of certain voices. Seen from standpoint epistemology, we are not able to present a 'whole truth'. This, however, does not devalue the potential of arts-based research. It precisely amplifies the urge for constant awareness towards social in- and exclusion in knowledge production.

References

Alexandra, D. (2008). Digital storytelling as transformative practice: critical analysis and creative expression in the representation of migration in Ireland. *Journal of Media Practice, 9*(2), 101–112.

Barone, T., & Eisner, E.W. (2011). *Arts Based Research*. Sage.

Booth, T., & Booth W. (2011). In the frame: Photovoice and mothers with learning difficulties. *Disability & Society, 18*(4), 431–442.

Botfield, J.R., Newman, C.E., Lenette, C., Albury, K., & Zwi, A.B. (2018). Using digital storytelling to promote the sexual health and well-being of migrant and refugee young people: a scoping review. *Health Education Journal, 77*(7), 735–748.

Boydell, K.M., Gladstone, B.M., Volpe, T., Allemang, B., & Stasiulis, E. (2012). The production and dissemination of knowledge: a scoping review of arts-based health research. *Forum: Qualitative Social Research, 13*(2), 32.

Burgess, J. (2006). Hearing ordinary voices: cultural studies, vernacular creativity and digital storytelling. *Continuum, 20*(2), 201–214.

Chen, S. & Schweitzer, R.D. (2019). The Experience of Belonging in Youth from Refugee Backgrounds: A Narrative Perspective. J Child Fam Stud 28, 1977–1990 (2019). https://doi.org/10.1007/s10826-019-01425-5

Chilton, G., & Leavy, P. (2014). Arts-based research practice: merging social research and the creative arts. In P. Leavy (Ed.), *The Oxford Handbook of Qualitative Research* (pp. 403–422). Oxford University Press.

Clark, A., Prosser, J., & Wiles, R. (2010). Ethical issues in image-based research. *Arts & Health, 2*(1), 81–93.

Collins, P.H. (1990). *Black Feminist Thought: Knowledge, Consciousness, and the Politics of Empowerment.* Routledge.

Darvin, R., & Norton, B. (2014). Transnational identity and migrant language learners: the promise of digital storytelling. *Education Matters: The Journal of Teaching and Learning, 2*(1), 55–66.

De Jager, A., Fogarty, A., Tewson, A., Lenette, C., & Boydell, K.M. (2017). Digital storytelling in research: a systematic review. *The Qualitative Report, 22*(10), 2548–2582.

Gubrium, A.C., Hill, A.L., & Flicker, S. (2014). A situated practice of ethics for participatory visual and digital methods in public health research and practice: a focus on digital storytelling. *American Journal of Public Health, 104*(9), 1606–1614.

Harding, S. (1992). Rethinking standpoint epistemology: what is 'strong objectivity'?. *The Centennial Review, 36*(3), 437–470.

Israel, B.A., Coombe, C.M., Cheezum, R.R., Schulz, A.J., McGranaghan, R.J., Lichtenstein, R., Reyes, A.G., Clement, J., & Burris, A. (2010). Community-based participatory research: a capacity-building approach for policy advocacy aimed at eliminating health disparities. *American Journal of Public Health, 100*(11), 2094–2102.

Johnson, L., & Kendrick, M. (2016). 'Impossible is nothing': expressing difficult knowledge through digital storytelling. *Journal of Adolescent & Adult Literacy, 60*(6), 667–675.

Jung, H. (2016). Fuzzy boundaries when using 'mental mapping' methods to trace the experiences of immigrant women in South Korea. In D. Warr, M. Guillemin, S. Cox, & J. Waycott (Eds.), *Ethics and Visual Research Methods* (pp. 31–44). Palgrave Macmillan.

Lambert, J. (2013). *Digital Storytelling: Capturing Lives, Creating Community.* Routledge.

Lenette, C., Cox, L., & Brough, M. (2015). Digital storytelling as a social work tool: learning from ethnographic research with women from refugee backgrounds. *The British Journal of Social Work, 45*(3), 988–1005.

Liebenberg, L. (2018). Thinking critically about photovoice: achieving empowerment and social change. *International Journal of Qualitative Methods, 17*, 1–9.

Livingstone S. The Challenge of Changing Audiences: Or, What is the Audience Researcher to Do in the Age of the Internet? European Journal of Communication. 2004;19(1):75-86. doi:10.1177/0267323104040695

McGuigan J. The Cultural Public Sphere. *European Journal of Cultural Studies.* 2005;8(4):427-443. doi:10.1177/1367549405057827

Mitchell, C., de Lange, N., & Moletsane, R. (2017). *Participatory Visual Methodologies.* Sage.

Mizock, L., Russinova, Z., & Millner, U. C. (2014). Acceptance of mental illness: Core components of a multifaceted construct. *Psychological Services, 11*(1), 97–104. https://doi.org/10.1037/a0032954

Pessar, P.R., & Mahler, S.J. (2003). Transnational migration: bringing gender in. *International Migration Review, 37*(3), 812–846.

Rice, C., LaMarre, A., Changfoot, N., & Douglas, P. (2018). Making spaces: multimedia storytelling as reflexive, creative praxis. *Qualitative Research in Psychology, 17*(2), 222–239. https://doi.org/10.1080/14780887.2018.1442694

Schrooten, M. (2020). Transnational social work: challenging and crossing borders and boundaries. *Journal of Social Work*, online first. https://doi.org/10.1177/1468017320949389

Smith, D.E. (1990). *The Conceptual Practices of Power: A Feminist Sociology of Knowledge*. University of Toronto Press.

Verschelden, G., Dehaene, J., Van Steenberghe, T., & De Droogh, L. (2019). Film as social change: from giving voice to giving a stage. In E. Huss & E. Bos (Eds.). *Art in Social Work Practice. Theory and Practice: International Perspectives*. Routledge.

Wang, C.C. (1999). Photovoice a participatory action research strategy applied to women's health. *Journal of Women's Health, 8*(2), 185–192.

Wang, Q., Coemans, S., Siegesmund, R., & Hannes, K. (2017). Arts-Based Methods in Socially Engaged Research Practice: A Classification Framework. *Art/Research International: A Transdisciplinary Journal 2* (2):5-39. https://doi.org/10.18432/R26G8P.

Warr, D., Guillemin, M., Cox, S., & Waycott, J. (Eds.) (2016). *Ethics and Visual Research Methods: Theory, Methodology, and Practice*. Palgrave Macmillan.

4

Autoethnographic playwriting and performance for self-healing and advocacy

Rogério Meireles Pinto

Introduction

This chapter focuses on how autoethnographic playwriting and performance can be used as research pursuits in social work. It lays out (1) a rationale for using playwriting and performance as a research method to engage in self-healing and to advance social change; (2) a case study including theoretical approach, research procedures, and dissemination; and (3) a discussion for future social work research and practice. Autoethnographic playwriting and performance provides a tool that researchers can use to explore the experiences of research participants.

Autoethnographic playwriting and performance as research

As a research method, autoethnography developed in the late 1990s (Ellis et al., 2011). As a more sophisticated method of postmodern social science, autoethnography became in the 2000s as 'the study, representation, or knowledge of a culture by one or more of its members' (Buzard, 2003, p. 61). Autoethnography has since become a confessional form of inquiry in which researchers embrace the realities of their lives while they deconstruct reality, power, and identities (Adams & Holman Jones, 2011, p. 108). Autoethnography has provided a space in the human sciences where the 'human' is of central interest and where the ethnographic method is the vehicle for writing stories, for excavating the past, for envisioning the future, and for investigating life in its totality (Bochner & Ellis, 2016).

The exploration of the self in playwriting and performance was solidly developed in the second half of the twentieth century, and it then took hold in the past 20 years alongside reality shows, YouTube, Facebook, and Instagram – all forms of expression that not only allow for but call for the exposure of the self in the public space (Pendzick et al., 2016). Autoethnographic playwriting and performance are investigational pursuits that echo experimental theatre, whose main focus is more on the *process* of acting than on the actual outcomes, be it the written play or the performance (Emunah, 2020).

The method of 'self-revelatory performance' was described by Emunah in 1983 (Emunah, 2015). For this chapter, self-revelatory performance is a genre of experimental theatre that encourages the actor/ethnographer to explore themselves and their process to find a relationship with the audience before, during, and after the performance. The term 'self-revelatory performance' has spun off; currently, it is referred to as auto drama, auto performance, memory theatre, testimonial theatre, autobiographical storytelling, confessional performance, solo autobiographical performance, theatre of the real, autobiographical drama self-referential theatre, and many others (Emunah, 2020).

Self-referential theatre conceptualised

Self-referential theatre is often pursued for therapeutic purposes, such as personal growth, healing, and/or problem-solving. For example, playwriting and performance of personal material may help to heal traumatic life events, substance misuse sequelae, and mental health difficulties (Heddon, 2008). However, self-referential theatre may also involve storytelling and/or dramatisation of real-life events and experiences without the explicit purpose of healing oneself (Emunah, 2015). This autobiographical pursuit can be used as a research method for non-therapeutic purposes, such as artistic production (for example, video, music, dance, performance), arts-based education, and advocacy. Self-referential theatre often includes both autobiographical content – personal aspects of one's life – and auto ethnographic content – positionalities, such as one's identified ethnicity, race, gender, and class. Self-referential theatre is a research method that calls for exploring 'trans locational positionality' (Anthias, 2008, p. 5) – an intersectionality framework used here to elevate our understanding of myriad social identities represented in the person of the playwright and the performer. Translocational positionality advances understanding of positional identities as ever-evolving in context and meaning, as being time-dependent, and also prone to inconsistency and ambiguity (Anthias, 2008). For non-therapeutic purposes, self-referential theatre is informed by socio-political approaches, and it often carries a social awareness and an advocacy agenda (Saldãna, 2003; Spry, 2010). Therefore, it resonates well with social justice-focused social work research.

Whether for therapeutic or non-therapeutic purposes, self-referential theatre has the potential to address issues concerning racial, ethnic, gender, and other social inequities when it is conceived as a socially, politically, and academically transgressive form of inquiry. As in any other form of theatre, the self-referential performance also has the purpose of entertaining the reader of a play or the audience for the performance (Schechner, 2013). Therefore, a balance between pursuing entertainment and efficacy is highly recommended, that is, 'did the work achieve its therapeutic and/or non-therapeutic goals?' Self-referential theatre as a form of inquiry would be designed to challenge academic inquiry and the patriarchal narrative of 'truth' found in academic books and journals. However, to accomplish self-healing and/or artistic purposes, educational and/or advocacy goals, self-referential performance must take the reader/audience beyond the linear recounting of personal stories. It is in the transformation of personal conflict that one can achieve self-healing and/or artistic, educational, or advocacy goals. These points are illustrated by the case study below.

Case study on self-referential theatre: Marília

Here, I use *Marília*, an award-winning play that I wrote and performed, as a case study of popular, community-based art interrogating intersecting issues related to immigrant rights in the US, gender identities and gender crossing, and issues of death and dying.

I was born, and I grew up, in Belo Horizonte, Brazil. I came to the US in 1987 at the age of 21. I lived in New York City for nearly a decade as an undocumented immigrant. I became a naturaliaed American citizen 13 years after my arrival. I wrote *Marília* between 2012 and 2014, and I performed the play at the 2015 United Solo Festival on Theatre Row in NYC, where it won Best Documentary Script. I also performed *Marília* at the Vrystaat Kunstefees, a culturally specific community arts festival in Bloemfontein, Vrystaat, South Africa, in 2016. I published excerpts of *Marília* in *Chelsea Station* magazine (Issue #3, 2012), and presented it as part of the Classical Theater of Harlem's *Playwrights Playground* (NYC, 2015).

Marília was written as a play because I felt that the story needed to be experienced live (not told), with audience participation. The set was conceptualised as representing the cemetery where the character of Marília was buried. Following the contours of autoethnographic writing, in *Marília* I recount my journey out of a childhood of poverty, sexual trauma, and domestic violence, living in southeast Brazil, parallel to the military dictatorship of 1964-1985. Undocumented in the US, I struggled but ultimately built a successful life as a US citizen and out gay.

In 1966, at the age of two, Marília was struck and killed by a bus outside the building where our family lived. I was then ten months old, as I slept unaware of the horror that would come to shape my life, as my parents and siblings would seek to accommodate the tragedy by assigning each other blame and by 're-conceiving' me, the infant boy, as a replacement for the girl they lost. My father, who had already sexually molested three of his daughters, began to groom me. "Am I a girl?" I wondered as I wrote the play. "Am I Marília?" I guessed as I performed on stage. Marília has been a comforting presence during my childhood and adolescence in Brazil and later during the cold, dark, lonely winters of New York, where I struggled to learn English, to find jobs and housing, and to deal with homophobic violence. Throughout my life, I have been shadowed, even at times inhabited, by my sister, Marília.

Research question

A qualitative method – autoethnography in the form of self-referential theatre – calls for a conceptual framework with the capability of describing and explaining the main variables required to answer a research question. Using an autoethnographic approach for exploring one's life, I propose that an open question be asked; in this example, 'What is the impact of the loss of my sister in my life and in that of my family members?' The main question is then followed by self-created prompts to illuminate the details needed to respond to the main question. I conceptualise those details as 'variables', such as cast of characters, behaviours, and allegories that lend meaning to the life of that person whose story is being told and performed.

For this case study, I chose the theme 'crossing borders and boundaries' to explore the many facets of my relationship with my sister Marília. These include examining how Marília and I have moved from one geographic space to another (from Brazil to the US) and from one emotional state to the next. Specifically, in *Marília*, I examine three forms of crossing, but not necessarily in any pre-determined order: (1) The playwright/actor, though assigned male gender at birth, narrates and re-lives the perennial questions, "Am I a girl? Am I my dead sister?" and ponders the possibility of crossing from boy to girl; (2) the playwright/actor remembers, evokes, and communes with the dead and in so doing invites the audience to cross that realm and dwell in the space of the dead; and (3) the playwright/actor recounts the decision-making process and the actual crossing from Brazil to the US. Thus, I evoke the current situation at our southern border where poor, vulnerable immigrants, even small children, are detained, imprisoned in cages, and often denied entry by the US Immigration and Customs Enforcement.

Conceptualisation

Grounded in my life experiences and my theoretical academic inclinations, I provide a summary of the specific concepts used to guide the writing and the performance of *Marília*.

Theater of the Oppressed

As a social work researcher, my approach to self-referential theatre is grounded in the work of Brazilian theatre artist and activist Augusto Boal (1931-2009), the founder of the *Theater of the Oppressed*. Boal drew on Freire's landmark work, *Pedagogy of the Oppressed* (Freire, 2000), and asserts that theatregoers ought to be 'liberated spectators' who are launched into action. Boal (1979) notes that revolutionary theatre, or productions that question the status quo, can help to reshape socio-cultural realities. Boal's work and the work I present here reflect concepts of popular education (Portuguese, *educação popular*), advanced by Brazilian educator and philosopher Paulo Freire (1921-1997), which uses lenses of class and political struggle to view possibilities for social change or social transformation.

Brazilian literary traditions

Marília reflects mid-19th-century Brazilian Romanticism, which often dwelt on morbidity and death. Subsequently, the essayist Euclides da Cunha (1866-1909) introduced to Brazilian art and thought a powerful strain of determinism, evident in *Marília* in the struggle of the protagonist and his family to both shape and evade a narrative that will forever hold and shape *them*: the circumstances of Marília's death, including their continual parsing of the question of blame.

Brazilian Spiritism

These concepts above are amplified by Brazilian Spiritism – religion, culture, and folklore. Spiritism is a popular philosophy and religion founded by the French educator Allan Kardec (1987), who suggested that human beings have immortal spirits that temporarily inhabit the organic, physical body. According to Spiritism, spirits may come back after death to dwell in and influence the physical world (Kardec, 1987). In *Marília*, audience members join the protagonist to converse with his dead sister as he seeks to understand and accept her death.

Solo drama

Marília also belongs to the tradition of the solo drama, which is often adopted by marginalised, migrating individuals to help them own and control their narratives. Examples of solo dramas from American theatre include *The Madness of Lady Bright* (Wilson, 1964), *The International Stud* (Harvey Fierstein, 1978), *My Queer Body* (Tim Miller, 1992), *Creative Fluid* (Tim Driscoll, 1998), *I Am My Own Wife* (Doug Wright, 2003), and *Buyer and Cellar* (Jonathan Tolins, 2013). Geographical and ethnic migrants, too, have a tradition of solo, often autobiographical drama. Most prominent in the US in recent years has been the stage work of John Leguizamo (b. 1964, Bogotá, Colombia). Similarly, *Marília* confronts myriad positionalities (race, ethnicity, immigrant status) and fears (death and fear of the immigrant).

Ethnographic methods

The creative practice behind *Marília* extends my social work scholarship, which is grounded in principles of community-engaged research, involving community members in all phases of the social work research cycle, from the specification of research goals to defining methods and procedures to the dissemination of findings (Pinto et al., 2013; Pinto et al., 2018). Therefore, this autoethnographic work required collecting data in the form of semi-structured interviews with several family members, friends, and neighbours willing to share observations about the phenomenon in question, the death of my sister. I conducted multiple interviews with my mother (my father died when I was seven years old) and my six siblings. I also had informal interviews with individuals who helped me contextualise the family's behaviours. Talking to individuals outside the immediate family helped me to control for social desirability (family members telling me what they thought I wanted to hear) and to abate any bias toward a less realistic set of events that led to my sister's death (Dempsey, 2010). The type of ethnographic data described here is acceptable and desirable in the pursuit of social scientific objectives (Nelson, 2013).

To answer the research question, 'What is the impact of the loss of my sister in my life and in that of my family members?' I also engaged in the analysis of written and visual data – historical and contemporary family photographs and the content of documents, such as personal letters and birth certificates. The two-year process involved reading, viewing, and analysing these data, following a semi-structured plan. The plan included telephone and in-person interviews in Brazil and the US. I also used email for follow-up questions and to exchange documents and photographs. In interviewing, I took the time to share and to talk about subjects that could shed light on the three types of crossing – namely, my *evolving* gender identities, immigration status, and explorations in the realm of death and dying.

As suggested in the autoethnographic literature, and more specifically in self-referential theatre, I found self-healing and a better understanding of my internal conflicts and those of my family's in the process of interviews and through myriad processes. This method has the potential to also help research participants to explore internal and familial conflicts. These processes included the actual writing, giving public readings to different audiences, rehearsing to root written experiences in my body, mind, and soul, and performances. The performance of *Marília* allowed me to share elements of my life, work through conflicts, and validate my experiences. Both the play and its performance are apparent outcomes of this project. The play is the end-product of the research, a way to both embody this experience and to disseminate it among people who can identify with it, and also to help 'others', with different life experiences, to develop empathy for the issues dealt in this research. Further, at the micro level, key accomplishments also included my personal growth and healing, and the development of problem-solving capacities.

On the macro level, informal evaluations – post-reading discussions and interviews with audience members – revealed that this project has engendered a sense of social awareness around the key elements of the play and the desire to participate in advocacy efforts. I have written and performed *Marília* as a work of popular, community-based art that can be a tool for social change. Through *Marília*, I interrogate contemporary issues related to immigrant rights in the US, gender identities and gender crossing as human rights, sexual molestation as a personal, and legal and socio-cultural matter, and personal physical safety as a human right. I encourage audience members to consider these matters as individuals and as community members. My audiences have become aware that accidents, such as Marília's, are preventable in low-income areas if we, as a society, can value research and practices that could prepare us to avoid them (for example, better transportation systems, more vital legislation around childcare for low-income families). Once aware of such issues, audiences are encouraged to 'launch into action' and engage in advocacy concerning child protective services and injury prevention.

Dissemination

Marília is expected to speak to anyone who has lost a loved one, to any boundary-crosser who has carried baggage from one place to another, and to anyone who has migrated from one identity to another. The play has the potential to speak to anyone who has unpacked their past, including unspoken or abridged truths that have nonetheless guided their existence and shaped their identities. Migrants have two lives – an 'old' one from which they never entirely separate, and a 'new' one they never fully adopt. We spend our lives crossing and re-crossing boundaries and, at each seeming point of rest, unpacking more and more of the question 'Who am I?' *Marília* has, and it will continue to open community members to contemporary ideas of the self as many-faceted, mutable, assuming different positionalities and suffering from many forms of oppression. What is it like to lose a child to drugs, to a police shooting, to a forced parent/child separation that may never be reversed, or to any accident or illness that you tell yourself repeatedly was preventable? Whom do you become? How do you live?

Implications and limitations for social work research and education

I have discussed how playwriting and performance can generate innovated outputs to reach and encourage diverse audience members to consider autoethnographic self-referential theatre – as individuals and as community members. I have assigned plays and other autoethnographic materials (for example, Ntozake Shange's *For colored girls who have considered suicide when the rainbow is enuf*) as required readings for social work students, and I recommend such readings to help students develop social awareness and begin the process of self-questioning and self-healing. Self-referential theatre and performance can help students to heal their selves and to prepare them to use their selves ('use of self') in social work practice. It may help students to envision creative ways to help their family and community members pursue strategies to solve the myriad biopsychosocial problems they face in their day-to-day lives and day-to-day social work practice.

Autoethnographic research is always grounded in the life experiences and academic/ theoretical inclinations of the researcher. In this case, the researcher is a social worker, playwright, and performer. Therefore, the conceptual framework for this project is reflected in both the research question and the themes. The case study used to illustrate the use of autoethnographic research in the form of self-referential theatre reflects the notion of translocational positionality (Anthias, 2008) – an intersectionality framework that expresses the uniqueness of the ever-evolving contexts and meanings of a person's life. In autoethnography, positionalities are explicit. By being explicit, and through a process of reflexivity, researchers may embrace vulnerability in order to convey their doubts, insecurities, and uncertainties, which inevitably emerge from the outset of any research project and which persist through both the conduct of the research and its public manifestations (Peshkin, 1988; Spry, 2011, p. 54), for example, in writing and performance.

My play *Marília* has been used here to illustrate the research concepts I think are the key to understanding self-referential theatre as a form of auto ethnography. My pursuit of self-referential theatre was done apart from my empirically-driven research. *Marília* represents arduous, time-consuming labour; writing a play is emotionally draining, and this type of labour, though intense and scholarly, does not always generate the conventional academic outcomes needed for promotion and tenure in social work. Nonetheless, *Marília* has been a marvelous journey that has helped me bring together the variables that make up the story of my life and the lives of my family.

References

Adams, T., & Holman Jones, S. (2011). Telling stories: reflexivity, queer theory, and autoethnography. *Cultural Studies–Critical Methodologies, 11*(2), 108-116. doi:10.1177/1532708611401329

Anthias, F. (2008). Thinking through the lens of translocational positionality: an intersectionality frame for understanding identity and belonging. *Translocations, 4*(1), 5-20.

Boal, A. (1979). *Theatre of the Oppressed*. Theater Communications Group.

Bochner, A., & Ellis, C. (2016). *Evocative Autoethnography: Writing Lives and Telling Stories*. Routledge.

Buzard, J. (2003). On auto-ethnographic authority. *The Yale Journal of Criticism, 16*(1), 61–91. doi: 10.1353/yale.2003.0002

Dempsey, N.P. (2010). Stimulated recall interviews in ethnography. *Qualitative Sociology, 33*(2010), 349–367. https://doi.org/10.1007/s11133-010-9157-x

Ellis, C., Adams, T. E., & Bochner, A.P. (2011). Autoethnography: an overview. *Historical Social Research/Historische Sozialforschung, 36*(4), 273–290. doi: 10.17169/FQS-12.1.1589

Emunah, R. (2015). Self-revelatory performance: a form of drama therapy and theater. *Drama Therapy Review, 1*(1), 71–85.

Emunah, R. (2020). *Acting for Real: Drama Therapy Process, Technique, and Performance* (2nd ed.). Routledge, Taylor and Francis Group.

Freire, P. (2000). *Pedagogy of the Oppressed* (30th anniversary ed.). Bloomsbury.

Heddon, D. (2008). *Autobiography and performance*. Palgrave Macmillan.

Kardec, A. (1987). *The Gospel According to Spiritism* (1st ed., trans. from original 1866). The Headquarters Publishing Co.

Nelson, C.K. (2013/1994). Ethnomethodological positions on the use of ethnographic data in conversation analytic research. *Journal of Contemporary Ethnography, 23*(3), 307–329. https://doi.org/10.1177/089124194023003003

Pendzick, S., Emunah, R., & Johnson, D.R. (2016). The self in performance: context, definitions, directions. In S. Pendzick, R. Emunah, & D.R. Johnson (eds.), *The Self in Performance* (pp. 1–18). Palgrave Macmillan.

Peshkin, A. (1988). *In Search of Subjectivity – One's Own*. Educational Researcher. https://doi.org/10.3102/0013189X017007017

Pinto, R.M. (2020). *Marília*. University of Michigan, School of Social Work. https://ssw.umich.edu/faculty/profiles/tenure-track/ropinto

Pinto, R.M., Spector, S., Rahman, R., & Gastolomendo, J.D. (2013). Research advisory board members' contributions and expectations in the USA. *Health Promotion International, 30*(2), 328–338. https://doi.org/10.1093/heapro/dat042

Pinto, R.M., Witte, S., Filippone, P., & Wall, M. (2018). Recruiting and retaining service agencies and public health providers in longitudinal studies: implications for community-engaged implementation research. *Methodological Innovations, 11*(1). https://dx.doi.org/10.1177/2059799118770996

Saldãna, J. (2003). Dramatizing data: a premier. *Qualitative Inquiry, 9*(2), 218–236. https://doi.org/10.1177/1077800402250932

Schechner, R. (2013). *Performance Studies: An Introduction* (3rd ed.). Routledge.

Spry, T. (2010). Call it swing: a jazz blues autoethnography. *Cultural Studies–Critical Methodologies, 10*(4), 271–282. https://doi.org/10.1177/1532708610365476

Spry, T. (2011). *Body, Paper, Stage: Writing And performing Autoethnography.* Left Coast Press.

Wilson, L. (1964). Madness of Lady Bright. Methuen.

5

Using photography to research the 'other': the validity of photography for social work research – a visual case study from China

Peter Szto

I'll know it when I see it.

(colloquial expression)

Introduction

This chapter will examine the role of arts-based approaches for social work research. Art is understood as the human impulse to express ideas, emotions, and experience through various forms such as painting, music, architecture, or poetry. The art seeks to reflect and convey cultural sensibilities, a spiritual zeitgeist, and artistic meaning. Art is important because the dominant discourse in social work research has privileged positivist-framed data to explain human experiences. Seeking to understand why social work education has largely ignored art as a tool of research that motivates his chapter. The art form of photography, in particular, is highlighted as a reliable and valid tool of social work research. Its advantages and disadvantages are examined based on the premise that seeing is critical to what one is trying to ameliorate. A case study based on in vivo field research in China is discussed to demonstrate the value of photographic inquiry. Specifically, China's floating population – the mass internal migration of Chinese labourers from rural to urban areas – is studied as an unprecedented socio-cultural phenomenon in need of a social work response. A visual study is appropriate to clearly see the floating population for its mitigation.

Case study: China's floating population

The phenomenon of China's floating population is unprecedented. Not well known outside of China, the term 'floating population' (流动人口) was first coined in the 1980s to describe the mass movement of people without permanent settlement (Solinger, 1999; Nielsen et al., 2004). Similar terms also include 'temporary migrants', 'state-sponsored permanent migrants', and 'non-migrant urban natives' (Fan, 2005). The unregulated migratory flow of labourers into urban centres began in the early 1980s when China's central government sought to invigorate its stagnant economy. The implementation of economic reforms unintentionally created wide-spread negative consequences in cities. Some 150–200 million labourers relocated illegally in search of better jobs, higher wages, and improved standards of living. The floating population is perhaps the largest internal migration in human history (Cai, 1996; Chang 1996; Goodkind & West, 2002).

When the People's Republic of China (PRC) was established in 1949 the new regime promised its citizenry cradle-to-grave social welfare provisions, that is, food, education, employment, health care, housing, etc. China's socialist ideals was called the 'Iron Rice Bowl' (鐵飯碗) and administered through a household registration system called *hukou* (戶籍謄本). The system was based on kinship and surname affiliation, place of birth, citizenship, and location. Its purpose was to restrict social mobility in order for the central government to dispense its social welfare resources in an organised way. If someone relocated but without proper *hukou*, they were denied benefits in the new location because they had moved illegally. The government believed that *hukou* was sufficient and sustainable and therefore banned social work in the early 1950s as a professional class of helpers. However, by the late 1970s, the Iron Rice Bowl policy was unable to provide social welfare benefits to all its citizens. The policy was no longer viable and economic reforms were necessary to boost productivity and wealth.

A key component of the government reforms was establishment of Special Economic Zones (SEZs) to spur growth through private enterprise and free-market capitalism.[1] The region surrounding Guangzhou was first targeted as an SEZ because of its close proximity to Hong Kong – considered one of the world's most free economies (see Figure 5.1). The SEZs began building factories and luring millions of labourers from the countryside promising higher wages, a better quality of life, and prosperity. But not everyone secured a good factory job. Many labourers were forced to eke out a living on the street as mendicants and entrepreneurs. By the early 2000s, the floating population had become highly visible in Guangzhou but, despite their ubiquity, they were officially unseen and therefore not considered a social problem. Why the perceptual gap between their clear street presence and apparent hiddenness? More importantly, how might social work research provide credible visual evidence to reduce the perceptual gap?

According to the International Federation of Social Workers (IFSW), the mission of social work is to promote 'social change, problem solving in human relationships and the empowerment and liberation of people to

Figure 5.1: Guangzhou is indicated by the red spot

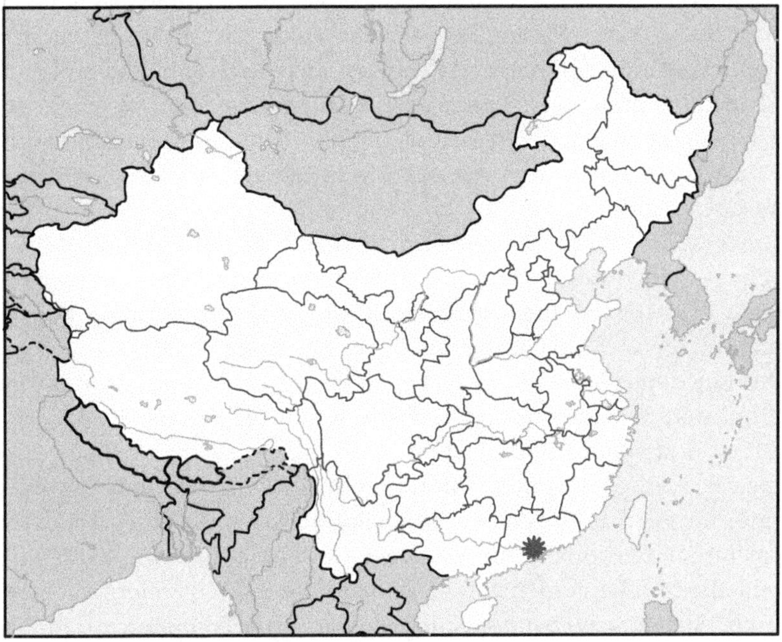

Source: http://china.strategicmanagement.net/china_travel.php

enhance well-being.'[2] Without a viable social safety net and effective social interventions, the floating population is highly vulnerable to exploitation, marginalisation, and disenfranchisement. The challenge for professional social work is to provide culturally appropriate social protections informed by reliable evidence. Documentary photography offers social work research the means to visualize what 'the floaters' look like, where they hang out, and what are their survival strategies in public places. I conducted two weeks of fieldwork in Guangzhou during the summer of 2005. Three research questions guided my research: (1) what do these internal migrants look like, (2) where do they hang out, and (3) how do they survive on the streets of Guangzhou? The purpose is to inform social work interventions based on credible visual evidence.

Arts-based research to affect change

Social work practice emerged in the late 19th century in response to many new social problems in America. Rapid urbanisation, unfettered industrialisation, and increasing secularisation were creating untold social problems – for example, racial and gender inequality, urban overcrowding, skid rows, hobos, and child labour exploitation, etc. Social work initially emerged as a first line of defence but gradually gained professional status in the 1920s – despite not having a clear set of values, specialised skills, nor coherent body of systematic knowledge. Professional identity has not come easy for social work. Tension between the validity of social work practice skills, a reliable method of service delivery, and epistemological grounding has shaped the profession to embrace the scientific method versus the arts. The viewpoint argued here is that the tension between science and art is a false dichotomy. Social work research can and should embrace both art and scientific methods.

Photography can lesson this tension because it includes both science and art. Photography was discovered in 1839 and provided the world a whole new way of seeing. For the first time it allowed observers to capture both the natural and social world with a high degree of reliability and accuracy (Szto, 2008). The camera's 'sober chronicling of the external world' (McCausland, 1939) proved an authentic and aesthetic way to document. Errol Morris (2011) also attributes photography's credibility to its authoritative and enigmatic rule over reality. Photography had the uncanny ability to produce images that looked just like reality. Soon after its discovery, artists, journalists, and portraitist bought cameras to photograph the social world around them. The academy, too, saw the potential of photography for research. Anthropology and sociology understood early the research value of photography (Collier & Collier, 1986; Banks & Murphy, 1999). For example, Evans-Pritchard (1902–1973) and Margaret Mead (1901–1978) adapted photography in their research (Edwards, 2015). More closely aligned to social work, Lewis Hine (1874–1940) used photography to document social problems. Hine's social photography was published in the premier social work journal of the day, the *Survey Graphic* (1921–1952). President Franklin D. Roosevelt also recognised the power of photography and hired Harry Hopkins, a social worker, to advance his New Deal policies through images. Between 1935 and 1944, the Farm Security Administration (FSA) produced 175,000 black-and-white photographs of the Great Depression.

Survey ceased publishing in 1952, bringing to an end a major source of visual information for social workers. The end of *Survey* did not stop sociologically oriented photographers – for example, Bruce Davidson, Sebastio Salgado, Mary Ellen Mark, and Diane Arbus – from documenting social problems. In 1998, social work professor, Daniel D. Huff, reminded the profession how the FSA photographers used images to impact social change. He also challenged the profession to once again use photography in social work research. More recently, Photovoice was developed in 1992 by Caroline Wang and Mary Ann Burris (1997) as a community-based participatory method. Putting cameras in the hands of subjects empowers people to photograph their own lived experience. Many social work researchers have since embraced Photovoice as a valid research method to evoke empathy, humanise social problems, and effect social change.

Methodology: the validity of visual inquiry

The most appropriate method to address research questions on the floating population is documentary photography as a means of observational analysis. Observations of everyday phenomenon aspire to a holistic understanding of events in their natural settings. In my visual study, the floating population was made visible using the camera to observe and document what they look like, where they hang out, and how they survive on the streets of Guangzhou. The premise of the study was that seeing a social problem is requisite to solving it. Ironically, social problems also persist in spite of reliable and valid visual evidence, or brute facts. Credible visual evidence, however, is necessary to correctly perceive social problems.

Why the bias against qualitative visual evidence? Richard Titmuss of the London School of Economics argued in the 1950s that statistical analysis offers the best means to objectively describe and explain social problems. He believed quantitative analysis was indispensable for clear-eyed seeing of problems. Statistical reasoning provided the best explanation on how discreet variables were causally related 'by falsifying a no-relationship hypothesis' (R. Titmuss, personal communication, n.d., p. 1). The quantitative approach required reducing the whole of reality into numbers, frequency, proportion, size, and scale. The reduction of the whole into parts, however, involves a loss of meaning. Quantitative methods have dominated social work research despite its limitation to holistically describe what phenomenon look like. Visual sociologist, Jon C. Wagner (2004) explains that 'no object of social inquiry can be fully understood without attending to' (p. 55) its visible qualities and that 'all objects of social inquiry have important material and visible dimensions' (p. 55). Visualising the floating population is important to understand their inherent material qualities.

A visual study of the floating population is important because a casual observer might assume all the floaters were vagrants, beggars, homeless, or a drain on society – rather than the unintended but direct consequence of policy. Visual evidence challenges these naïve assumptions of what the floaters look like, where they hang out, and their survival strategies.

Field work

I was awarded a research grant in 2005 to conduct fieldwork in Guangzhou, China. My fieldwork involved daily walks documenting the floating population. In the spirit of street photographers Walker Evans, Helen Levitt, Bruce Davidson, Garry Winogrand, and Lee Friedlander, I sought to capture the immediacy and intensity of chance encounters. The randomness of Guangzhou's street life required reflexive reaction to document floating population.

I began the fieldwork by looking without my camera as I strolled. After two days I felt more comfortable and started wearing my camera to take pictures. Since all cities have their own unspoken rules and vibe it was important to initially take a flaneurist's posture. Each successive day I gained increased sensitivity to the rules and learned how to photograph unobtrusively. Staying focused was critical to identify the visible and invisible floating population amidst Guangzhou's hustle and bustle. Reflexive analysis was necessary to anticipate when to press the shutter and capture that 'decisive moment'. Reflexivity required blending into the street as to appear hidden just like the floating population. The better I was camouflaged the better I could photograph the floating population. I wanted to gain an emic perspective through immersion. A stealthy posture was key to getting an authentic visual story.

In street photography an unspoken dialogue exists between 'subject' and 'observer-of-subjects'. The dialogue functions 'to articulate submerged realities' (Pink et al., 2004, p. 1) undetected at first glance. The dialogue requires split-second decisions on all aspects of camera operations: angle composition, exposure, distance-to-subject positioning, and subject selection. In social work parlance, making decisions on what to photograph or not to photograph, entailed an acute sensitivity regarding 'person-in-environment' (Karls, 1997). What is that person doing? Why are they doing it? How did they get to this particular spot? Some social situations also required the suspension of disbelief to honour and respect individuals' human dignity.

Visual evidence

I took approximately 1400 digital photographs of Guangzhou's floating population. These 1400 bits of data tell a compelling story but obviously are too many to share here. I have selected six photographs to share as credible visual evidence. They represent in visual form what the floating population looked like, where they hung out, and how they survived on the streets of Guangzhou. Accompanying each photograph is a brief narrative regarding context plus a short personal commentary.

Figure 5.2 is a middle-aged male begging in the gutter. He is lying on his right side in a busy street intersection. Many walked right past him and even more ignore him while headed to their destination. The man's right arm is outstretched holding a small plastic container for passersby to give him money. Most appear not to notice him and calmly stroll by without donating anything into his plastic cup. I witness scenes like this throughout Guangzhou, but this grabbed my attention because of where he was begging – he was literally in the gutter. I also found telling his deep tan. Long exposure to Guangzhou's intense sub-tropical sun will give you a tan. Finally, it was hard to believe that anyone would subject themselves to the bright midday sun just to beg. I took several photographs of this man to disprove my disbelief.

Figure 5.2: Mendicant – *Man in the Gutter*

Source: Author.

Figure 5.3: Entrepreneur – *Two Street Vendors*

Source: Author.

Figure 5.3 documents two young men presumably selling fake CDs. Copyright abuses and selling counterfeit CDs was pervasive in China. These two fly-by-night street vendors were holding trays full of CDs and standing ready for a quick get away if public security officers came by.

Selling contraband on the street is illegal in China but, because so many were doing it, it was near impossible for local authorities to stop the illicit activity. Ironically, if you look closely, just to the right of the two men is a public security officer sitting under the tree. His shirt and shoulder insignia reveals his identity. Interestingly, the officer is glancing away and seemingly unaware of their illegal activity, or intentionally chooses to ignore them. Not seeing this illegal activity reinforces the perception that the floating population were invisible.

Figure 5.4 is a woman selling exotic animal parts with a child on her lap. She is squatting on a short stool waiting for a customer. I spotted her in Guangzhou's Qing Ping Market famous for wholesale herbs and spices. She is selling different herbs and assorted animal hoofs, tusks, and bone parts, presumably for medicinal purposes. The hacksaw to the right of her foot is for cutting animal bones into smaller pieces. This woman selling bone parts was a rare scene although indicative of the floating population's entrepreneurial spirit.

Figure 5.5 is a blind street musician playing traditional Chinese music. The man was playing with passion and purpose. To me his playing sounded pretty good. He apparently understood the strategic value of his location since it was in a high foot traffic area. Some passersby did put small change into his tin can, but not many. I thought it was interesting that he could not see who was giving money but that the donors could see him.

Figures 5.6 and 5.7 are two persons sleeping in public. These two were visible to others while they appear invisible through sleep. Figure 5.6 is a sleeper sitting upright on a corner bench. Despite the city's loud hustle and bustle, the woman is fast asleep. She is also wearing a light jacket which was odd in the 90-plus degree heat and humidity. Figure 5.7 is a scene of bags piled on the floor on an overpass walkway. The bags appear innocuous but, on closer examination, one can see ten toes sticking out. Obviously, the toes belong to a person under the bags. These two photographs are good examples of social camouflage.

Conclusion

This chapter explored the reliability and validity of photography as a tool of social work research. Bias in social work research favouring quantitative methods at the expense of arts-based approaches was examined in terms of advantages and disadvantages. A visual case study on China's floating population was presented to demonstrate the validity and usefulness of photography for social work research. An advantage of photographs – or visual evidence – is how they provide indisputable proof on the existence of the floating population regarding what they look like, where they hang out,

Figure 5.4: Entrepreneur – *Animal Parts*

Source: Author.

and their survival strategies. Photographs of the floating population provide a clear advantage rather than merely relying on descriptive statistics alone. The visual case study affirmed the value of documentary photography to make visible what was difficult to see. Photography enhanced understanding of the floating population's visible qualities to promote a holistic perspective.

Figure 5.5: Music – *Blind Musician*

Source: Author.

Figure 5.6: Sleeper I

Source: Author.

Figure 5.7: Sleeper II

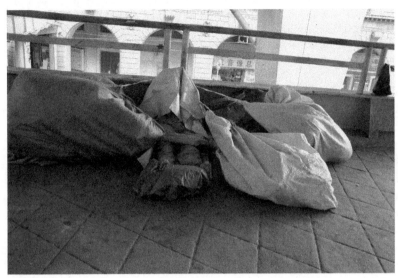

Source: Author.

One can see how person-in-environment impacts the quality of life of the floaters. The photographs captured both the individual and their surrounding milieu. Finally, the role of visual aesthetics, on the part of social work researcher and viewers, was also significant to persuasively convey their life situations.

The use of photography is not a panacea for all research studies. A limitation of this visual case study is the collection of evidence at a specific point in time. The photographs only represent what I saw for two weeks in July 2005, and only then. The visual data was also limited to the one city of Guangzhou – albeit a reliable representative sample of the floating population vis-à-vis a SEZ. A missing comparative perspective would be visual evidence from other major cities like Shanghai, Beijing, or Chongqing. A longitudinal study at Guangzhou would also be prudent to account for possible missing data. What does the floating population look like during the other three seasons? Photography also requires adept camera handling skills and aesthetic sensibility. These skills can be acquired but not necessarily natural to all social work researchers. It might involve time to learn and practice. A final disadvantage of photography involves ethical issues. The social work researcher must be sensitive to the role of informed consent, especially in a cross-cultural and international context. It is highly recommended to become familiar with country-specific regulations and guidelines on the use of photography in social research and, in particular, photo release forms for public domain subjects.

Notes

[1] In 1978, the 3rd Plenary Session of the 11th Communist Party of China Central Committee met and decided to establish SEZs. The first SEZs established in 1989 were: Shenzhen, Zhuhai, and Shantou in Guangdong Province, Xiamen in Fujian Province, and the entire island of Hainan.

[2] http://ifsw.org/policies/definition-of-social-work/

References

Banks, M., & Murphy, H. (Eds.) (1999). *Rethinking Visual Anthropology*. Yale University Press.

Cai, F. (1996). Causes, trends, and policy of population migration and the floating population. *Chinese Journal of Population Science, 8*(2), 179–191.

Chang, S. (1996). The floating population: an informal process of urbanisation in China. *International Journal of Population Geography, 2*, 197–214.

Collier, J., & Collier. M. (1986) *Visual Anthropology: Photography as a Research Method*. University of New Mexico Press.

Edwards, E. (2015). Anthropology and photography: a long history of knowledge and affect. *Photographies, 8*(3), 235–252.

Fan, C. C. (2005). Interprovincial migration, population redistribution, and regional development in China: 1990 and 2000 census comparisons. *The Professional Geographer, 57*(2), 295–311.

Goodkind, D., & West, L. (2002). China's floating population: definitions, data and recent findings. *Urban Studies, 39*(12), 2237–2250.

Karls, J.M. (1997). The use of the PIE (person-in-environment) system in social work education. *Journal of Social Work Education, 33*(1), 49–58.

McCausland, E. (1939). Documentary Photography. *Photo Notes*, January 1939, 1-2.

Morris, E. (2011). *Believing Is Seeing (Observations on the Mysteries of Photography)*. Penguin.

Nielsen, I., Smyth, R., & Zhang, M. (2004). Unemployment within China's floating population: empirical evidence from Jiangsu survey data. www.buseco.monash.edu.au/units/aberu/papers/unemployment-china-floating-population.pdf

Pink, S., Kurti, L., & Afonso, A. (Eds.) (2004). *Working Images: Visual Research and Representation in Ethnography*. Routledge. www.personal.psu.edu/wxh139/Quality.htm

Solinger, D.J. (1999). China's floating population: implications for state and society. In R. MacFarquhar & M. Goldman (Eds.), *The Paradox of China's Post-Mao Reforms* (pp. 220–240). Harvard University Press.

Szto, P. (2008). Documentary photography in American social welfare history: 1897–1943. *The Journal of Sociology & Social Welfare, 35*(2). https://scholarworks.wmich.edu/jssw/vol35/iss2/6

Titmuss, R. (n.d.) Personal communication.

Wagner, J. (2004). Constructing credible images: documentary studies, social research, and visual studies. *Visual Studies, 47*(12), 1477–1506.

Wang, C., & Burris, M. (1997). Photovoice: concept, methodology, and use for participatory needs assessment. *Health, Education, & Behavior, 24*(3), 369–387.

6

Mixed arts-based methods as a platform for expressing lived experience

Orna Shemer and Eitan Shahar

'A joint fate' was the topic chosen by the co-researchers, young adults with disabilities, as one of the topics of the research that they wanted to study in-depth. In the preparatory meeting concerning collection of data on the topic they discussed that many songs, some of which are protest songs, were written by people who shared a joint fate and the desire to change their situation in society, like Bob Marley. Therefore, they decided that this would be the topic they would study by writing poems.

In the research meeting, they invited the co-researchers to work in groups and to find people among them who shared a fate and to express this in a song/poem that they would present. The data that were collected included the poems, the discussion about them, and the ways in which people participated in the discourse.

We used poems, stories, plays, photographs, cards, and other methods in the participatory action research (PAR) that we undertook together with young adults with disabilities. The study explored their lives in preparatory programmes for independent living which were run by the NGO, Gvanim. In our research, we explored together the meaning participation in Gvanim's programmes had for the young adults. By employing different artistic instruments, we had a varied platform, which allowed the young adults to connect and to express their meaningful knowledge – their knowledge from experience, expressed through arts. Turning life experiences into expert and meaningful knowledge from which theoretical insights could be formulated and actions that can have social impacts designed, was made possible via art. The art served as the foundation for the psychological–mental–morale activity, through which expansion of creativity that renews knowledge creates channels for the expression of the knowledge and forges social ties, which make exchange of knowledge possible.

The research design

This study was a PAR study in which the researchers work together with the co-researchers in a repeated cooperative and spiraled process of collection of knowledge, analysis, and action (Arieli et al., 2009). The study was designed to deepen 'knowledge from experience', which is created from personal experiences of the group members. The research participants were young adults coping with different disabilities (psychological crises, autism, or physical and sensory disabilities), who were integrated into programmes run by the NGO, Gvanim, and were living together in the community.

The NGO Gvanim provides services to over 1700 people with disabilities in more than 25 programmes, which include specialisation in the field of young adults between the ages of 18 and 35. Gvanim aims to facilitate service users' achievement of self-realisation, as people and as citizens, and to integrate into society in an active and contributing manner. The programmes make it possible for their participants to gain experience in different life roles and to undergo significant processes in personal, group, and community aspects.

Fourteen people, who are involved in Gvanim's programmes and six employees, who fill different roles, participated in the research. The group met ten times – once a week – in one of the activity centres belonging to the NGO. Some of the meetings were facilitated by the head-researchers and most of them by co-researchers. Later, some of these members formed a team that took part in analysis and presentation of the data.

'Lived experience' / 'knowledge from experience' as a research design that redefines what is 'knowledge'

This study faced two central challenges, connected to knowledge.

The basis of the knowledge: This study was mainly based on the desire to present lived experience by relating to the co-researchers as "experts by experience." Expertise from knowledge is a relatively new term in the field of social services that has raised questions concerning the strength and nature of the concept that neither defines kinds of knowledge, nor the criteria for its acquisition (McLaughlin, 2009). Moreover, when the concept is ascribed to people with disabilities – whose mental or emotional state can influence their decision-making – the validity and clarity of the term may be weakened and destabilised even more.

The study aspires to include the authentic voices of people whose voices are rarely heard and, even if they are heard, are usually interpreted by others who, as a result, blur their authenticity (Walmsley & Johnson, 2003). This study was based on the PAR understanding that young adults bring new and important knowledge that is based on their life experiences. Furthermore, they are able to present a picture of their complex realities, which allows for the construction of plausible theories (Sullivan, 2006). We assume that arts can help to capture this complex picture. By assuming that the young adults had the ability to be co-researchers, it was possible to design a PAR study in which they chose the topic of the research and collected the data. Furthermore, some of them were active partners in interpreting the data and in presentation of the research results.

Presentation of the knowledge as arts-based data: Knowledge is traditionally transmitted via spoken or written words, through familiar and accepted terminology. At times, lived experience is not expressed in a clear and coherent manner even though it is deserving of attention, brings new information, and contributes to our knowledge. Due to its nature, lived experience is often characterised by conversational, descriptive terminology, which is expressed in a narrative and emotional manner. This is subjective knowledge; it is often intuitive, and it does not match well-known, positivistic, rational, and coherent theories and facts. It is understood from examples, attitudes, and stories and is often expressed in powerful, indirect, metaphorical, visual, or implied ways. At times, it needs to be mediated (Shemer, 2019). Therefore, this type of knowledge is perceived as less relevant, valid, logical, and legitimate.

The critical perception of the hierarchy of knowledge (Yarbrough, 2020) motivated us to find a variety of expressions that would make it possible to extend and present knowledge in a clear, accessible, and deep manner. As a result, from an epistemological aspect, the use of art allowed us to work on a legitimate stage and laid a foundation for an interpretive discourse, which invites a rich discourse.

The rationale for using an arts-based mixed-methods approach

The use of art as a means of study that is inclusive and expresses lived experience: Lived experience can be expressed in a myriad of ways. The most frequent ones are stories, examples, descriptions of feelings, and expression of thoughts accumulated during life's experiences. The content and style in which the knowledge is presented testifies to its strength and to its great wisdom. The use of arts opened possibilities for the expression of insights in a number of ways, since, at times, words may actually impede or narrow complex multifaceted expression. The ability to work in abstract, flexible, and free ways, from inner expression and via the imagination, expands the ability to embody knowledge that, as a rule, is excluded and latent. It is difficult for young adults with disabilities, especially those who are limited in speech, to express themselves and their emotions and they often feel a lack of confidence in their knowledge. In this study, they were given the equal opportunity to express themselves through the endless possibilities found in art – an instrument for emancipatory expression.

PAR is included under the umbrella of inclusive research methods (Walmsley & Johnson, 2003) and anti-oppressive research methods (Strier, 2006). Since the artistic creations of the 'research participants' are presented in a direct and respectful manner to the audience, this leaves the power in the co-researchers' hands, without the mediating interpretation of researchers, who may distort their meanings.

Art provides a rich platform for expression of knowledge, including critical knowledge: On the one hand, art offers a wide range of styles of expression. On the other hand, the richness of possible interpretations creates an opening of an unmined pool of kinds of knowledge. The encounter with creating art, and reflecting upon it, can create something new that will take place, due to the subjective encounter between the creator, via her/his creation and the people who look at it, via their experiences. It will always be an unexpected encounter. Moreover, the universal language and the indirect dimension of art makes it easier to transmit critical messages that perhaps would not be expressed in other ways, especially by minority populations (Sullivan, 2006; Huss, 2013).

Art as strengthening partnership: The use of artistic instruments extended the channels of communication between the research participants. Through making room for the expression of emotions and experiences in multiple ways, closeness and solidarity can sprout. In this way, partnership can develop between the creators and, later on, between the creators and the people who viewed their work.

Research instruments as a basis for a 'transitional space' that arouses action

During the research meetings, together with the co-researchers, we employed several artistic methods to create an intimate and productive 'transitional space' (Friedman et al., 2016) for undertaking the study and enhancing the co-production of knowledge between researchers and research participants. This transitional space invites the creation of a joint social space for a change in awareness, through encounters with the other (Friedman, 2011). The shared art processes are a necessary stage for the creation of the stage of action, which is an inseparable part of the progress of the action research.

Our acquaintance with the co-researchers and the development of the group process made it possible for us to choose appropriate methods and to understand how to make the methods accessible to some of the research group. Since half of the meetings were organised by the research participants, together with us, we could encourage them to use different artistic means that they liked.

Here is a description of some of the methods we used to collect data, for interpretation, and for presentation of the results.

The play and the role play

In the research, we used instruments taken from the world of theatre. For example, one meeting dealt with the meaning of partnership for the young adults, in which they were asked to remember a personal experience of partnership they had in their life. The participants were divided into small groups and each member shared her/his story, while the group members asked questions in order to better understand the story. In the next stage, each group chose one of the memories that reflected for them a story of partnership, and they prepared a play to present in the big group. After the presentation of each play, there was a group discussion, which made it possible to learn about the experience of partnership in depth.

The process of writing and performing plays opened a reflexive and experiential discourse about narrative, which required group cooperation. The plays sharpened the patient and inclusive coping of the participants, who have disabilities (physical handicaps, problems with speech, problems understanding certain content). As a result, nobody was left out and everyone expressed her/himself in her/his own way and, thus, contributed to the group knowledge base. Each play earned applause and serious consideration in terms of its contribution to understanding joint experiences.

Photovoice

One of the concepts that the group wanted to study was 'independence' and its meaning for the young adults. We used photographs that the young adults took, found in their personal photo albums, or found in other sources. Each member added an original text or another text that they chose (a headline, a metaphor, a quote). Big, colour prints were made of the photographs that were chosen and they were taped to sheets of big white paper.

Before the meeting, we hung the photographs on the wall, which created a group exhibit on the theme of independence. At the beginning of the meeting, the participants were asked to walk around and look at the photographs, like in an exhibit in a gallery. During the next stage, each co-researcher presented her/his photograph with the text.

At the end of the round, everyone was asked to walk around all the photographs and to personally respond to them, by saying a word or a sentence, or via a graphic element. This process of expressing, observing and discussion enlarged the repertoire of pathways to expressing knowledge.

Singing and music

Singing and music were used throughout the study, as instruments for creativity and personal expression of the participants and as instruments we used which for presenting the research in interactive meetings and afterwards. The musical creations aroused significant responses to topics, such as identity, belonging or not belonging, weakness and power. One of the participants – a young adult – is an artist, who composed songs about the content of the study. These songs became the 'topic songs' or organising metaphors for theoretical elements.

Use of creative writing and statements as an expression of personal and collective narratives

The progression of the research meetings created a variety of texts made by the young adults who participated in the study. The meetings were taped and transcribed. During the joint work of analysis, undertaken together by the head-researchers and co-researchers, we discerned authentic sentences and statements of personal narratives, attitudes, emotions, and meanings concerning the experiences of the young adults with disabilities.

These statements were compiled into a literary creation, which used metaphors and quotes from philosophers and proverbs. These texts were put up in exhibition so that people could hear about the research. Most of the statements were put on a table, on the floor, or were printed on one page. Each participant chose a statement and shared a personal story that connected to living with a disability. In this way, the people interested in the study and observers of the study became partners in the research and the knowledge became interactive.

The young adults and Gvanim are planning on publishing a book, *An Illustrated Statement Book*, inspired by the statements of lived experience of the young adults living with disabilities. The book is an initiative of the co-researchers and, through this book, they emphasise the need to connect to the wider public and influence its stigmatic stances toward people with disabilities.

Looking at the research results: second degree accessibility

The research produced several interesting findings about the lives of young adults with disabilities. In terms of the research process, this study transformed the position of the co-researchers from a status of 'research population' to partners in excavating and constructing the knowledge. We conceptualised this shift in position as 'accessibility in the second degree'.

In contrast to accessibility in the first degree, which focuses on matching and arranging communication channels, functioning, and activity for people with disabilities, accessibility in the second degree expresses the critical call of the young adults for a change in consciousness. A change in their consciousness concerning themselves – concerning their power and resilience – and a change in the consciousness of their surrounding society, concerning perceptions and behaviours that decrease the abilities and dreams of people with disabilities. From their understanding, only action around this change will lead to a transformation in the reality in their lives. As a result, for example, they developed a 'proverb's' workshop that was described above.

Conclusions about the use of arts-based methods in research

Over the years, arts-based research has led to continued discourse about the essence of knowledge and research (Leavy, 2020). Traditional and conservative perceptions have delayed acknowledgement of its qualities and advantages. However, it is important to discuss such methods in order to deepen and negotiate their basic assumptions and advantages. For example, we found that using arts-based methods helped unpack processes of knowledge creation and transitional spaces within which knowledge can be created and it helps to demonstrate that knowledge can appear in different ways and represent different realities. Art also has the ability 'to grasp' or to disseminate knowledge and express it in ways that other methods cannot.

Another finding was that artistic methods serve as a meeting point between emotional and cognitive insights, as well as between the universal, cultural, and the personal perspectives on the experience. Therefore, their power is found in the expression of the individual's phenomenological experience within the structural context (Huss, 2013). Offering a variety of forms of artistic expression gave the co-researchers a chance to find a medium through which they could express themselves subjectively and authentically, and also to find their collective narratives in a variety of ways and to actively engage and contribute to people who were interested in the study's results.

Another element was the sense of playfulness and pleasure that the art gave, as well as providing social interaction and sense of empowerment and meaningful experience. This secondary benefit makes it a suitable choice to integrate empowerment as well as research. In our study, we saw the co-researchers laugh, make new friendships, create alone and with others, and expand their imaginations and artistic powers. This is very important as it makes the research context more pleasurable and people more motivated to contribute to the research. In continuation of this, the art was an equitable experience, despite the disabilities some participants live with. The use of different artistic means, throughout the research process, made it possible for everyone to express themselves more using the means that were most comfortable, clear, and accessible for them. If the study had only employed verbal means (group discussions, personal interviews, or questionnaires), it is clear to us that there would have been co-researchers who would not have been at their best using this mode. This could have even led to them experiencing being silenced due to their difficulty in expressing themselves in words. We believe that the arts helped make the findings more accessible to those interested in the research. Presentation of the research via songs, stories, photography, or activity extended the research's ability to reverberate among more people and to arouse different responses.

We also saw that the arts-based methods relaxed the hierarchy between the head researchers and the co-researchers. An experience was created in which we all could engage in the joint creativity. This study was a creation that could be expressed in many ways, and one in which the researchers did not have ownership over the method or the knowledge that was produced. We were positioned as partners in this journey while simultaneously being the leaders of the research who integrated and organised it. This led us to 'walk on a tightrope' and was a new experience for us, as researchers. The relaxing of the relations made it possible for us to often engage in reflexivity, which helped us maintain this position.

Ethics. The significance of engaging in ethical work accompanied us throughout the study and became intensified, due to our use of art. For example, we dealt with the ethics of inclusiveness concerning accessibility of artistic instruments for all the participants. In order to ensure inclusiveness, we organised things ahead of time so that the young adults who had trouble expressing themselves – physically, verbally, or psychologically – received help from us or from Gvanim employees who participated in the study. For example, we wrote things down for them or helped them physically present their work and move around. We also made ourselves available between the meetings, so that we could support them and relate to content that the study aroused.

Another example of an ethical issue connects to ethics of copyright concerning the publication of artworks and ethics of research connected to the discussion about the art products. All the participants signed a consent form that we gave to them and explained to them. Specifically, we asked the young adults for their permission to present and/or to write about their personal creations at conferences or in articles. If they agreed, we gave them the choice whether their works would be published with their name or whether a pseudonym would be used. Related ethical considerations connected to maintaining the partnership, which is expected in participatory research (Khanloua & Peter, 2005). We dealt with this in the writing and reflexive discussions that we held between us in order to remain aware of the power relations in the study.

In conclusion, in this research the numerous ways of employing art proved that lived experience is valid and new knowledge. It compensated for the disabilities that impeded research when only words were used and it turned this study into a creative, colourful, inspiring, touching, and connecting endeavour. The developing process made it possible for us to deepen the content and to hear critical content from the young adults.

References

Arieli, D., Friedman, V.J., & Agbaria, K. (2009). The paradox of participation in action research. *Action Research, 7*(3), 263–290.

Friedman, V.J. (2011). Revisiting social space: relational thinking about organizational change. In A.B. (Rami) Shani, R.W. Woodman, & W.A. Pasmore (Eds.), *Research in Organizational Change and Development* (Vol. 19, pp. 233–257). Emerald.

Friedman, V.J., Sykes, I., Lapidot-Lefler, N., & Haj, N. (2016). Social space as a generative image for dialogic organization development. *Research in Organizational Change and Development, 24*, 113–144.

Huss, E. (2013). *What We See and What We Say: Using Images in Research, Therapy, Empowerment, and Social Change.* Routledge.

Khanloua, N., & Peter, E. (2005). Participatory action research: considerations for ethical review. *Social Science & Medicine, 60,* 2333–2340.

Leavy, P. (2020). *Method Meets Arts. Art-Based Research Practice* (3rd ed.). Guilford Press.

McLaughlin, H. (2009). What's in a name: 'client', 'patient', 'customer', 'consumer', 'expert by experience', 'service user' – What's next? *British Journal of Social Work, 39,* 1101–1117. doi:10.1093/bjsw/bcm155

Shemer, O. (2019). *A Story About Learning from the Participation and the Non-Participation of People Living in Poverty.* ATD Fourth World UK. https://atd-uk.org/2019/04/15/in-the-paths-of-participation-learning-from-not-sharing-with-people-living-in-poverty/

Strier, R. (2006). Anti-oppressive research in social work a preliminary definition. *British Journal of Social Work, 40*(6), 1908–1926.

Sullivan, G. (2006). Research acts in art practice. *Studies in Art Education, 48*(1), 19–35. DOI: 10.1080/00393541.2006.11650497

Walmsley, J., & Johnson, K. (2003). *Inclusive Research with People with Learning Disabilities: Past, Present, and Futures.* Jessica Kingsley Publishers.

Yarbrough, D. (2020). 'Nothing about us without us': reading protests against oppressive knowledge production as guidelines for solidarity research. *Journal of Contemporary Ethnography, 49*(1), 58–85. DOI: 10.1177/0891241619857134

7

Arts-based methods to support and reveal new mothers' and families' experiences: a positive parenting and feminist approach

Lucía Hervás Hermida

Introduction

The situation of families and the transition to new motherhood are experiencing deep changes globally. Parental roles and family models are transforming from traditional ones. There is a growing concern about family needs and family's socialising and educational function, which has led to the development of the positive parenting approach and family support measures, focusing on supporting parenting roles for optimal child development.

But, what are mothers' needs and challenges within their parenting role? What is their perspective of what parenting means? We have observed that despite the advances made in terms of women's rights and equality, motherhood still has profound implications for women's lives and identities, as it is related to strong social expectations. Usually, maternal care is undertaken from within the physiological and medical frameworks, but such care rarely takes into account the emotional, relational, and cultural aspects of the transition to motherhood. In fact, cultural representations mostly show an idealised image of motherhood, making real mothers' first-hand experiences invisible.

From an intersectional feminist perspective, there is the need to develop new references and the collective imagination of what being a mother means. What kind of models of motherhood do we want to create? What could be the role of arts-based methods for understanding the needs of new mothers and family support?

This chapter will present a research project set in Spain which focused on exploring and evaluating arts-based support for new mothers and families (Hervás Hermida, 2018). The programme is in response to the Comprehensive Plan for Family Support 2015–2017 (Council of Ministers of Spain, 2015) and is focused on addressing the socio-cultural dimensions of reproduction and nurturing. This chapter will focus on arts-based methods to evaluate an arts-based intervention program (McNiff, 1998). Its assumption is that arts-based methods can better evaluate an intervention that is based on the artist.

Researching the impact of art therapy for mothers and families as a way to support positive parenting using arts-based methods[1]

The Comprehensive Plan for Family Support 2015–2017 (2015), drafted by the Council of Ministers of Spain, offers a diagnosis of the situation of Spanish families, and the need for coordinated actions that include both psychosocial and prevention measures. This document was developed within the framework of the European family support strategy, established in 2006 by the Council of Ministers of Europe (2006) with *Recommendation REC (2006) 19 on Policy to Support Positive Parenting*.[2]

This strategy emphasises the importance of educational and preventative programmes that focus on parental competencies as a way to enhance child development (Rodrígo López, 2015). For that purpose, art therapy has be found to be suitable, looking at the possibilities that offer a creative group framework as well as using images as pathways to explore family dynamics (Hogan, 2003, 2015, 2020; Proulx, 2003; Riley & Malchiody, 2003; Kerr et al., 2011; Hoshino, 2015; Hogan et al., 2017).

The project sought to know the possibilities of using art therapy for new mothers and families as a form of psychosocial intervention, focusing on the development of art therapy methods that are effective as a way to support positive parenting. From the feminist perspective, a focus on the mother´s personal experiences and women's empowerment was also included, as well as a cultural focus on contemporary artistic expressions of motherhood.

The chosen approach for this research was a plural methodology. This research combined the evidence-based practice paradigm, as well as the constructionist, feminist, and postmodern postulates, with a special emphasis on evaluation as a way to create guidelines for informed practice (Gilroy, 2006; Gilroy et al., 2012). Art and visual methods were included not only to raise evidence, documentation through images and films, but also to enhance a deep understanding of processes and dynamics through artistic ways of knowing.

Three complementary studies have been undertaken:

- A consultation with experts in which we have asked experienced art therapists about their practice with mothers and families using arts.
- A multiple case study, in which two cycles of intervention have been conducted and evaluated, in three different settings: in the educational, social, and health fields.
- A curatorial study, a sample of artwork made by contemporary artists, about their experience of motherhood.

In this chapter I will focus on the last two, where visual methods have played a fundamental role.

The multiple case study

This practice-based study followed a spiral process inspired by action research (Elliott, 1986). It included two intervention cycles in the educational, social, and health fields, which were evaluated in three stages: previous assessment, implementation, and final evaluation. The reflections and findings from each cycle led to conclusions applicable to the next one, until finally we arrived at more consistent conclusions. Data analysis and triangulation of all the cases were then compared, regarding the construction of guidelines for practice.

The evaluation was approached from different perspectives, looking at the complexity of art therapy interventions, focusing on participants' experiences and images as witness to the process. We included two questionnaires, before the beginning and after the end of the process, and followed the process using field diaries and observation sheets. Several focus groups and interviews were also conducted. All of these together created a rich basis for the evaluation.

The arts-based approach was included in order to document and reveal the creative and interactive process with photographs and films, and as a form of evaluation including two specific techniques to create collective knowledge within the focus group sessions, explained below (see Figures 7.1–7.4).

The 'basket' evaluation technique:[3] a very simple drawing technique, in which participants are asked to think metaphorically of the experience of the workshop as some kind of 'fruit collection'. The drawing of the basket symbolises what they have acquired, the 'fruits' of the experience. During the last session, they are asked to reflect visually on which aspects of the experience have been 'fruitful' for them, and which have not, so they would remove them from their basket. Normal paper, crayons, and markers can be used for this purpose. Some evocative questions can be posed. What does the basket look like? Is it a big basket or small one? Hard or soft? This all provides information about their personal experience. A direction to include both verbal expressions and drawing can be explicitly given.

After finishing their drawing, they are invited to share their drawings and reflections with the group, as the beginning and catalyst of the focus group. It is important to note that, in this manner, participants can feel free to conduct a deep self-introspection, and then decide what they want to share with the group. When listening to other participants' statements, resonance usually occurs, expanding their perspectives.

The collective development of a creative mind map of the experience: during the conversation within the focus group, participants are invited to portray their thoughts on a big paper. The same markers and crayons can be used for this purpose, encouraging participants to develop a spontaneous and

Figure 7.1: Details of "The basket" and mind map art based techniques

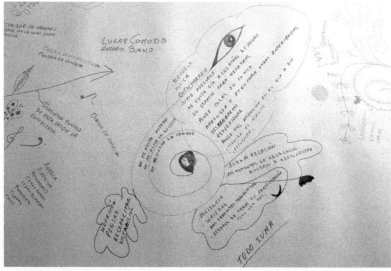

Source: Images included were created by parents in the art therapy interventions undertaken in Aranjuez and Calpe during the years 2015–2017.

Figure 7.2: Details of "The basket" and mind map art based techniques

Source: Author.

Figure 7.3: Details of "The basket" and mind map art based techniques

Source: Author.

Figure 7.4: Details of "The basket" and mind map art based techniques

Source: Author.

quick 'not thinking too much' kind of drawing and mapping. This way the ideas that emerge during the conversation can be expressed through drawings, scribbles, and concepts, resulting in a visual mind map of the focus group experience.

The curatorial project

The research culminated with a curatorial study through the collection and selection of images made by contemporary artists who have explored their motherhood. The sample included a selection of seven artists: Ana Casas Broda, Trish Morrissey, Natalia Iguíñiz Boggio, Ana Álvarez Errecalde, Cristina Llanos, Elinor Carucci, and Offmothers collective (Susana Carro Fernández, Elena de la Puente, Natalia Pastor, Roxana Popelka, Blanca Prendes, Gema Ramos, and Eugenia Tejón) (Hervás Hermida, 2018).

This study focused on the creative and expressive potential of the arts as a way of articulating maternal experiences. It is halfway between a documentary study and a creative process, following the rhizomatic process of a/r/tography as a reference (Irwin et al., 2006).

This study also underpins the social dimension of motherhood, dealing with an issue frequently overlooked by the dominant culture. Women artists have traditionally had little presence in art history (Bartra, 1987; Nochlin, 1988; Lopez Fernandez Cao, 2000), and so representations of motherhood have been dominated by male perspectives that portray an idealised vision of motherhood. The imaginary concerning motherhood shows a very restrictive model, with only young, feminine, white, and nourishing women: stereotypes that operate to maintain socially acceptable models of motherhood and make the experiences of many different real women invisible (Morant, 1998, in Mannay 2015). This curatorial project was aimed at women's art recognition, as well as to illuminate alternative realities regarding motherhood, as proposed by Llopis (2015).

Following the art sample, images and artists' processes were analysed around possible contributions to arts-based interventions, as a way to communicate and elaborate on experiences of motherhood. It is interesting how the issues that emerged were consistent with the literature and the findings of the previous practice-based study, regarding women's needs and difficulties in their transition into motherhood. Themes arising included the ambivalence of the experience of their motherhood, feelings of isolation and loss, tensions about their changing body, intimate space, concerns in relation to the children, and conflicts within their own work and life as women.

Three creative and expressive processes have been synthesised from the analysis of the artworks:

(1) Portraiture: the artwork functioning as a way to capture and witness to maternal experiences.
(2) Poetic recreation: the artwork as a shift in reality through metaphors.
(3) The ability to experience cathartic release through the visual use of irony and humour, where the artwork has meaning as both a re-signification and catharsis.

Beside these three processes, the sample of professional artwork provided innumerable and evocative possibilities. The images in the sample were used with the groups both as images for projection and elicitation processes, and as material from which to elaborate on one's own work, through creative appropriation. This experience found that art is equally useful for the individual elaboration of maternal experiences, as well as for the communication of its social and cultural aspects, as the use of images have an important subversive impact.

On the group level, sharing the observation of the images enabled participants to produce empathy and resonance, as well as to generate new models of motherhood, opening a space for dialogue and collective creativity. As stated previously in the work of Hogan (2016), the practice of art therapy as a culturally critical practice can have a social dimension, as it favours visualisation, enables us to question absolute truths about social constructions of motherhood, and promotes participants' empowerment.

Summary of findings: contributions of arts-based methods to understanding the impact of art therapy on positive parenting

The conclusions of the research show how the creative experience can serve as a catalyst for the expression of mothers' issues, fostering an awareness of their situation and needs, as well as serving for the exploration of attachment patterns and family dynamics, in a process that moves participants towards self-knowledge, mutual knowledge, and the development of autonomy and empowerment by questioning hegemonic norms of motherhood. The use of arts-based methods as part of a multiple research evaluation programme has shown this method as being able to capture this.

The results have been useful in developing methods and techniques, focusing on what participants valued explicitly, and allowing us to establish the basic principles for practice that was developed in previous publications (Hervás Hermida, 2018, 2020). The conclusions join previous feminist literature on arts therapy (Hogan, 2003) and emphasise the potential of art language and group creation for mutual support and the development of parental and resilience skills, as well as the significance of the role of the art as mediator of the process of indirectly expressing silenced narratives of the difficulties of motherhood. The chapter hopes to provide a protocol or potential method that can be adjusted to additional similar situations.

Final reflections

Arriving at the end of the chapter, I would like to reflect on my role as researcher being part of the process, taking as reference the heuristics approach, which emphasises the relationship and personal motivation of the researcher with the subject, focusing on the human experience (Douglass & Moustakas, 1985; Moustakas, 1990). Following the model proposed by the A/r/tography (Springgay, Irwin, & Kind, 2005; Leggo & Irwin 2013) the research has developed in the intersection between my three roles as artist, researcher, and therapist (teacher, in their model). This triple role was sometimes complex to hold. Sometimes I could hardly take any images during the process, so the photos taken as static shots were definitely a great help.

The fact that I myself am a mother and an artist has been a very important fact that participants highly valued, and this aided me in having a greater understanding, but also resulted in my having a strong emotional involvement in the work. Personal therapy and supervision was then necessary for me to keep a clear focus on the participants' needs.

It is important to emphasise the importance of the participants' involvement, as informants but also as an active part of the research process, which does have therapeutic and empowering implications. In that sense, the use of different sources and techniques of data collection has allowed a deeper understanding of the phenomenon from multiple perspectives – understanding developed not only from a cognitive perspective but also from visual, relational, and emotional perspectives, creating a complex and embodied knowledge explored through collective reflection. Art and visual techniques, as empowering ways of knowing, are capable of making visible what would be difficult to generate through other means.

To conclude, visual methods have shown themselves as being useful to the construction of new symbolic models regarding motherhood. This would consist not only in the revision and deconstruction of the existing belief systems, but in the active construction of the collective imagination through arts-based methods. We have seen how art is capable of facilitating processes of emotional expression and construction of knowledge that are meaningful beyond the art therapy setting.

Notes

[1] Project developed as my PhD research in the Autonoma University of Madrid, 2018.

[2] Positive parenting there refers to parental behaviour based on children's needs: behaviour that is nurturing, empowering, and non-violent, and enables full development of the child.

[3] This technique was learned from Juan José Díaz, Gestalt therapist and trainer.

References

Bartra, E. (1987). *Mujer Ideologia y Arte*. La Sal.

Council of Ministers of Europe (2006). *Recommendation REC (2006) 19 on Policy to Support Positive Parenting*.

Council of Ministers of Spain (2015). *Comprehensive Plan of Family Support 2015–2017*.

Douglass, B.G., & Moustakas, C. (1985). Heuristic inquiry: the internal search to know. *Journal of Humanistic Psychology, 25*(3), 39–55.

Elliott, J. (1986). *Investigación-Acción en El Aula*. Valencia.

Gilroy, A. (2006). *Art Therapy, Research and Evidence-Based Practice*. Sage.

Gilroy, A., Tipple, R., & Brown, C. (2012). *Assessment in Art Therapy*. Routledge.

Hervás Hermida, L. (2018). *Art Therapy for Motherhood and Families. A Way to Support Positive Parenting*. PhD. Universidad Autónoma de Madrid.

Hervás Hermida, L. (2020). Art therapy for motherhood and families as a way to support positive parenting. In Hogan (Ed.), *Therapeutic Arts in Pregnancy and New Parenthood*. Routledge.

Hogan, S. (2003). A discussion of the use of art therapy with women who are pregnant or have recently given birth. In S. Hogan (Ed.), *Gender Issues in Art Therapy* (pp. 148–172). Jessica Kingsley Publishers.

Hogan, S. (2015). Mothers make art: using participatory art to explore the transition to motherhood. *Journal of Applied Arts & Health, 6*(1), 23–32.

Hogan, S. (2016). *Art Therapy Theories: A Critical Introduction*. Routledge.

Hogan, S. (Ed.). (2020). *Therapeutic Arts in Pregnancy, Birth and New Parenthood*. Routledge.

Hogan, S., Sheffield, D., & Woodward, A. (2017). The value of art therapy in antenatal and postnatal care: a brief literature review. *International Journal of Art Therapy, 22*, 4.

Hoshino, J. (2015). Getting the picture: family art therapy. In D.E. Gussak & M.L. Rosal (Eds.), *The Wiley Handbook of Art Therapy* (pp. 210–220). Wiley & Sons.

Irwin, R.L., Beer, R., Springgay, S., Grauer, K., Xiong, G., & Bickel, B. (2006). The rhizomatic relations of a/r/tography. *Studies in Art Education, 48*(1), 70–88.

Kerr, C., Hoshino, J., Sutherland, J., Thode Parashak, S., & McCarley, L.L. (2011). *Family Art Therapy: Foundations of Theory and Practice*. Routledge.

Leggo, C., & Irwin, R.L. (2013). A/r/tography: always in process. In P. Albers, T. Holbrook, & A. Flint (Eds.), *New Methods of Literacy Research* (pp. 150–162). Routledge.

Llopis, M. (2015). *Maternidades subversivas*. Txalaparta.

Lopez Fernandez Cao, M. (2000). La creación artística: Un difícil sustantivo femenino. In M. Lopez Fernandez Cao (Ed.), *Creación artística y mujeres: Recuperar la memoria* (pp. 13–48). Narcea.

Mannay, D. (2015). *Visual, Narrative and Creative Research Methods: Application, Reflection and Ethics*. Routledge.

McNiff, S. (1998). *Art-Based Research*. Jessica Kingsley Publishers.

Moustakas, C. (1990). *Heuristic Research. Design, Methodology and Applications*. Sage.

Nochlin, L. (1988). *Women, Art and Power and Other Essays*. Thames and Hudson.

Proulx, L. (2003). *Strengthening Emotional Ties Through Parent-Child-Dyad Art Therapy: Interventions with Infants and Preschoolers*. Jessica Kingsley Publishers.

Riley, S., & Malchiodi, C.A. (2003). Family art therapy. In C.A. Malchiodi (Ed.), *Handbook of Art Therapy* (pp. 362–374). Guilford Press.

Rodrígo López, M.J., Maíquez Chaves, M.L., Martín Quintana, J.C., Byrne, S., & Rodríguez Ruiz, B. (Coord.). (2015). Manual práctico de parentalidad positiva. Madrid, Síntesis

Springgay, S., Irwin, R.L., & Wilson Kind, S. (2005). A/r/tography as living inquiry through art and text. *Qualitative Inquiry, 11*(6), 897–912.

SECTION II

Using arts-based research to listen to, and give voice to, children in social work

8

"I don't like the cameras in the house. They're looking at us all the time": the contribution of Photovoice to children in a post-hospitalisation programme

Arielle Friedman and Hila Zaguri Duvdevani

> Just to show something, anything, in the photographic view is to show what is hidden.
>
> (Sontag, 1973, p. 94)

Introduction

The present chapter examines how the use of Photovoice contributes to children in special education programmes in a post-hospitalisation programme. The Photovoice project allows these children to express their voices and points of view through photography, as well as their feelings and thoughts regarding the photographs they have taken.

Photovoice with children

Photovoice was developed by Wang & Burris (1994) as a method where researchers provide participants from disadvantaged or excluded populations with cameras for them 'to record and to reflect their needs, promote dialogue, encourage action, and inform policy' (p. 171). This technique offers the users a reflective possibility to examine their world and study their surroundings in an effort to represent it and create change as part of the practice of personal and social empowerment. According to the researchers (Wang & Burris, 1994), the Photovoice method is based on the idea that the participants are experts regarding their own lives; they are partners and cooperators in the knowledge construction process and free to express the topics they see as significant for them. The method is based on three main aims (Wang & Burris, 1994; Wang, 2006): to allow people to document and reflect their own and their community's points of strength and weakness; to promote a critical dialogue as well as knowledge and inner examination of important topics through a group discussion of photographs; and to reach excluded populations and make their voices heard (through pictures) among policy makers.

In the second decade of the 21st century, many studies were published dealing with Photovoice in public health, education, the social sciences, and other areas (for a detailed account see: Tsang, 2020). Recent studies with children undertaken around the world have shown that Photovoice is an effective method for children of addict parents in Israel to express secrets and negative feelings (Malka et al., 2018); a means of expressing their concerns regarding their health, such as obesity, in the US (Cahill & Suarez-Balcazar, 2012); it also had a beneficial effect on the comprehension of care-givers regarding the life experiences of chronically ill children in Australia (Drew et al., 2010); another example is that it allows for expression of fear of abandonment by abandoned or orphaned children in Sierra Leone (Walker & Early, 2010); another example shows how it allows for expression of feelings of safety or lack thereof in their natural surroundings in a comparison between children in high and low socio-economic statuses in South Africa (Adams et al., 2017); another example uses Photovoice as a means of expression in societies where children's right to express themselves, share and make their voices heard through their personal stories told through pictures, is unclear with respect to orphaned children with HIV in Uganda (Fournier et al., 2014). From the above, we see that Photovoice is particularly effective with populations suffering from verbal difficulties based on different reasons – age-related, cultural, marginalisation, or due to difficult or traumatic experiences (Malka et al., 2018). Photovoice helps children expand and develop their voice. For example, a study with preschool children found that photographic work with this age group enhances the children's achievements and improves their proficiency in both verbal expression and visual literacy (Friedman, 2018).

We see from this that Photovoice can help make children's experiences manifest to themselves and to others.

The present project

The population of the present project includes eight children, five boys and three girls, aged 9–15, living in a post-hospitalisation residential treatment programme, and studying in special education frameworks. The children are at different developmental levels, both cognitively and emotionally. Some suffer from emotional disorders and have serious behavioural issues, and all come from at-risk family backgrounds. The study involved working with these children with Photovoice, including photographs taken by the participants and personal and group discussions regarding the photographs and their meanings for them.

The research question was: does Photovoice contribute to the empowerment of children in such an educational setting? The second question was: does this tool drive a change in policy and practice in this boarding school?

The photographic process was accompanied by one of the researchers working with each of the children on an individual basis, including three rounds of topics, lasting 90 minutes on average for each participant. Each individual photographic process was followed by a discussion regarding the photograph taken and the reasons for choosing the specific object is depicted. The conversations were documented in the researcher's diary. The entire research process lasted six months.

The Photovoice method photographic work model

The suggested model (Figure 8.1) includes five stages. The pre–project stage, before the actual photography process with the children, includes preparation for the work in collaboration with the educational–therapeutic framework.

The work with the children includes three stages along two axes – individual and group-based (to be explained later).

The final stage is a return to the system/institution, including the conclusions from the entire process in an effort to create a change.

Figure 8.1: A diagram of the Photovoice process

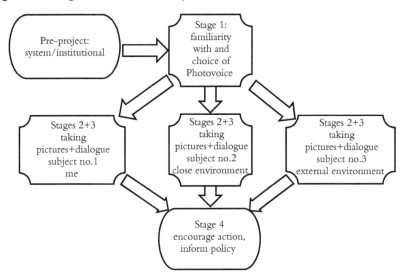

A detailed description of the process and examples of the children's work

The pre-project system/institutional stage

- Defining general research aims and questions.
- Applying to the management for permission to use Photovoice, including dealing with the relevant ethical issues.
- Defining the target population together with the therapy staff and receiving the children's personal details (for example, background, therapy they have undergone).
- Creating a varied group.

This preparation stage is crucial, as it necessitates gaining the management's trust as well as the staff's assistance in supporting the children throughout the process, allowing the care-giver to receive the necessary space.

For example, in the institution where the Photovoice took place, there was a main meeting with the management where we explained the process. Permission was granted on condition that, given their backgrounds, the children's faces would not be shown in the photographs. Next, a meeting with the social worker took place, including a discussion of potential participants, in light of the therapeutic process they are undergoing. Finally, Photovoice was presented to the institution's staff, gaining their support.

Stage 1: children's acquaintance with Photovoice and choosing to participate

- Exposure to the educational–therapeutic process: the children become acquainted with the planned process and choose whether or not to participate. They are allowed to leave at any point or join in the next stages.
- Deciding on setting and rules: the order of the following meetings, seating arrangements, discussion management, photo presentations, and choosing a new topic, creating a safe space and enabling space for all participants to express themselves both through photos and orally.
- The children understand that their photographic creations will be presented at an exhibition at the institution as well as to the therapeutic staff.
- Becoming familiar with the work model. The instructor presents the programme to the children.
- A basic familiarity with the camera.
- Exposure to photographs: the children choose photographs from different genres and present them to the group.
- Choosing the first topic for their photographs within the general topics – me, the close environment, the external environment.

At the beginning of Stage 1, the Photovoice instructor presents the children with the photographic process and all its stages. They explain that the work is both individual and group-based; the children will present their photographs, discuss them and then go out again to do individual work with the instructor while taking the photograph, followed by a joint discussion with the instructor and the therapist regarding one of the photos they had taken. It is emphasised that the photos will be presented to the entire institution at the end of the process. The manner of doing this (for example, an exhibition) is decided upon through group dialogue.

At the end of this stage, the children decide whether to continue with the process. At this stage, the discussion rules are decided on by the group. The group meeting is structured in the following manner – photo presentation by the children, feedback, and reflection from the group, choosing another sub-topic based on the model, and going out for another round.

Each of the children is asked to present personal photographs of family or friends. They become acquainted with different photographic genres they are familiar with, such as internet photos or family albums. To connect the children to the world of photography, they receive a general explanation of the camera and its basic operation only.

This stage serves as a basis for the entire process with the children for two reasons. First, this is the stage where they choose whether to become part of the process, and the therapist emphasises that it is a choice-making process. The rationale is that children in residential treatment programmes are usually denied the right to choose when taken out of their homes. To create a process placing them at the centre, they must join it of their own free will, thus becoming involved in and devoted to the process.

The second reason is that this is the stage where the Photovoice instructor exposes the children to the work process – the tool, the stages, and the cyclical model. The children understand how to operate the camera at a basic level as well as the model's topics, to simplify them into sub-topics that they will later choose.

The instructor explains that choosing the topics will take place from the personal level to the family to the group and external community levels and that each topic in each cycle represents a general topic, from which the group will decide together on a common sub-topic. For example, in the topic selection process in the institution described here, the children decided to choose the sub-topic of 'hobbies' under the topic 'me'. The sub-topics change in number and essence according to the children's choice. Other topics were, for example, places I like/dislike in the boarding school; external environment outside the school; and the community and environment where I live.

Stage 2: the children going out to take photos and the therapist documenting in his/her diary

- Photographed documentation of the topic decided on in Stage 1.
- Individual accompaniment of each child during the photography process, including a dialogue regarding subject choice, why it was chosen, how to take the photo, and so on.
- The therapist documents the entire process in their diary.

At this stage, the individual axis of child and therapist takes place, with both determining a pre-set leisurely time for the round of photographs, according to the selected topic. The child takes the photos they had decided on based on the group decision in the previous meeting, receiving assistance from the instructor only on how to use the camera, not the essence of the photography, as the photos need to be authentic with no external interference to meet the child's needs in the best way possible. After the photos have been taken the therapist asks the child why they had decided to take those photos as part of the current topic, documenting the dialogue in their diary. The participants sometimes took low-quality photos, but the researcher decided not to recreate the photos with them, in order to preserve their authenticity.

Stage 3: returning to the group and selecting the next topic

- Each child presents the photos from the first topic picked by the group (they can choose what to present, if anything).
- Creating a reflective discourse regarding group members' personal photos.
- Documenting in writing the children's words regarding their individual or group process with the photographs.
- Choosing a new sub-topic for photography within the topics.

At this stage, the group gathers again. The children present the photos they have chosen to show to the group, and the group reacts to each child's photo, asks questions, and raises associations. The instructor then reminds the group of the cyclical topic model (personal/close environment/external environment), asking whether the children wish to remain with the same topic or move to a new one. The children understand how to move from abstract topics to photographable sub-topics and that not every topic can easily be made into a photograph.

At this stage we can detect a developing group discourse. The children learn from each other and get glimpses into each other's world. The instructor

Figure 8.2: An example of the 'me' topic, 'hobbies' sub-topic

Note: The photo shows a puzzle box on a sofa in the house's common space. T., a 14-year-old boy, suffers from morning tantrums caused by medication side effects. He finds it almost impossible to discuss his difficulties, rather acting them out. Regarding the photo, he said: "I like doing puzzles all the time. It calms me down in the morning."

must be aware of the group process and keep the space open and enabling, as the process includes personal exposure for each child in the group.

Stage 4: exposing the photographic process to the institution's staff and policy makers and analysing it

- Exposing the photographic process and discussing its conclusions in front of and together with staff members (for example, an exhibition, a joint album).
- Motivation for action – identifying children's needs and changing educational and therapeutic practices according to reports of experiences, discomfort, or distress evident in the children's photographs or verbal expressions.

At this stage, the internal group process is presented to the institution's staff and management. The children must be prepared for this exposure. The therapist has an important role at this stage. They must make sure that the

Figure 8.3: An example of the 'close environment' topic, 'places I like in the boarding school' sub-topic

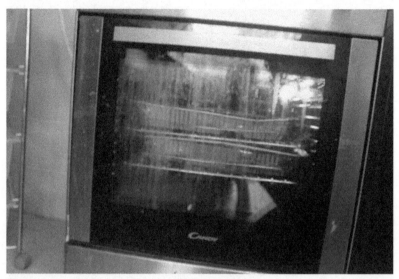

Note: The photo depicts an oven in the boarding school kitchen. This photo was also taken by T. (above), and like Figure 8.2, was pre-planned and marked in his notebook as the second place to photograph. T. chose to photograph several objects and appliances as representing the kitchen for him. Following a discourse where the therapist explained about action and products, he replied that he wants to photograph one of the appliances in action. They made dinner together, and he photographed the oven while it was working.

exposure does not harm the children and is carried out through the right platform for the group and the institution and that the photographs actually make a change in action and therapy practices vis-à-vis the children.

Examples of therapeutic and systemic results following the children's photos

- Following Figure 8.2 (jigsaw puzzle), the staff decided to use puzzles to calm this boy down and open the day in a calm, positive manner, allowing him to do puzzles in the morning hours.
- Following Figure 8.3 (the oven), the staff realised conclusively that the child suffers from emotional eating and constructed a personal emotional-nutritional programme for him.
- Following Figure 8.4 and 8.5 (surveillance cameras), the principal was exposed to the photographs and the children's point of view and disconnected all the surveillance cameras in the institution.

- Following Figure 8.6 (shower drain), the staff decided to work with the boy and help him face his fears of taking a shower, creating a system making his shower experience a positive one.
- Following Figure 8.7 (bird's nest), the staff began discussing the possibility of keeping pets in the boarding school. An animal-based therapist was hired and, later on, worked with this girl using a parrot.

Figure 8.4 & 8.5: An example of the 'close environment' topic, 'places/objects I don't like in the boarding school' sub-topic

Figure 8.4 & 8.5: An example of the 'close environment' topic, 'places/objects I don't like in the boarding school' sub-topic (Continued)

Note: The photos show the boarding school's surveillance cameras. One (on the right) is on the girls' floor and the other (on the left) on the boys' floor. The photos were taken by A. and Y. A. was undecided regarding the 'places I don't like' sub-topic for a long time. He consulted the staff, saying that he could not agree with a negative topic, as they were encouraged by the school to think positively. It was decided not to push him to photograph a theme he was uncomfortable with. Two weeks later he began the process again, saying that he has an idea for an object he dislikes in the house, asking to photograph the surveillance cameras, saying "I don't like the cameras in the house. They're looking at us all the time." Y, A.'s sister, also mentioned following this that she feels this way, adding, "They're looking at us all the time and punishing us when we do things that are wrong." The topic of security cameras set off a serious discussion among the children, and more children began to photograph the cameras as areas and objects they do not like in the institution.

Figure 8.6: An example of the 'close environment' topic, 'places/objects I don't like in the boarding school' sub-topic

Note: This is the shower on the boys' floor, with the drain at the centre of the photo. The photograph was taken by N., who knew in advance what he wanted to photograph, saying that T., his brother, helped him plan before the session. Regarding the choice of photo, he said: "I'm afraid of the shower. I often don't want to shower because of the water going out." In the discussion following the photographic session, the boy said he was afraid of falling into the drain hole and asked where the water goes.

Figure 8.7: An example of the 'external environment' topic, 'Saturday walk' sub-topic

Note: This is a photo of a bird's nest on the playground equipment. The photo was taken by R., who said, "Last time we were here, I got scared of the pigeon and wanted to break its nest because it scared me, but now I understand, after the staff members explained it to me, that this is its home." R. shared that she has been following this nest since the former walk, guarding it, and asked the staff to go back and check whether the nest was safe. When asked why she chose this photo specifically to describe her external environment, R. said, "I feel this is my nest only, like a dog or a cat other children have at home, and we're not allowed to have a mini-zoo at the boarding school."

Conclusion

The Photovoice model of working with children in institutions such as the one described in this chapter may serve as a tool for educational and therapy staff in these institutions, based on the belief that the educational-therapeutic process is incomplete without the children's voice. Photovoice provides the children with a way to express their private experiences, needs, and troubles within ecological circles of day-to-day physical life. Because photographs are spatial, they enable us to capture experiences of space, allowing both children and staff to discover and understand these in a process-based manner. The suggested model also allows the therapist to win the child's trust and receive a glimpse into his/her world, thus strengthening the connection between them and making the therapeutic process better for both parties.

This project included children with limited verbal ability, partly due to mental and emotional difficulties. Circumventing the verbal issue by using a visual means of expression (that is, photography) through the Photovoice process is the strength of the educational-therapeutic process described, in addition to strengthening the children's verbal ability by sidestepping it. Through engaging in reflective individual and group discussions regarding their photographs, the children developed verbal abilities they had not had previously. They experienced the use of correct expressions and a wider emotional spectrum, developed language among themselves, and a willingness to share personal experiences and areas of interest. Thus, the children gained from this research method and were participants in defining the subjects of concern for them.

Clearly, the focus of the Photovoice model is on empowerment, participation, reflexivity, and social change. However, says Switzer (2019), Photovoice alone cannot bring about social change. A similar concern is expressed in a meta-analysis of 37 Photovoice studies from across the world. Catalani and Minkler (2010) claim that 'although photovoice is often conceived of as a community intervention, its impact at the community level has not been well described or assessed' (p. 447).

However, the Photovoice programme described in this chapter addresses these concerns in the context of this residential treatment programme. Following the entire Photovoice process, the management took significant decisions to make changes in personnel and set new regulations, new therapeutic policy, and practice for the children's benefit.

References

Adams, S., Savahl, S., & Fattore, T. (2017). Children's representations of nature using photovoice and community mapping: perspectives from South Africa. *International Journal of Qualitative Studies on Health and Well-being, 12*(1), 1333900. doi: 10.1080/17482631.2017.1333900

Cahill, S.M., & Suarez-Balcazar, Y. (2012). Using Photovoice to identify factors that influence children. *Internet Journal of Allied Health Sciences and Practice, 10*(2), 1–6.

Catalani, C., & Minkler, M. (2010). Photovoice: a review of the literature in health and public health. *Health Education & Behavior, 37*(3), 424–451.

Drew, S.E., Duncan, R.E., & Sawyer, S.M. (2010). Visual storytelling: a beneficial but challenging method for health research with young people. *Qualitative Health Research, 20*(12), 1677–1688.

Fournier, B., Bridge, A., Mill, J., Alibhai, A., Kennedy, A.P., & Konde-Lule, J. (2014). Turning the camera back: a photovoice project with Ugandan children who are orphaned and living with HIV. *Sage Open, 4*(2), 2158244014530997.

Friedman, A. (2018). To 'read' and 'write' pictures in early childhood: multimodal visual literacy through Israeli children's digital photography. *Journal of Children and Media 12*(3), 1–17.

Malka, M., Huss, E., Bendarker, L., & Musai, O. (2018). Using photovoice with children of addicted parents to integrate phenomenological and social reality. *The Arts in Psychotherapy*, *60*, 82–90.

Sontag, S. (1973). *On Photography*. Farrar, Straus & Giroux.

Switzer, S. (2019). Working with photo installation and metaphor: re-visioning photovoice research. *International Journal of Qualitative Methods*, *18*, 1609406919872395.

Tsang, K.K. (2020). Photovoice data analysis: critical approach, phenomenological approach, and beyond. *Beijing International Review of Education*, *2*(1), 136–152.

Walker, A., & Early, J. (2010). We have to do something for ourselves: using Photovoice and participatory action research to assess the barriers to caregiving for abandoned and orphaned children in Sierra Leone. *International Electronic Journal of Health Education*, *13*, 33–48.

Wang, C.C. (2006). Youth participation in photovoice as a strategy for community change. *Journal of Community Practice*, *14*(1–2), 147–161.

Wang, C., & Burris, M.A. (1994). Empowerment through photo novella: portraits of participation. *Health Education Quarterly*, *21*(2), 171–186.

9

Arts-based research work with migrant children

Genevieve Guetemme

'Migrant children represent a significant share of the refugee population' (IOM & UNICEF). Many are growing up in bleak conditions, surrounded by poverty and violence. Education is widely recognised as a mean to foster successful integration, but it is not always available or is sometimes too formal with a focus on the values, norms, and experiences of the native population.

This can lead to migrant children and ethnic minority pupils gradually developing a sense of inferiority, irrelevance, and resentment (Szalai, 2011, p. 67).

Fieldwork supports the importance of informal arts-based education by showing that:

> Almost all youths enjoyed taking part in certain remedial and recreational educational activities. For most of them, participation in a wide range of off-site activities, such as language courses, football and basketball, music, painting, and break-dance classes, was a source of excitement.
>
> (Daskalaki & Leivaditi, 2018)

Such engagement in combined educational and recreational activities has therefore led many educators to turn to art as a facilitator for learning, socialising, understanding a difficult past, and exploring new directions for the future.

During the last 20 years, many artists have been contributing to these arts-based educational experiments. They are convinced that art has a role to play in providing a wider and more complex vision of reality. Then too, researchers have recognised art as a legitimate and useful methodological approach (Greenwood, 2012) to explore the acquisition of knowledge and social inclusion (Jindal-Snape et al., 2018). Arts-based research (ABR) uses art as a methodological research tool in its data generation, analysis, interpretation, and representation. It also presents art as a theoretical and practical way to address social research questions.

This chapter will focus on ABR methodology to explore the experience of migration by children. It is based on the description and analysis of two experiments led in Orléans (France) with two Syrian refugee artists – Diala Brisly and Manar Bilal. And it is linked with the heuristic approach of Childhood Studies, which places the expression of young people at the heart of the system. The idea is to present artworks and art activities that enable the children to describe, express, and communicate their thoughts, help them consolidate their identity, and tell their story – knowing that these stories are often objectified by the strategies of politicians, media, or educators. This study will analyse the role of art workshop's techniques (drawing, writing, photography) to enhance the dialogue between the researchers and a usually mute migrant population (only narrowly defined by its administrative status, education, or state of health).

Understanding ABR

This chapter provides an opportunity for understanding new qualitative research paths based on art practice and in line with the current break from the positivist paradigm (Pentassuglia, 2017, p. 3). First called ABER (arts-based education research) by Elliot Eisner (1981) and later ABR by Shawn McNiff (1998), this research methodology sets new approaches in the educational and social fields to open up to new questions and to new ways of communicating experiences and phenomena that are almost impossible to describe with words (Greenwood, 2012). It relies on 'all practices that use artistic processes as a way of investigation and knowing. [It favours] an interdisciplinary perspective [and] is becoming a preferred way to understand the complexity of social phenomena' (Lincoln & Guba, 1985). The idea is to highlight teaching and learning processes through 'embodied ways of knowing' (Barbour, 2011) with the 'total' involvement of the researcher in the setting that needs understanding. This method shifts the focus onto corporeal, unsaid, and sensible experiences, while reaffirming the very close and necessary link that grows between arts and public life. It wishes to rethink artistic intervention as a means 'for social transformation through the critical analysis of social values that are inherent in works of art' (Clark, 1996, p. 35).

But some consider ABR unscientific and unreliable, so it is unfortunately usually still marginalised. Monica Pentassuglia notes: 'Although some authors highlighted the importance of this type of research, there is still a poor scientific understanding of this process' (Pentassuglia, 2017, p. 2). This may be because communication and dissemination of findings have not conformed to the traditional texts and are therefore still frowned upon in the scientific field: ARB 'takes place as a "parallel" research path' (Pentassuglia, 2017, p. 10).

According to the literature on ABR summed up by Pentassuglia, the learning and research process is based on the collection of embedded data and construction of knowledge utilising four main methods:

(1) *Narrative inquiry* or *narrative method*: qualitative interviews using either storytelling or not in order to observe the participants' life. It works as a lens on their habitus and provides evidence of their experience.

(2) *Poetry research*: using poetry as a form of representation.

(3) *Music research*: music used as a key instrument to interpret and study social reality.

(4) *Performance studies*, using theatre as a research process for data collection and expression.

Following that line of thought, we note that both experiments described in this chapter combine narrative, photography, and painting in order to reach three main objectives:

- collect data on migrant children's meaningful experiences and inner world;
- highlight practical approaches dedicated to migration that arouse interest in children while developing self-awareness;
- build a tool-kit for teachers interested in tackling migration with children (whether migrants themselves or not).

Our hypotheses are that:

- ABR develops the subjective and cultural understanding of migration (away from the mediatic ideological focus on political, legal, or diplomatic representations).
- ABR highlights the power of complex artistic representations as models leading to new educational practices linked to migration.

The aim of these two arts-based workshops is to show how 'hybrid empirical, interpretive, and naturalistic theory-building practices' (Rolling & Haywood, 2013, p. 5) become informative and ethical sources of knowledge, ways of thinking, and methods for developing actions in order to promote integration and education. The experiments encompass arts and languages in their capacity to develop a co-constructive dynamic between migrant children and local communities.

Two artists' workshops using ABR's methods to explore children's migration

Two Syrian artists – photographer Manar Bilal and illustrator Diala Brisly – were invited by the faculty of education in Orléans (France) to lead a set of art workshops in different educational contexts. Both artists had been working with children in refugee camps in Jordan, Lebanon and Turkey, before being granted refugee status in France.

I mainly worked with children, especially with the wounded and those who were traumatized by the war. It was about giving them psychological and social support to help them keep a little hope, cope with the living conditions in the camps and dream of a better tomorrow.

(Brisly, 2016a)

Brisly currently continues her collaboration with German charity *Zeltshule,* which sets up and manages school tents in the Bekaa valley in Lebanon. She regularly sends large and colourful canvases to transform a tent into a special corner within the grey and dusty environment of the camp. The idea is to use the canvases to help identify the tent as a different place, far from the war, destruction, poverty, and uncertainty of life and inspire children to enter and learn.

Bilal's two-day workshop was conducted with a class of 28 primary school children (age group 9–10) of multicultural background (European, North and Central African). It was run with the school teacher during school time, and with the active participation of 12 master's student trainee teachers from the Orléans's Faculty of Education (Bilal, n.d.). The trainee teachers contributed to the planning of the two sessions in the class, summarised the data, and wrote the activity report.

Brisly's workshops were run every day during a full week with (1) evening sessions open to anyone interested (master's students and staff) in the art department at the Orléans's Faculty of Education, (2) day-time sessions

Figure 9.1: School-tent, Lebanon, 2016

Source: © Diala Brisly.

Figures 9.2 & 9.3: Year 5, Jean-Zay Primary school, Orléans, 2018

Source: Author.

inserted in the master's degree programme on 'vulnerable children' and 'multiculturalism', (3) one session with 12 unaccompanied young migrants was run during a language course organised by a local charity.

Both artists used storytelling techniques to expose and debate:

- the living and educational conditions of migrant children in refugee camps;
- the posture of the host (in transit and arrival countries);

Figure 9.4: Zataary camp, Jordan, 2014

Source: © Manar Bilal.

- the role of art to improve language learning and social inclusion;
- the responsibility of the artist/researcher to analyse and develop innovative pedagogy.

Both artists began their workshops by sharing their personal story (in English, as their knowledge of French was very limited) and insisted on the educational issues in refugee camps.

In his workshop, Bilal then encouraged the French children to tell their own story of newcomers or old-timers in France. He presented a set of pictures from Zataary Camp (Jordan) and suggested starting a dialogue through fictional meetings with the Syrian children from the pictures. Next, photos taken by Bilal in the camp and by the French school-children themselves on their playground – were downloaded on the computer and French children pasted in Bilal's shots while Syrian children were digitally included in the French context. The digital manipulations bought the French children (migrant or not) to reflect on their living conditions and educational opportunities.

Brisly's sessions, in their different forms, invited students, trainees and experienced teachers, migrants and asylum seekers, to a collaborative project consisting of painting a mural together that would be sent to Lebanon. This allowed all participants to feel included in a place (Orléans), in a group (of diverse but like-minded people), and into a federative and generous project.

Both artists' interventions focused on openness with migrants and non-migrants who were encouraged to appreciate (compare, analyse, valorise)

Figure 9.5: French boy playing with a small Syrian girl

Source: Anonymous.

Figure 9.6: Details of the canvas painted with the students of the INSPE-CVL (Orléans), March 2020

Source: Author.

their own situation and share their experience. The artists insisted on their need, as a migrant, to express their feelings and multicultural identity in order to rebuild themselves:

When I moved to Istanbul, I had contradictory feelings about lots of things. I felt guilty and lonely not being in Syria. Later, when I came to Beirut, I was doing voluntary work with refugees and I was with friends. I could do things to distract myself.

(Brisly, 2016b)

They also used narrative as a lens on habitus and experience. Brisly presented for example, some aspects of the children's life in the camps and also revealed the role that art played in easing their day-to-day routine. Art did indeed help children in the camps to express themselves, to understand their past, and to prioritise education's power to build their future (bearing in mind that many of the refugee children are still not in school). She also admitted that it helped her to justify her own exile by making it useful, both in Syria or the refugee camps and in France.

Brisly's and Bilal's stories do the work of introducing emotional and irrational connections between themselves and the workshop participants. In Syria they helped neutralise the misery of the migrant children with photography and drawing. Making them paint or jump, climb and fly in the wind did help take their minds off their situation. In France, the storytelling brings mainly awareness and energises the debate in order to help everyone learn about each other and develop empathy. Storytelling does so with stories based on recurrent themes such as the escape route: climbing up on a fence or high in the sky. The stories take into account the weight of the world, but also present space for the children to dream and thoughts of how to reach a safer place − even imaginary − like the image of the boy selling cotton candy:

He's a kid but he's selling things for other kids because he has to make a living […] I drew this boy happy. I can't find a solution for him but I want him to be happy anyway. He will keep working, he doesn't have any solution.

(Brisly, 2016b)

The story reveals the infinite potential of lightness against the terrible reality of war, far from the death of parents, of brothers and sisters and friends. Far from the destroyed houses, the harrowing journeys to cross borders. It shows the power of art to understand the present and look towards a future − hopefully a happy one. Aimed at teachers, this story presents a possible entry for multicultural and child-focused, humane education that goes well beyond learning a language. It pushes the representation of migration away from the ideological models linked to border control, activism, political, legal, or diplomatic strategies, towards subjectivity and cultural dialogue. These methods allow us to radically rethink the social and educational role of art as a transformation tool for the migrant children as well as their hosts.

Figure 9.7: Diala Brisly, *Child Labour*

Source: © Diala Brisly, created for *Zayton and Zaytonah* magazine.

Discussion and results

Afterwards, the master's degree students – as future professionals in educational environments likely to welcome migrant children – gave some feedback on the workshops, focusing on three points: the storytelling, the choice of ABR to explore the experience of migration, and the personal impact of the workshops on migrants and non-migrant participants.

The storytelling

The artist's life stories, in transit as well as in different host countries, captivated the audience. Although migration is very well documented by journalists, charity workers, volunteers, and the migrants themselves, with texts and photographic or video posts on social media, it is commonly reduced to superficial and stereotypical knowledge. Here, the personal and direct account gave the migrant a face and a name. They revealed migration as a personal journey and shared very intimate memories. More stories emerged – as described by French photographer Marie Dorigny when commissioned by the European Parliament to produce a photo report on Middle Eastern refugees:

> My mother left in exodus in front of the Germans in 1940, I thought about that during the whole report. My mother was traumatized by it all her life [...] I wonder what these women and children are going to be like [...] I'm ashamed. It's terrible to see history repeating itself and to tell ourselves that we are not up to the task.
>
> (Dorigny, 2016)

This first-hand encounter with migrants brought the participants to reflect on themselves and on their own stories. Most of them (middle-class, white, young women, aged 23–25, coming from rural or small French towns) had only a very theoretical knowledge of migration and Orléans's Faculty of Education does not currently include any teacher training regarding first- and second-generation migrant children in mainstream French schools:

> I think a dialogue was established between the artist and the students, and this dialogue that was at the very heart of the course made the students learn a lot about life in general and about possible interactions between people of different cultures.
>
> (student testimony)

The students became part of the artist narrative. The focus on children made sense and became a big motivational factor for the participants. Children and students of whatever background were all excited to assist both artists for the creation of the fresco or for setting a photographical dialogue:

> Participating in the making of a fresco to be sent to Lebanon made me realise that drawing is not always a question of technique but also of intention. It was so interesting to hear the artist talk with such passion, eloquence and sometimes philosophically about her art.
>
> (student testimony)

The story about the children's need for colours brought forth real empathy. According to Brisly, there is no colour in the camps. Dust and bright light make everything grey. Her story told about the children's fascination with colours in Lebanon as they were repetitively covering themselves – hands and clothes – with paint. She insisted therefore in bringing as much colour as possible into the fresco, to make the European participants realise how the colourful tent would work like an anchor, helping the children escape from their constant state of disorientation, separation, and loss.

ABR method

The second intention of the workshop was to present ABR as a professional educational tool aimed at reducing discrimination and exclusion of refugee and migrant children in host countries. The students witnessed the arts-based research method, with a focus on narrative, as a contribution to inclusive teaching and as an introduction to critical though on social representations and values:

> Working on migration through art is very interesting because one can convey different messages in a different form: messages that would be impossible to convey in writing or in speech. For the fresco, we did not have to write our thoughts, but our pictures said a lot about our understanding and engagement.
>
> (student testimony)

The workshops revealed art's ability to meet Syrian children – photographically – or to help them attend 'school' in Lebanese camps with 'tent art', as Brisly called it. They had the power to transport the French children/students into a different place in order to consider:

- the role of school in life;
- the role of art (and storytelling) as a teaching tool;
- new methods for language learning;
- the link between the arts and public life with paradigmatic representations of migration in contemporary arts that would tell us a lot about migrant children;
- the importance of participatory practices to explore complex questions touching on multiculturality and politics such as border crossing, exile, identity;
- the need for social and intercultural dialogue, as required by the action plan of the European Commission aimed at facilitating the integration of migrants into the education and training system of member states, from kindergarten to university.

The students, teachers and educators understood the broad impact of the workshops in mainstream schools as well as in informal education as a response to the migrants' need to express themselves, using pictures as a way to make contact with others – wherever and whoever they are. The participants described ABR as an ethical practice, able to reveal a necessity (such as to give migrant children a voice and a sense of belonging), and a method (art used to create the conditions for dialogue).

Personal development

The workshops showed that tackling migration through educational art programmes could contribute to language, social, and cultural learning. However, on a more general level, the children as well as the students – whether migrants or not –all learned to communicate with each other via pictures and were able to describe their mutual development. Art helped them building a bridge between themselves and their environment: 'Thanks to these workshops, I realised that culture goes further than what we know and what we see around us; it also includes every experience we have lived, whether pleasant or not, important or not' (student testimony). As an artist and as a newcomer herself, Brisly shared drawings, words, and thoughts on what she called 'best memories' to describe the things that make one's core. This worked with the group of unaccompanied minors who attended her workshop with a local charity. The focus was on language learning, but it also led to mutual discovery. They realised that:

- Although not fluent in French (the artists and themselves), they had a lot to say and that French words were undeniably introduced and memorised.
- The written texts (stories) produced to accompany the pictures did reveal a lot of unsaid and usually repressed emotions.
- Expression of the self was key to helping participants become aware of their own goals and therefore led to reconstruction and integration.

For the students who were experiencing their first personal contact with migrants, the workshops caused them to consider charitable commitments and trainee teachers started to see the professional necessity (and difficulty) of favouring openness and inclusion when standing between cultures.

Artistic representation of migration

More theoretically, the workshops offered some insight into ABR's ability to focus on the concept of collage as a paradigm for representing migration. In Bilal's workshop the collage was digital, while with Brisly it was pictorial, and added many different contributions within one piece of artwork. In both cases, the collage had the power to act against disorientation and loss with playful associations and magical juxtapositions revealing the unbroken link between history, imagination, and expression. The two workshops indeed used collage as a method to connect values and emotions and, as a matter of fact, to question the collisions between cultures, systems, and interlocutors, at every stage of the creative process, which mirrored the multiple encounters within every migrant's journey.

This reflects on French philosopher and art historian Georges Didi-Huberman's view of collage as a wartime practice: interweaving the dramatic past of the war with the perspectives of exile (2009). Greco-Romans referred to "helping words" as those that help us deal with strong feelings and stressful situations (Hubert, 2015, pp. 71–73).

These ageless discourses, able to piece together the disparate was, according to Didi-Huberman, central to Brecht's exploration of the educational value of visual montage during the war – with his *ABC* published after the war, in 1955. Walter Benjamin – another famous exile – also recommended collage as a way to switch from terror to action and retain a certain level of innocence:

> [Collage makes the viewer] deliciously naïve, which does not mean stupid or ignorant [...] [but like] the scientist, the thinker or the artist [...] able of playing despite the difficulties, working, creating, rediscovering the gesture of learning, constantly reopening to pleasure.
> (Didi-Huberman, 2009, p. 216)

Such naivety allows the children to develop their knowledge, their speech, their values, and their feelings, while accepting the need to 'see everything through the lens of conflict, transformation, gap, alteration' (Didi-Huberman, 2009, p. 191). It allows them to wander through an unstable space-time, marked by isolation and exclusion, without forgetting the dream of an 'open', 'abundant', 'colourful' world.

Conclusion

Built on refugee camps' life narratives, the exploratory workshops led by migrant artists Manar Bilal and Diala Brisly, with the vital reflexes of those who cross spaces and cultures, showed how heterogeneous interactions allowed French children of various origin, as well as students and teachers, to connect. The artists' ideas were also to create a toolbox for educators, school representatives, and social workers to use to improve their understanding of art as a laboratory for deciphering a changing society.

Both artists' interventions used storytelling to initiate a research aimed at understanding the way students and children – refugee or not – reflect on migration and learn about themselves and about one another. They also presented the collage with its ability to piece together collections of thoughts. They were able to engage with new audiences and created surprise while they also presented art's ability to question and refine teacher training with 'embedded' didactic skills. This was in line with the principle of an 'integrated curriculum' organised 'to show the connectedness of things, while an interdisciplinary curriculum is organised in ways that reinforce the separate and discrete character of academic disciplines' (Clark, 1996, p. 35).

These teaching and learning experiments align with current initiatives in education: prioritising concepts and processes, exploring transdisciplinary fields, and using art as a transformation tool. The aim is to develop more inclusive, equitable child-focused practices, for the 'promotion of lifelong learning opportunities for all' (United Nations, 2015).

Both artists revealed the way arts-based research can help – in line with the constantly evolving field of social sciences – to understand life experiences in a multifaceted world with strategies based on sensory perceptions and emotions. These workshops are examples of artistic communicative and interpreting tools, aimed at exploring our world's ambiguities, liminalities, and complexities, while bypassing verbal expression.

References

Barbour, K. (2011). *Dancing Across the Page*. University of Chicago.

Bilal, M. (n.d.) www.manarbilal.com/

Brecht, B. (1955). *Kriegsfibel*. Eulenspiegel Verlag.

Brisly, D. (2016a). *BBC Newsnight*, April 7. www.youtube.com/watch?v= ZyYPATXpdjw

Brisly, D. (2016b). Diala Brisly: Paintings of hope for Syria's children. *BBC Magazine*, March, 19. www.bbc.co.uk/news/magazine-35847632

Clark, R. (1996). *Art Education: Issues in Postmodern Pedagogy*. National Art Education Association.

Daskalaki, I., & Leivaditi, N. (2018). Education and hospitality in liminal locations for unaccompanied refugee youths in Lesvos. *Migration and Society: Advances in Research*, *1*(1), 51–65. www.berghahnjournals.com/ view/journals/migration-and-society/1/1/arms010106.xml

Didi-Huberman, G. (2009). *Quand les images prennent position. L'Oeil de l'histoire*, 1. Editions de minuit, Collection Paradoxe.

Dorigny, M. (2016). Visa pour l'image: les femmes réfugiées dans l'objectif de Marie Dorigny. *France info culture*, December 6. www.francetvinfo.fr/ culture/arts-expos/photographie/visa-pour-l-image-les-femmes-refugiees-dans-l-objectif-de-marie-dorigny_3340431.html

Eisner, E. (1981). On the differences between scientific and artistic approaches to qualitative research. *Educational Researcher*, *10*, 5–9.

European Commission (2020). Education and migrants, in Education and Training. https://ec.europa.eu/education/policies/european-policy-cooperation/education-and-migrants_en

Greenwood, J. (2012). Arts-based research: weaving magic and meaning. *International Journal of Education & the Arts, 13* (Interlude 1). www.ijea.org/v13i1/

Hubert, V. (2015). Foucault educateur: un art de l'écriture et un modèle d'autoformation. *Le Télémaque*, Presses universitaires de Caen. www.cairn.info/revue-le-telemaque-2015-1-page-71.htm

IOM – UN Migration (2018). *Addressing the Needs of Migrant Children.* https://eea.iom.int/sites/default/files/publication/document/7-IOM-Addressing-needs-migrant-children.pdf

Jindal-Snape, D., Davies, D., Scott, R., Robb, A., Murray, C., & Harkins, C. (2018). Impact of arts participation on children's achievement: a systematic literature review. *Thinking Skills and Creativity, 29*, 59–70. https://doi.org/10.1016/j.tsc.2018.06.003

Lincoln, Y., & Guba, E. (1985). *Naturalistic Inquiry*. Sage.

McNiff, S. (1998). *Art-Based Research*. Jessica Kingsley Publishers.

Pentassuglia, M. (2017). 'The Art(ist) is present': arts-based research perspective in educational research. *Cogent Education, 4*(1), 2. https://doi.org/10.1080/2331186X.2017.1301011

Rolling Haywood, J. Jr. (2013). *Arts-Based Research Primer*. Peter Lang.

Szalai, J. (2011). *Contested Issues of Social Inclusion Through Education in Multi-Ethnic Communities across Europe*. EDUMIGROM.

UNICEF (2020). *Latest Statistics and Graphics on Refugee and Migrant Children.* www.unicef.org/eca/emergencies/latest-statistics-and-graphics-refugee-and-migrant-children

United Nations (2015). *THE 17 GOALS"- The 2030 Agenda for Sustainable Development, 2015* https://sustainabledevelopment.un.org/?menu=1300

10

Using creative art research approaches to assess arts-based interventions with children in post-disaster contexts

Julie Drolet, Nasreen Lalani, and Caroline McDonald-Harker

Introduction

Creative art research approaches are gaining in popularity in recent years and are increasingly being used in social work, health, and other disciplines (Vanover et al., 2018). Arts-informed approaches can serve as expressive therapies, and have been successfully applied in psychotherapy, counselling, and rehabilitation for decades (Malchiodi, 2005). Creative art research approaches expand the domain of qualitative inquiry and enable social science researchers to incorporate and utilise arts-based methodologies to better understand human behaviour, perspectives, and experiences (Leavy, 2017). Arts-based scholarly research is located in the creation of art, based on extensive artistic training, while arts-informed research is used to express the experiences, perspectives, and emotions of research participants (Shannon-Baker, 2015). Arts-informed research mainly focuses on the advancement of knowledge rather than merely the production or creation of artwork or art craft for this purpose. It facilitates the possibility of establishing deeper and genuine human connections by capturing different perspectives and expressions due to its expressive qualities (Leavy, 2017).

Art and creative methods in social work research are consistent with the philosophy, mission, and values of the profession (Peek et al., 2016). Shannon (2013) discusses several key components of social work research that includes active community participation, understanding of the local contexts, mutual dialogue and understanding, and facilitating social change leading to empowerment, equality, and social justice. The profession of social work strongly values and respects the inherent worth and dignity of all people (IFSW & IASSW, 2004), and arts-informed creative research approaches provide an ethical platform to inquire about the lived experiences of individuals and communities (Jarldon, 2016). Arts-informed approaches allow social workers to learn how service users develop their inner strength by recognising 'the inherent worth and dignity' of an individual person

(Foster, 2012). Arts-based and arts-informed research approaches assist research practitioners in engaging participants to create a narrative of their story or experience using art. By doing this, it invites participation and the expression of diverse perspectives, and provides an empowering experience for both participants and researchers (Jarldorn, 2016).

This chapter highlights the significance and application of creative art research approaches using a 'Youth Paint Nite' activity with children and youth in a post-disaster context in Alberta, Canada. The chapter discusses the methodologies, practices, and outcomes of using creative art research approaches in the study *Alberta Resilient Communities (ARC): Engaging Children and Youth in Community Resilience Post-Flood in Southern Alberta*. The ARC project was launched following the 2013 floods that devastated communities in southern Alberta, Canada.

Context: Alberta Resilient Communities (ARC) project

On June 20, 2013, an intense weather system involving thunderstorms and heavy rainfall caused rivers in the southern half of the Canadian province of Alberta to overflow their banks. This resulted in catastrophic and unprecedented flooding, whereby 32 states of local emergency were declared. The Canadian Armed Forces were deployed to help evacuate 175,000 people, making the event one of the largest evacuations and costliest disasters in Canadian history (Mertz, 2016). Numerous communities were flooded and completely evacuated, five fatalities occurred, and extensive damage was caused to homes, businesses, roads, and critical infrastructures due to this disaster (Pomeroy et al., 2016). The town of High River, a rural community just south of the city of Calgary, was hardest hit by the flood. All 13,000 residents were evacuated upon orders by the government of Alberta (Geddes, 2014). The southern Alberta floods severely affected many individuals, families, and communities, especially children and youth. This population faced unique challenges due to their dependence on adults; the various physical, psychological, and social factors related to their developmental stage; and the lack of adequate child/youth-centred resources available post-disaster (Kousky, 2016). However, children and youth also have the capacity to be resilient in the face of adversity and can act as powerful catalysts for change and recovery in their families and communities in post-disaster environments (Drolet, et al., 2015).

A collaborative research team was created to better understand the experiences of children, youth, and their adult allies (parents/guardian) and community influencers who deliver services and programmes in flood-affected communities during the flood response and recovery. The goal of the ARC project was to better understand the social, economic, health, cultural, spiritual, and personal factors that contribute to resiliency among children and youth while empowering them and their adult allies and communities to enact resilience building strategies (Drolet, et al., 2015). The project used creative art research approaches to engage children and youth to create a shared understanding of their perspectives and lived experiences. Art drawings, clay modelling, colouring/painting, digital stories, and arts-informed approaches including a 'Youth Paint Nite' were adopted. By using creative art research approaches, we were able to generate meaningful conversations with children and youth in an interactive and child/youth-friendly way. These approaches put the voices and experiences of children and youth at the centre of the research process, empowering children and youth in their post-disaster recovery. An in-depth understanding of children and youth's perspectives and lived experiences and perspectives is necessary to inform disaster management strategies to foster community resilience.

Significance of creative art research in disaster contexts

In disaster contexts, creative art research offers a way for children to make sense of their experiences, to express their loss and grief, and to actively engage in their own healing process (Orr, 2007). Disaster recovery is a long-term process that brings social and economic challenges (Drolet, 2019). Rebuilding homes, social disruptions, and financial losses result in a difficult transition for disaster-affected families and their children (Felix, et al., 2013). Evidence suggests that creative arts and play are children's natural medium for self-expression; allow children to express thoughts and concerns that may be difficult to verbalise; and serve as a powerful medium for the cathartic release of feelings and frustrations (Frost, 2005). These strategies also assist trained adults to determine the nature and causes of such behaviours and enable them to create a meaningful connection with the children and their grief. Evidence suggests that using art as a participatory research method allows the participants to engage in a creative manner, foster community building, and generate a collective sense of self-empowerment (Literat, 2013). However, researchers need to be cautious and trained in using arts-informed strategies with vulnerable children and youth, especially in a disaster context.

Arts-based and arts-informed approaches have been used in multiple research studies including dance (Snowber, 2002; Travis & Deepak, 2011; Vanover et al., 2018), traditional crafts (Huss, 2009), photo voice (Jarldorn, 2016), narrative writing (Lentin, 2000), auto/ethnography (Kolker, 1996), performance (Mienczakowski et al., 2002), short film (Foster, 2009), poetry (Szto et al., 2005), music (Daykin, 2008), fashion shows (Barry, 2017), and sculpture, collage, and painting (Van Son, 2000; Foster, 2012). These creative approaches provide research practitioners with a new and unique lens to better understand existing and emerging social phenomena, and to develop strong relationships and connections in diverse ways. Creative art research approaches with children and youth serve as effective tools for empowerment, engagement, and building partnerships that contribute to positive social change in post-disaster contexts (Peek et al., 2016). The use of arts-based and arts-informed research methods continue to evolve and develop. O'Donoghue (2015) argues there are not enough resources to educate and train new researchers to practise arts-based research. Greater clarity is needed to define arts-based approaches and how to use them appropriately in research to avoid presenting any risks or harms to participants. The non-linear and expressive nature of arts-informed research can appear complex and messy, presenting a challenge for new researchers to translate their findings into concrete research outcomes (Cole & Knowles, 2011).

Methodology: Youth Paint Nite

The ARC project organised a 'Youth Paint Nite' to explore the lived realities of children and youth (ages 10–16) affected by the flood in the town of High River, Alberta. The 'Youth Paint Nite' as an arts-informed research activity was created to engage children and youth in guided conversations about their flood experiences and to learn what factors promote their resilience. The 'Youth Paint Nite' activity was designed as a child/youth-friendly and child/youth-centred event where children and youth shared their post-disaster experiences in a familiar, fun, and friendly environment. The activity was followed by a qualitative interview guide and a survey questionnaire that measured resilience using Child and Youth Resilience Measure (CYRM-28) scale. The child and youth resilience measure was completed by participants during a break when the painted canvases were drying. The results from this study are discussed in Drolet et al., 2018. In this chapter we present and discuss the methodology of using an arts-informed 'Youth Paint Nite' activity.

The 'Youth Paint Nite' was organised in collaboration with the Boys and Girls Clubs (BGC) of the Foothills in the town of High River, Alberta, a charitable organisation dedicated to the personal development and growth of children and youth. Participant recruitment was led by the BGC, in partnership with a community-based researcher. A recruitment poster and a letter of initial contact was shared with those who expressed an interest in the activity. Research ethics approval was obtained through the University of Calgary Conjoint Faculties Research Ethics Board prior to collecting data. Parental consent forms and child/youth assent was obtained prior to the 'Youth Paint Nite' activity by having both the parent and the child/youth sign an informed consent form. Parents and children and youth were also asked to sign a media consent form. There was no potential for coercion or undue influence as the 'Youth Paint Nite' was a voluntary activity made available free of charge to participants. Participants were advised that if and when they wished to end the research or certain aspects of the research, all data collected would be destroyed, and a debrief session would be provided to explain that termination has no impact on the participant's relationship with any community partner or any other institution. In addition, the confidentiality of the data was maintained by removing all identifying information. Photographs of the artwork created during the painting activity were captured using an arts-informed research approach.

The painting activity was organised for two hours on a weeknight at the BGC where the participants normally meet. Fifteen young people participated in the event, including children and youth between the ages of 10 and 16 years who were living in the flood-affected communities of High River, Okotoks, and the surrounding Foothills region of Alberta, Canada. Practitioners and service providers of the BGC were present and available to provide translation support (for example, Spanish, Tagalog) for participants and their parents and/or legal guardians if required. During the 'Youth Paint Nite' participants were invited to paint a canvas using a step-by-step approach along with the instructions provided by a professional artist educator. All the painting supplies and materials were provided free of charge along with refreshments to the participants. The participants were invited to engage in conversations with the researchers about their experiences during the 2013 flood while they were painting. A separate interview conversation guide was developed to lead the conversations with children and youth about their flood experiences and the ongoing post-disaster recovery efforts. Some of the guiding questions included: What would I need to grow up well here in High River? Did you know what was happening when the flood occurred? What kinds of things are most challenging for you growing up here? Did the challenges growing up here change for you after the flood? Can you think of anything good that happened because of the flood? Three researchers were present to engage in conversations with the participants and detailed notes were taken, which were then analysed for themes.

The painting activity provided an opportunity for self-expression, active participation, and use of imagination while reflecting on lived experience. The conversations during the activity allowed child/youth participants to illustrate some of the ways in which they were affected by the flood and subsequent evacuation. Flood was described as "an experience" and "a shock that it actually happened". Some child/youth participants stated that they "didn't know what a flood was" prior to the event. Further, the flood was described as "stressful" and "tiring" for some. Child/youth participants were evacuated from their school and were unable to contact their parent(s) or family members. The challenging nature of having experienced the flood and the aftermath of recovery was discussed in the conversations held during the painting activity. Those challenges included damage/loss of homes and displacement, transportation challenges, financial struggles, and feelings of isolation, loss, and grief. Most child/youth participants spoke about the loss of their homes and schools, which were destroyed and needed extensive remediation due to damage and contamination from the flood. Some of the child/youth participants lost all their personal belongings, and some lost contact with many close friends as a result of the flood. Unemployment was also identified as a recovery challenge as many community members lost their jobs due to the flood. Interestingly, some child/youth participants expressed a lack of desire to talk about the flood as they had become fatigued by such discussions, which they felt were constant and never ending. Many of these child/youth participants either stated that they simply did not want to talk about it, or that they did not remember the flood very well.

Child/youth participants also shared several positive experiences that resulted from the flood, such as having the opportunity to stay with family and friends, attending a new school, making new friends, and enjoying new stores and buildings in their community. Participants appreciated the role and importance of social networks, particularly family and friends, and stated that it helped them overcome the difficulties they faced in their everyday lives post-disaster. Findings also showed that child/youth participants who were directly involved in post-disaster recovery efforts and had opportunities to help others experienced increased happiness, joy, and a spirit of service in helping others. Child/youth participants were also directly involved in emergency preparedness initiatives, such as the creation of emergency kits that contain clothes and first aid materials, as well as learning about new technology and social media apps to help better prepare for disasters in their community. These findings demonstrate that children and youth play an important role and service during post-disaster recovery processes, in many ways contributing to their own and their communities' resilience. Children and youth bring new perspectives and understandings to post-disaster recovery, demonstrating the need to build upon their lived experiences to strengthen and improve disaster preparedness initiatives and efforts.

Discussion

Creative art research approaches allow children, youth, and their families to express their unique experiences and perspectives in an innovative manner (Fraser & Al Sayah, 2011). Disaster studies demonstrate that children and youth require different forms of physical, social, mental, and emotional support than adults in disaster contexts (Peek, 2008). Creative art research approaches can assist in enhancing young people's resilience, helping them to prepare so that they and their families might respond and recover well when disaster strikes from a preventive lens (Ronan & Towers, 2014). The 'Paint Nite' activity provided an opportunity for self-expression, active participation, and the use of imagination while reflecting on lived experience. By adopting a painting activity, a space was created to engage participants in conversations about their flood experiences. The research partnership for the 'Youth Paint Nite' between the BGC and the academic research team facilitated the recruitment and engagement of child and youth in research. Since flood recovery is ongoing, partnering with local community champions and organisations played a key role within the community during the recovery process. The BGC's primary mandate is a commitment to sustained child and youth engagement and, therefore, the 'Youth Paint Nite' aligned well with the organisation's overall goals and objectives.

Moreover, the 'Youth Paint Nite' assisted in planning and formulating goals for meeting the long-term recovery needs of children and youth through targeted programming. The project demonstrated a collaborative effort in finding alternative solutions to disaster recovery processes and in ensuring the inclusion of children and youth as essential parts of the research process. The collaborative and iterative approach used in the research also engendered multiple sources of data collection and analysis methods, resulting in rich findings and multiple ways for knowledge translation and mobilisation. These activities allowed the researchers to go beyond traditional research approaches to answer the research questions, as well as build on collaborative community efforts while empowering children and youth through the research process. These methods also allowed us to build upon existing resources in the community, develop partnerships, and create new opportunities for children and youth to learn, share, and participate in disaster recovery in their community.

Study limitations

Along with all the benefits of using arts-informed research with children and youth, there were some limitations with the methodology. There is a possibility that the data may reflect what the child/youth participants wished to convey in conversation, as opposed to what they actually felt and experienced. In fact, there was a reluctance on the part of some of the child/youth participants to engage in discussions about their feelings and experiences of the flood. The highly structured nature of the art activity, using a group format led by an artist educator facilitator, may not have been well suited to each child/youth participant's needs or preferences. Yet, it is quite likely that child/youth participants were drawn to a 'Youth Paint Nite' because art activities are often perceived as interesting and fun by children and youth. A more general limitation of using arts-informed approach with children and youth is that some may perceive that they are not creative or artistic, and therefore may not feel comfortable participating in an art activity.

Conclusion

Arts-informed and community-based research approaches can be used as innovative research strategies to generate a mutual dialogue and engage children and youth to share and learn about disaster recovery and resilience experiences. The arts-informed activities appealed to children and youth, while also serving as a recreational and leisure activity post-disaster. It was particularly important to partner with a local community organisation and service providers who had an existing relationship with community members to honour their sustained community efforts. This approach presents a promising pathway for ethically engaging children and youth in post-disaster recovery research. Social work researchers, social scientists, and practitioners are encouraged to use arts-informed creative research approaches with children and youth to learn about their perspectives and experiences in disaster recovery and in partnership with community agencies and organisations.

References

Barry, B. (2017). Enclothed knowledge: the fashion show as a method of dissemination in arts-informed research. *Forum: Qualitative Social Research, 18*(3), 145–167. doi:10.17169/ifs-18.3.2837

Cole, A.L., & Knowles, J.G. (2011). Drawing on the arts, transforming research: possibilities of arts-informed perspectives. In L. Markauskaite, P. Freebody, & J. Irwin (Eds.), *Methodological Choice and Design* (pp. 119–131). Springer.

Daykin, N. (2008). Knowing through music: implications for research. In P. Liamputtong & J. Rumbold (Eds.), *Knowing Differently: Arts-Based and Collaborative Research Methods* (pp. 229–243). Nova Publishers.

Drolet, J. (Ed.) (2019). *Rebuilding Lives Post Disaster*. Oxford University Press.

Drolet, J., Cox, R., & McDonald-Harker, C. (2015). *Alberta Resilient Communities*. http://arcproject.ca

Drolet, J., McDonald-Harker, C., Fulton, A., & Iliscupidez, A. (2018) Art-informed research with children and youth in a post-flood community. *The International Journal of Social, Political and Community Agendas in the Arts, 13*(3), 39–50.

Felix, E., You, S., Vernberg, E., & Canino, G. (2013). Family influences on the long-term post-disaster recovery of Puerto Rican youth. *Journal of Abnormal Child Psychology, 41*(1), 111–124.

Foster, V. (2009). Authentic representation? Using video as counter-hegemony in participatory research with poor working-class women. *International Journal of Multiple Research Approaches, 3*(3), 233–245.

Foster, V. (2012). The pleasure principle: employing arts-based methods in social work research. *European Journal of Social Work, 15*(4), 532–545.

Fraser, K.D., & Al Sayah, F. (2011). Arts-based methods in health research: a systematic review of the literature. *Arts & Health, 3*(2), 110–145.

Frost, J.L. (2005). Lessons from disasters: play, work, and the creative arts. *Childhood Education, 82*(1), 2–8.

Geddes, L. (2014). 15 compelling images of High River in the 2013 flood. *Global News*, June 16. http://globalnews.ca/news/1338253/ 15-compelling-images-of-high-river-in-the-2013-flood

Huss, E. (2009). A case study of Bedouin women's art in social work. a model of social arts intervention with 'traditional' women negotiating western cultures. *Social Work Education, 28*(6), 598–616. doi: 10.1080/ 02615470903027298

IFSW & IASSW (2004). *Ethics in Social Work, Statement of Principles*. www. iassw-aiets.org/wp-content/uploads/2015/10/Ethics-in-Social-Work-Statement-IFSW-IASSW-2004.pdf

Jarldorn, M. (2016). Picturing creative approaches to social work research: using photography to promote social change. *Aotearoa New Zealand Social Work, 28*(4), 5–16.

Kolker, A. (1996). Thrown overboard: the human costs of health care rationing. In C. Ellis and A.P. Bochner (Eds.), *Composing Ethnography: Alternative Forms of Qualitative Writing* (pp. 132–159). Alta Mira Press.

Kousky, C. (2016). Impacts of natural disasters on children. *The Future of Children*, 73–92.

Leavy, P. (2017). *Research Design: Quantitative, Qualitative, Mixed Methods, Arts-Based, and Community-Based Participatory Research Approaches*. Guilford Publications.

Lentin, R. (2000). *Israel and the Daughters of the Shoah*. Berghahn Books.

Literat, I. (2013). 'A pencil for your thoughts': participatory drawing as a visual research method with children and youth. *International Journal of Qualitative Methods, 12*, 84–98.

Malchiodi, C.A. (2005). Art therapy. In C.A. Malchiodi (Ed.), *Expressive Therapies* (pp. 16–45). Guilford Press.

Mertz, E. (2016). Top 10 most costly disasters in Canadian history for insurers. *Global News*, July 7. http://globalnews.ca/news/2810070/ top-10-most-costly-disasters-in-canadian-history-for-insurers

Mienczakowski, J., Smith, L., & Morgan, S. (2002). Seeing words-hearing feelings: Ethnodrama and the performance of data. In C. Bagley & M.B. Cancienne (Eds.), *Dancing the Data* (pp. 34–52). Peter Lang Publishing.

O'Donoghue, D. (2015). On the education of art-based researchers: what we might learn from Charles Garoian. *Qualitative Inquiry, 21*(6), 520–528.

Orr, P.P. (2007). Art therapy with children after a disaster: a content analysis. *The Arts in Psychotherapy, 34*(4), 350–361.

Peek, L. (2008). Children and disasters: understanding vulnerability, developing capacities, and promoting resilience – An introduction. *Children Youth and Environments, 18*(1), 1–29.

Peek, L., Tobin-Gurley, J., Cox, R.S., Scannell, L., Fletcher, S., & Heykoop, C. (2016). Engaging youth in post-disaster research: lessons learned from a creative methods approach. *Gateways: International Journal of Community Research and Engagement, 9*(1), 89–112.

Pomeroy, J.W., Stewart, R.E., & Whitfield, P.H. (2016). The 2013 flood event in the South Saskatchewan and Elk River basins: Causes, assessment and damages. *Canadian Water Resources Journal/Revue canadienne des ressources hydriques, 41*(1–2), 105–117.

Ronan, K.R., & Towers, B. (2014). Systems education for a sustainable planet: preparing children for natural disasters. *Systems, 2*(1), 1–23.

Shannon, P. (2013). Value-based social work research: strategies for connecting research to the mission of social work. *Critical Social Work, 14*(1), 102–114.

Shannon-Baker, P. (2015). "But I wanted to appear happy": How using arts-informed and mixed methods approaches complicate qualitatively driven research on culture shock. *International Journal of Qualitative Methods, 14*, 34–52.

Snowber, C. (2002). Bodydance: enfleshing soulful inquiry through improvisation. In C. Bagley & M.B. Cancienne (Eds.), *Dancing the Data* (pp. 20–33). Peter Lang Publishing.

Szto, P., Furman, R., & Langer, C. (2005). Poetry and photography: an exploration into expressive/creative qualitative research. *Qualitative Social Work, 4*(2), 135–156.

Travis, R., Jr., & Deepak, A. (2011). Empowerment in context: lessons from Hip-Hop culture for social work practice. *Journal of Ethnic & Cultural Diversity in Social Work, 20*, 203–222.

Van Son, R. (2000). Painting women into the picture. In A. Byrne, & R. Lentin (Eds.), *(Re)searching Women: Feminist Research Methodologies in the Social Sciences in Ireland* (pp. 214–236). Institute of Public Administration.

Vanover, C., Jones, B.D., Shanae, J., Hand, E., Anguiano, A., Miller, T., & Knobloch, K. (2018). *Chicago Butoh: Visioning Research Informed Dance and Theatre.* University of South Florida, Faculty Publications. https://digital.usfsp.edu/cgi/viewcontent.cgi?article=4796&context=fac_publications

SECTION III

Arts-based research as a way for researchers and community members to understand communities

11

Murals and photography in community engagement and assessment

Holly Feen-Calligan, Elizabeth Barton, Julie Moreno, Emma Buzzard, and Marion Jackson[1]

This chapter describes the painting and assessing of a mural on a corner food store in a large urban Midwest centre in the US, a city that was once a thriving industrial centre. In recent years, however, reductions in the manufacturing industry have resulted in unemployment, poverty, population loss, abandoned properties, and business closures – notably, full service grocery stores. Residents express frustration and bitterness at having to depend only on 'corner stores' selling mostly junk food, tobacco, and alcohol.

Currently, the city's residents, known for their grit and resilience, have begun repurposing many abandoned properties with vegetable gardens and public art. Grass-roots efforts have been working in concert with non-profit organisations like Groundworks Gardens and the Soup Kitchen Ministries (pseudonyms) to make healthier food options accessible to residents. Murals and other public artworks enliven the environment and the spirits of residents and contribute to the city's revitalisation.

Midwest University, located within the city, has partnered with these and other non-profit organisations in mutually beneficial service-learning, internship, and research relationships. An important mission of the university is community outreach and support, and service-learning and research initiatives are integrated within various departments and courses in the university. One such university initiative is CitySeed, a programme established to build sustainable food systems on the university's campus and in the city, in part, through the 'Healthy Corner Store Project'. The setting in this chapter is one corner store with which CitySeed collaborated. The store desired to change its image in the neighbourhood by promoting healthy eating and proclaiming its fresh food options to residents. To accomplish this, the assistance of another university programme, ArtsCorps, was elicited to paint a mural on the store to represent the healthy changes in products the store desired to promote.

ArtsCorps was established by arts faculty and faculty from other disciplines who were interested in service-learning (integrating community service into curricula to achieve learning outcomes). ArtsCorps helped identify local arts projects for which the helping hands of service-learners and volunteers could make a critical difference. ArtsCorps was envisioned as a tool to help revitalise the city through the arts using four interrelated components: service-learning, research, volunteerism, and public forums (i.e. opportunities for sharing projects, dialoguing about needs, and next steps through presentations and town hall style meetings).

Photography is used by ArtsCorps to (1) document community events and research activities; (2) disseminate research findings through exhibits and conference presentations; and (3) help students examine their contributions in art–based service-learning assignments. Photovoice techniques were used in the food store mural painting for evaluation purposes and to elicit the perspectives of mural participants.

Photovoice and community murals

Photovoice puts cameras in the hands of community members who record elements of their lived realities. Originators of Photovoice denote three benefits of the method: to enable individuals to record their community's strengths and concerns, to promote critical dialogue about personal and community issues, and to reach policymakers (Wang & Burris, 1997).

The benefits of Photovoice parallel common goals of social work, and Photovoice has been used by social workers for therapeutic and research aims (for example, Malka et al., 2018; Mitchell et al., 2019). Photovoice methods help make community strengths and needs explicit, as well as provide a methodology for descriptive evaluation (Catalani & Minkler, 2010). Photovoice facilitates individual empowerment and can lead to action and advocacy (Foster-Fishman et al., 2005). Our particular project was inspired by Carlson et al.'s (2006) use of Photovoice methods in a lower income African American community where residents were asked to photograph aspects of their neighbourhoods that they were proud of, as well as things they would like to change to inspire healthy living.

Community murals

Murals also have a rich history in representing community identities and strengths (Delgado, 2000; Kapitan et al., 2011). Today, notable mural programmes worldwide such as Artolution (n.d.) use artist-led collaborations with communities experiencing crisis to facilitate positive social change and mental health (World Health Organization, 2020). Currently, in the US, collaborative mural programmes such as Mural Arts Philadelphia (n.d.); specifically its Porchlight Program, report positive impact on residents' perceptions of neighbourhood including affecting collective efficacy, aesthetic quality, and behavioural health stigma (Tebes et al., 2015). Mural Arts Philadelphia published a replication manual and assessment guidelines (Ansell et al., 2013), which can assist similar collaborations in other communities. Social workers with knowledge and skills in working with communities and marginalised groups have the background to use murals to mobilise community participation while emphasising community strengths (Delgado & Barton, 1998).

Mural and Photovoice methods in the food store mural

A mini-grant from the state's art council funded a local artist to facilitate a mural on the food store in collaboration with ArtsCorps, CitySeed, and other community volunteers. The mural was intended to represent the healthy lifestyle neighbourhood residents would like to have, and to promote the community garden planned for the adjacent empty property the following spring.

For two weeks prior to painting, a poster was placed inside the entrance to the food store, describing the future mural and inviting participants. Customers (largely local residents) were invited to write what they would like to see on the building and in their neighbourhood. Many ideas were listed and sketched. The first session (of the eight-week Saturday mural sessions) consisted of examining the ideas by sketching some of them on the sidewalks in non-permanent format. Participants were asked, How do you want to represent yourself? What's great about this neighborhood? What's great about you? What would you like to see changed? (See Figure 11.1.)

Artist Halima Cassells determined that open books and notebooks could showcase the different ideas suggested: 'a healthy block is a clean block', fruits and vegetables, a healthy diet; the names of neighbourhood organizations and the businesses across the street (see Figure 11.2). ArtsCorps volunteers assisted Cassells by aiding residents who were less familiar with painting. Over the eight weeks, the mural evolved to reflect additional ideas of store customers and passersby, some who painted one time, others who returned multiple times until the mural was completed. Members of a bicycle club who were riding by stopped and returned to paint themes related to exercise and socialisation during each subsequent week.

A clipboard was available for participants to sign in and list their contact information if desired. Although individuals shot photographs using mobile phones or digital cameras, ArtsCorps offered disposable cameras to participants with the request to 'record your experiences with painting the mural'. Cameras were to be returned each week to an art therapy intern and ArtsCorps volunteer who labelled them with the name of the person who used the camera so that the camera could be given to the same individual the next week. Individuals were selected to receive cameras based on what seemed to be their investment in the painting (i.e. not someone who stopped briefly, but someone who spent time participating and showed interest in

Figure 11.1: Painting the food store

Source: authors.

Figure 11.2: Detail of food store mural

Source: authors.

the project). One camera was given to the bicycle club to share. Additional cameras were distributed to the lead artist, the store owner, and two other individual participants. ArtsCorps consent forms were explained to and then signed by all participants giving their permission to publish their photos and statements about their experiences.

The mural began on the front wall facing a high-traffic street, and quickly expanded to the side walls as well as the garage behind the empty lot. The season ended with each person signing the mural. Fall chrysanthemums were planted as a reminder that a vegetable garden would be coming in the spring.

The cameras were collected on the last day and were taken to a pharmacy for photo processing and duplication. Also, on the last day, ArtsCorps volunteer and MFA Media Arts student Angela Moriera conducted video interviews with participants about their experiences. Excerpts from three statements are:

> The mural create[d] positiveness…When we first started it was a plain white building. We let the people in the neighborhood know that, 'this is what your neighborhood is about: beauty and keeping it clean and healthy…'
>
> I think it gives people hope that it just don't [sic] always have to be one way. It can change, and people can change with it…You look at it and it just inspires you; it don't [sic] need no words or no explanation. You can tell that people actually cared enough to come out here take their time and change [the city] a little bit at a time; even though it's just a little bit, it's still a change; that's what we need.
>
> It's not tagging; it is something positive…Instead of a building just sitting abandoned, being an eyesore, it looks pretty when you add color. People just come by like strangers, and say, 'oh I love it' and they thank us. They… say, 'Thanks for adding this, beautifying our neighborhood, our block.'

Analysis of the photographs

Plans to review the photographs with the participants the following week did not materialise. The bicycle club was participating in an event, and others did not attend. Therefore, the photos were returned to individual participants without the opportunity for group discussion. The first author made arrangements with a participant from the bicycle club to return and discuss photographs. When she arrived at the meeting place on her bike, it had started to rain, and she was concerned about getting back home before a bigger storm hit. She later texted that she liked the photographs and asked if there were 'any more pictures of us?' Photographs from the author's camera were forwarded. A number of photographs of the mural were subsequently posted on the bicycle club's Facebook page.

A conversation about photographs did take place between community residents and ArtsCorps volunteer, Laura. In Laura's opinion, the mural reflects an antidote to "the broken window syndrome." She said:

> When you have one broken window everything goes down, bit by bit. When you have a mural like this and its beautiful, things progress… Once we got this done, people started coming by, asking what was going on, tooting their horns going past, the owner came out and asked us, could we paint the back? Building after building after building, soon … this whole area that will be repainted…[and] something done by the community will be respected by the community.

Some of the other photos were assembled to make a poster that was taken to the food store along with a small paper journal onto which people could record their thoughts, like a guest book at an art exhibit. One of the store employees helped the first author mount the poster at the bottom of a bulletin board inside the store. The comment book was also pinned to the bulletin board with a pen attached. Three weeks after leaving the poster and comment book the first author returned to see what had been written. She found the book was missing and that a single photograph had been cut out of the foam core board. Store owners did not know when the book went missing, nor had they noticed anyone cutting the foam core to remove the photograph.

Perspectives from service-learners

In the university's art therapy programme, service-learning is a pedagogy used to help achieve learning outcomes related to extending a sense of social responsibility and social justice in art therapy practice. The assessment of these learning outcomes is achieved in part through students' written and artistic reflections during the class. Students are asked to complete a minimum number of written reflections that can be illustrated with photographs of their service-learning activities. Concurrently, students create a semester-long work of art that reflects their learning in service-learning, by photographing their art week-to-week to document their process and growth. Often photographs help students recall moments of insight or changing perspective or to help objectify otherwise intangible experiences.

Findings drawn from the mural process and Photovoice

Throughout the food store mural painting project/sessions, ArtsCorps faculty met regularly to discuss the project, and the photographs were reviewed during one meeting. On a basic descriptive level, we noted what was there. More than 30 different people from infants to older adults, Black and White, male and female appear in the photographs. Activities were interpreted as painting, helping, sharing, mixing, observing, smoking, cooking, eating, watching, standing, playing, dancing, cleaning, planting. There were objects: bikes, cars, ladders, brushes, paint cans, trays, water bottles, garbage bags. Images on the mural included fruit, vegetables, designs, words: the name of the city and the bike club, names of area block clubs and businesses; symbols: peace sign, cross, Egyptian cross of life, and images from the locale: house, cow head, man on a horse, bikes, stroller. The mural was colourful; 20 colours were counted. The process is also apparent; in some of the photographs evidence of chalk sketches show beneath the paint.

The photographs and video interviews, researchers agreed, provide evidence of moving towards one of the goals of ArtsCorps, to 'revitalize the city through the arts'. The photographs were also useful to help ArtsCorps document community building, as evidenced by interactions between people who had not previously known one another and who worked together on a common goal. People from different groups, local residents, store employees, the bicycle club, ArtsCorps volunteers, university interns and faculty, and the lead artist worked collaboratively to contribute to the food store mural. Interactions such as these reflect the spirit of service-learning and corroborate what students have said about the benefits of service-learning: meeting and learning from people different than themselves.

Individual and community transformation

Evidence that the photographs were valued by the individual participants seemed demonstrated by the fact that each photographer wanted his or her photographs, additional photographs were requested, and they were posted on the bicycle club's Facebook page. The removal of the photograph from the food store poster suggests the photo must have had some value. The question, 'are there any more photos of us?' seems to reflect the sense of pride voiced in the interviews on the last day of painting as one member explained, "the mural painting uplifts not just the community but each one of us".

Laura's statement is consistent with Timm-Bottos' (2006) acknowledgement of 'the elevated positive affect that is associated with community art making. Celebrating what is working today within each individual [shows] the potential this creativity can manifest in the world' (p. 19). Rossetto (2012) similarly wrote that engagement in practices like mural making can help participants to 'deepen their relationship to society while simultaneously practicing social action' (p. 25). The food store mural seemed to provide membership a collective effort to make a difference in the city. Lead artist Halima Cassells emphasised each individual's capacity: "you are the one that you have been waiting on. It is as easy as envisioning it and then just deciding to do it. Be empowered" (video interview).

The mural itself resulted in a dramatic aesthetic improvement on one eastside street corner. The ability to point to a tangible difference made possible through the hands of volunteers seemed empowering. Photographs of the mural 'like all photographs that people take and keep... are much like "mirrors with memory" serving as markers of what (and who) has mattered most' (Weiser, 2004, p. 23).

Reaching policy makers

A third goal of Photovoice is to reach policy makers – people with power to leverage resources. While we were painting, an article written by the district's state representative was published in a local newspaper inviting families from her city (where we were painting) and the wealthy white adjacent suburb to discuss common interests and goals. The first author emailed her in response, and invited her to see for herself a project in which people from both cities were working together for the common good. She quickly arranged to speak with us and view the mural. The meeting resulted in her support of arts-based initiatives in her district.

Photos of the mural were also posted on a bulletin board inside busy restaurant across the street from the food store (where customers could observe the activity) Along with the photos, comment cards were pinned to the bulletin board encouraging customers to comment. One of the comments was from a journalist, congratulating our efforts. Although we are not aware of any publications written by this journalist on the subject of our mural, the potential exists for reaching policy makers through something as old-fashioned as a bulletin board.

Challenges, lessons learned and recommendations

Although ArtsCorps regularly documented community and service-learning projects, the food store mural project did not recruit participants specifically to participate in research. Future community arts projects are now planned, with evaluation components often including Photovoice and consideration of intended outcomes.

The food store mural painting project used Photovoice methods but fell short of discussing the photos with all the photographers. While there was much interest in painting, there seemed to be less priority placed on discussing the photographs after the project ended. Participants shot photographs every week with their own cameras or with the disposable cameras distributed by ArtsCorps. The photographs seemed to have meaning to the photographers in terms of reflecting individual and social identity. To the researchers, the photographs served to document the efforts of a corps of volunteers; they have been used in scholarly presentations to illustrate revitalising the city through the arts, to engage community members, and to promote individual and community health. Owners of the food store report that "the customers love [the mural]; they love the flowers; they ask us if we did it."

As described in several publications, Photovoice can enable individuals to record their community's strengths and concerns and promote critical dialogue about personal and community issues (Wang, 1999; Purcell, 2007). Social workers interested in Photovoice are directed to Strack et al.'s use (2010) of a logic model to guide Photovoice planning to produce individual-community level change.

Note
[1] The authors wish to thank mural artist Halima Cassells, media artist Angela Moriera, and art therapy graduate student Meah Tweh for their contributions to the project.

References
Ansell, S., Matlin, S.L., Evans, A.C., Golden, J., & Tebes, J.K. (2013). *Painting a Healthy City: The Porch Light Program Replication Manual.* City of Philadelphia Mural Arts Program.

Artolution (n.d.) *2019 Annual Report.* www.artolution.org/

Carlson, E.D., Engebretson, J., & Chamberlain, R.M. (2006). Photovoice as a social process of critical consciousness. *Qualitative Health Research, 16*(6), 836–852. https://doi.org/10. 1177/1049732306287525

Catalani, C., & Minkler, M. (2010). Photovoice: a review of the literature in health and public health. *Health Education and Behavior, 37*(3), 424–451. https://dx.doi.org/10.1177/1090198109342084

Delgado, M. (2000). *Community Social Work Practice in an Urban Context: The Potential of a Capacity-Enhancement Perspective.* Oxford University Press.

Delgado, M., & Barton, K. (1998). Murals in Latino communities: social indicators of community strengths. *Social Work, 43*(4) 346–456.

Foster-Fishman, P., Nowell, B., Deacon, Z., Nievar, M.A., & McCann, P. (2005). Using methods that matter: the impact of reflection, dialogue, and voice. *American Journal of Community Psychology, 36*(3/4), 275–291. https://doi.org/10.1007/s10464-0058626-y

Kapitan, K., Litell, M., & Torres, A. (2011). Creative art therapy in a community's participatory research and social transformation, *Art Therapy: Journal of the American Art Therapy Association, 28*(2), 64–73. https://doi.org/10.1080/07421656.2011.578238

Malka, M., Huss, E., Bendarker, L., & Musai, O. (2018). Using photovoice with children of addicted parents to integrate phenomenological and social reality. *The Arts in Psychotherapy, 60*, 82–90. https://doi.org/10.1016/j.aip.2017.11.001

Mitchell, C., Linds, W., Denov, M., D'Amico, M., & Cleary, B. (2019). Beginning at the beginning in social work education: a case for incorporating arts-based approaches to working with war-affected children and their families. *Journal of Family Social Work, 22*(1), 63–82. https://doi.org/10.1080/10522158.2019.1546949

Mural Arts Philadelphia (n.d.). www.muralarts.org/

Purcell, R. (2007). Images for change: community development, community arts and photography. *Community Development Journal, 44*(1), 111–122. https://doi-org.proxy.lib.wayne.edu/10.1093/cdj/bsm031

Rossetto, E. (2012). A hermeneutic phenomenological study of community mural making and social action art therapy. *Art Therapy, 29*(1), 19–26. https://doi.org/10.1080/07421656.2012.648105

Strack, R.W., Lovelace, K.A., Davis Jordan, T., & Holmes, A.P. (2010). Framing photovoice using a social-ecological logic model as a guide. *Health Promotion Practice, 11*(5), 629–636. https://doi.org/10.1177/1524839909355519

Tebes, J.K., Matlin, S.L., Hunter, B., Thompson, A.B., Prince, D.M., & Mohatt, N. (2015). *Porchlight Program Final Evaluation Report.* https://medicine.yale.edu/psychiatry/consultationcenter/Images/Porch_Light_Program_Final_Evaluation_Report_Yale_June_2015_Optimized_tcm798-218966.pdf

Timm-Bottos, J. (2006). Constructing creative community: reviving health and justice through community arts. *The Canadian Art Therapy Association Journal, 19*(2), 10–26. DOI: 10.1080/08322473.2006.11432285

Wang, C. (1999). Photovoice: a participatory action research strategy applied to women's health. *Journal of Women's Health, 8*(2), 185–192.

Wang, C., & Burris, M.A. (1997). Photovoice: concept method and use for participatory needs assessment. *Health Education and Behavior, 24*(3) 369–387. https://doi-org.proxy.lib.wayne.edu/10.1177/109019819702400309

Weiser, J. (2004). Phototherapy techniques in counseling and therapy: using ordinary snapshots and photo interactions to help clients heal their lives. *The Canadian Art Therapy Association Journal, 17*(2), 23–53. https://doi-org.ezproxy.bgu.ac.il/10.1080/08322473.2004.11432263

World Health Organization (2020, October 10). *World Mental Health Day: Addressing Mental Health in Emergencies.* World Health Organization. www.who.int/bangladesh/news/detail/10-10-2020-world-mental-health-day-addressing-mental-health-in-emergencies

12

Forum theatre as participatory action research with community workers

Mike de Kreek, Eltje Bos, and Margareta von Salisch

A new practice: neighbourhood teams

In Amsterdam, just like in 87 % of all municipalities in the Netherlands, integrated neighbourhood teams have been installed as an answer to the reform of the welfare state. During the last decade, the social domain has gone through its strongest change since 1945. Transitions by new national acts and policies have gone hand in hand with decentralisation, which has transferred most responsibilities in the social domain to municipalities, accompanied by less financial means. On the local level, these changes have been translated by municipalities into policies, responsibilities, interventions, and a repertoire that requires strong changes in the professional behaviour of all stakeholders.

One of the newly implemented practices consists of interdisciplinary neighbourhood teams focussed on empowerment of people or families who are dealing with multiple challenges in their lives. Professionals from elder care, youth care, community development, and welfare organisations need to collaborate while they attempt to reconcile various professional perspectives on a specific problematic situation. At the same time, there is a shift for many professionals from solving problems for clients towards empowering the clients to solve problems themselves, based on their own strengths or their network. Most of the structural transitions and implementations might be finished; however, the transformation in professional behaviour following these changes, is just starting to develop.

Despite a series of training courses in various methods, the Amsterdam neighbourhood team professionals strongly felt a need to deepen their experiences with situations in which the contact with a client or family had somehow stagnated. Together with the Amsterdam University of Applied Sciences (AUAS) they developed a form of participatory theatre through which they could – and still can – research critical situations in order to contribute to both practice theory and practice development.

Forum theatre as vehicle for action research

The municipality of Amsterdam asked the research institute of the Faculty of Social Work and Law to help the neighbourhood teams to research their experiences in critical situations. The aim was to increase sharing of knowledge, to develop intervention methods, and to provide tools for situations where contact with a client or family had stagnated. The professionals formulated the following research question: What and how can we learn from unravelling situations in which contact with clients has stagnated?

The search for a design for the research and learning trajectory was based on the following starting points: (1) professionals have a considerable amount of tacit knowledge; (2) professionals like to learn from each other; (3) reflection on difficult situations supports professional learning; (4) new knowledge arises in co-creation by professionals; (5) researching ongoing practice is part of professional development and continues throughout the professional career.

In order to achieve in-depth understanding, it was important to focus not only on the issue at hand, but also to address the beliefs, attitude, and values of the professionals involved. These factors are often hidden and need to be excavated, just like tacit knowledge in order to be useful. To access these more covert aspects and to facilitate co-creation, creative research methods were found in the approach of forum theatre, a method developed in Brazil (Boal, 1979).

In a forum theatre performance, the participants are expected to participate in unravelling a painful situation by continuously substituting one of the actors who can then divert the scene into a better direction. Doing so, the group experiments with all kinds of factors that affect the situation: including beliefs, attitudes, and values, but also verbal and non-verbal behaviours.

Through joint reflection after the performance, the participants investigate what the most desirable alternatives for action would be. If forum theatre is applied in combination with the systematic retention of the insights that are developed together, it can be labelled as participatory action research. Indeed, some books on action research describe the researcher as a cultural animator, a role that is close to that of a theatre maker (Tacchi et al., 2003).

This applied form of forum theatre with neighbourhood teams firstly consisted of preparing a performance by finding a critical situation that was rehearsed in order to emphasise its complicating elements in the interaction. Secondly, the participatory theatre show was repeatedly played and reflected upon afterwards by the participants. Thirdly, the useful insights were internalised in one or more additional performances by the participants and collected in a guideline document.

A central element in the second round of the theatre work was that professionals in the audience could stop a scene at any time and replace the person who played the professional in the stagnating contact with a client or family. Accordingly, the participants playfully experimented with roles, beliefs, potential solutions, language, behaviour, and attitude. They discovered that the crux is that both verbal and non-verbal alternatives are involved, not only unleashing rational, but also embodied professional experience and personal beliefs that are hard to self-define. We argue that this kind of knowledge co-creation can complement more traditional practice research methodologies and can be especially useful for social work teams to evaluate and research challenging situations in their practices.

The participatory research in action

The overall method of the applied form of forum theatre consisted of (1) determining the case, (2) performing the participatory theatre, and (3) elaborating the insights. The complete process was supervised by an action researcher who combined dramaturgical and animation skills.

Phase 1: determining the case

The preparation of the case consisted of three steps: (a) the research topic, (b) the ownership, and (c) the case. Each part was guided by collectively determining the answer to a question. For the research topic (step 1a) the question was: 'What wants to be investigated?' Together, the participants agreed to be searching for a kind of stagnation that was recognisable and urgent enough for everyone to explore further in the coming meetings.

For the step of ownership (step 1b) it was important for someone to step forward on the invitational question: 'Who wants to investigate a situation of stagnation based on his or her own experiences?' Menar, one of the professionals, volunteered, because she was unsure how to establish contact with a family who were confronted with multiple problems and negative experiences with another professional.

When selecting a specific case containing a critical situation (step 1c), the question was: 'Which concrete, existing situation lends itself to being further explored?' Menar's case consisted of an extensive and complex family story that stretched over a period of more than a year. The father and mother, each with a different cultural background, had an 11-year-old son with behavioural problems in school and a two-year-old toddler with physical and mental disabilities. The father was a frequent criminal offender and in jail for ignoring traffic fines. The parents were married against the will of their families, and they had nowhere to fall back and get support concerning their huge debts. Their contact with many professionals, including probation officer, hospital staff, parental support, and the neighbourhood team, had made them critical towards professionals in general. It also became clear that

Menar had taken over the family from a colleague in whom the family had lost confidence and against whom it had filed a complaint.

During Menar's story, the interaction with the colleagues and the action researcher, several questions came up that Menar wanted to investigate further. One of them was: 'How can I not only support her, but also point out her duties towards the children (which is also my task), without losing her?' Together with the action researcher, Menar chose to play and deepen a scene with the focus on this challenge of establishing contact with and gaining the trust of the mother.

Phase 2: performing the participatory theatre

The phase of the actual sessions of participatory theatre consisted of four steps: (a) the staging, (b) the rehearsal, (c) the participatory performance, and (d) the collective reflection. In the staging step (2a), a playable script of the chosen situation was discussed and developed with Menar's questions about establishing contact in mind. The action researcher and Menar did this in such a way that both verbal and non-verbal mechanisms possibly causing stagnation were expressed. The aim was to get as close as possible to the real situation in which contact was *not* established.

During the rehearsal (step 2b) the scene was performed by Menar, being the owner of the case, playing herself, and an actor as the mother for a few colleagues, social work professionals, as the audience. The dramaturgical skills of the action researcher were aimed at supporting, scrutinising, demonstrating, and amplifying. Now and then the action researcher asked the colleagues to tell both actors how they experienced the scene. When Menar said she reached the same kind of feeling as in the real situation, they established that they were on the right track. They rehearsed until both actors had internalised all non-verbal and verbal interactions that made the stagnation mechanisms tangible.

The participatory performance (step 2c) started with an introduction to the whole neighbourhood team by the action researcher and a warming-up exercise in which the participants made verbal and non-verbal contact with each other. This provided relaxation and a safe atmosphere for the rest of the session. Then the complete scene was first played by Menar and the actor without interruptions. There was a short discussion facilitated by the action researcher who also introduced the method allowing other participants to substitute for one of the actors. When replaying the scene, the other participants were invited to call 'stop' and take over the role of Menar in order to introduce alternative ways of action.

Collective reflection (step 2d) started in between the performances. The action researcher continuously wrote down questions, reactions, and insights on a flipchart. The scene was replayed repeatedly, each time examining what participants experienced and what could be improved in a next performance. This repetition came to an end naturally, when nobody thought anything was left to improve in successfully establishing contact with the mother. After this, each participant filled in an individual reflection form, which was the basis for a collective final reflection process.

Phase 3: elaborating on the insights

The participatory action research covered two steps for elaborating on the insights gained from the theatre process: (a) contemplating the insights, and (b) further developing the insights.

Contemplation of the insights (step 3a) was an important step in the third phase. A set of rather raw data was available in the form of notes on flipcharts and completed individual reflection forms. As is, these were not helpful to make the insights useful for others. However, the group of participating professionals wanted to internalise their preliminary insights by replaying the scene in a new rehearsal meeting. These rehearsal performances – without interruptions this time – were based on the 'best' alternatives for verbal and non-verbal action of the professional that had been developed/discovered in phase 2. During the debriefing after these performances, more general building blocks for professional verbal and non-verbal behaviour were collected, grounded in the joint insights. These building blocks were developed into a thorough description afterwards by the action researcher with two of the professionals.

The resulting description was shared with all the participants in the participatory theatre as an important summary of lessons learned, but had to be developed further (step 3b). The text was deemed to be incomprehensible for professionals who had not been present at the theatre meetings. Moreover, the lessons learned had not yet been compared with existing communication methods available for professionals. In response to this, the action researcher teamed up with another researcher to enrich the description into a guidelines document containing the case description, parts of the reflection notes, and some excerpts of responses by the participants. In this document they also incorporated reference to existing methods for motivational conversations and dealing with resistance. The guidelines and the developed forum theatre approach formed the basis for new trainings for other neighbourhood teams.

Research findings

The research question was formulated as: What and how can we learn from unpacking situations in which contact with clients has stagnated? The current chapter cannot include the full guideline in phase 3, but we will focus on the research findings closely related to the theatre sessions in phase 2.

Research findings: what have we learned?

A striking point that arose during the performances in phase 2 was that the mother (i.e. the actor) was only willing to engage in the conversation after real contact had been established. Two important and common reactions of professionals were revealed that obstruct this. Firstly, the professionals discovered that they were often inclined to defend themselves against the aggressive verbal behaviour of the mother, by repeating the difficulties she experienced earlier with other involved professionals. Secondly, professionals were tempted to shift the conversation to one of the aims of the neighbourhood team too early in the interaction, for example focusing on the well-being of the children. They called this 'the repair reflex' (Rollnick et al., 2009), leading to a situation in which the mother remained an aggressive victim.

As a result of discovering these obstructive reactions, the professionals realised that the aggressive verbal and non-verbal attitude of the mother was in fact a scream for attention and request to be heard. Asking a question such as 'How do you manage to run your family, despite all the problems?' enabled the mother to tell the story about her situation, both about things that went well and problems that she faced. In the unfolding conversation, the mother shared how proud she was of her son and her relationship with her husband. This was regarded as a turning point in establishing a new form of contact with the mother, in which there was space for mutual understanding and trust.

In the dialogues that followed, the professional was able to carefully address what the mother or the family might need help with. Questions like 'What keeps you awake at night?' and 'What do you hope for in the future?' were good starting points to identify the main challenges in her family's life. A collaborative relationship started to develop in which the professional could explain what the role of the neighbourhood team could and could not be. During this process, the professionals considered it crucial that they had to continuously attempt to address the mother regarding her own responsibility with questions like 'Who from your surroundings do you trust and could we ask them to think along with us?'

Research findings: what have we learned?

The first performances of the scene in phase 2 were meant to illustrate and discover why contact with the mother had stagnated. In order to achieve this, verbal and non-verbal mechanisms were identified and amplified in the rehearsals. It took courage to perform the scene in this way, especially for Menar, who made herself vulnerable doing so. That courage contributed to uncovering the two unproductive reactions in the aggressive conversation.

Furthermore, it took courage of all participants to try to improve their actions by playing the role of the professional in front of an aggressive mother. The skilled actor contributed to search of alternative verbal and non-verbal professional behaviour, by showing – in the role of the mother – that she would remain aggressive until someone really tried to make genuine contact with her.

According to the professionals, the way the action researcher directed the participatory theatre facilitated an effective way of exploring the stagnation and the options for change.

One of them said, "Working this way, made me really experience what effects the reaction of a professional can have on a parent in such a situation." Another commented on seeing the 'repair reflex' in action with: "This will never happen to me again." It was noted that the insights found during the performances were not completely new, but were, in fact, available in method books and practice research. However, that did not mean that the professionals could have read a book and followed a training course to change their approach. On the contrary, they wanted to investigate their experiences with complex cases more deeply in order to close the gap between 'knowing' and 'practising', and to connect between emotional and cognitive understandings

Conclusions: reflections on forum theatre as creative research methodology

On a more methodological level we reflect on what key characteristics play a role in forum theatre applied as a method for action research. Four criteria are crucial for ensuring the quality of this kind of research: affective aesthetics, practical relevance, methodological rigour, and ethical responsibility.

Affective aesthetics

The affect triggered by participatory theatre has a strong evocative power that uncovers other forms of intelligence beyond rational or verbal intelligence. Professionals also have other resources related to experiential knowledge, such as emotional intelligence, imagination, and social intelligence (Muijen & Brohm, 2018). Participating in theatrics encourages the imagination of possible future interactions that seemed previously unimaginable (Kreek & Bos, 2017). This enables participants to move into the perspective of 'the other' in new ways, which nurtures their empathy to other views and triggers reconsideration of their own views (Nussbaum, 2010). Moreover, the positive emotions participants experience in performing theatre together expands their frame of reference and fuels their willingness to care for others, including each other (Fredrickson, 1998).

Methodological rigour

Rationally verbalised characterisations by professionals about their actions are often limited to what they think their work ought to look like (Argyris & Schön, 1974). Using arts, such as participatory theatre, improves the credibility of the research, because it also exposes and combines their actual behaviour in situations, which tends to be tacitly stored in other forms of intelligence. During each performance in phases 2 and 3, these data were collectively expressed, collected, interpreted, and incorporated in an adjusted subsequent performance. Obviously, some participants preferred verbal actions and others non-verbal ones, which resulted in the group combining and experimenting with both. Across the performances, the participants systematically eliminated or retained aspects of their actions, jointly developing a new action repertoire. In a process towards saturation (Bryman, 2012), they arrived at an optimal performance in phase 2 and a set of validated building blocks in phase 3, leaving a trail of flipcharts behind that made their journey transparent.

Practical relevance

We argue that this chapter illustrates that deepening practical situations with the help of theatre provides more realistic insights, than doing a series of interviews or a traditional training. In this kind of participatory arts-based research, the practical relevance is strongly secured in the co-creation that characterises the whole process (Fouché, 2015). The professionals, the actor, and the action researcher formed a research group. The entire group was involved in the articulation of the research question, the choice of method, the case selection, the data collection, the analysis, the interpretation, and the conclusions. They had strong ownership of all these steps and could apply the research insights directly in changing their practice. This also illustrates the practical relevance of a new learning strategy like forum theatre for situations in which these professionals want to deepen their experiences.

Ethical responsibility

Transformative learning is about confronting unproductive implicit and explicit beliefs and the frames of reference behind them. This is not easy in a strictly rational way, because it concerns unlearning old beliefs and acquiring new ones (Kara, 2015). In a playful environment like forum theatre, three elements facilitate this process: (1) everyone joins in experimenting with new roles, beliefs, and actions, (2) the existing social order and its inequality are suspended, and (3) everyone interacts without constraints or prejudice. In this sense, to be part of the forum theatre was a personal decision of the professionals, because they left familiar ground and exposed their uncertainty (Engeström et al., 2015).

In the case described here, stimulated by the dramaturgical skills of the action researcher, the professionals discovered how, in their actions, the aims of their organisation tended to overrule the first needs of their clients. Similarly, the skills of the actor, who sensed this 'repair reflex', forced them to rediscover the importance of mutual understanding and contact. One could imagine how the voice of the client could be further strengthened by involving them in one or more of the phases, but during this first experiment with theatre the professionals regarded this to be unethical.

References

Argyris, C., & Schön, D. (1974). *Theory in Practice: Increasing Professional Effectiveness*. Jossey Bass.

Boal, A. (1979). *Theatre of the Oppressed*. Pluto Press.

Bryman, A. (2012). *Social Research Methods* (4th ed.). Oxford University Press.

Engeström, Y., Kajamaa, A., Lahtinen, P., & Sannino, A. (2015). Toward a grammar of collaboration. *Mind, Culture, and Activity, 22*(2), 92–111. https://doi.org/10.1080/10749039.2015.1024326

Fouché, C. (2015). *Practice Research Partnerships in Social Work – Making a Difference*. Policy Press.

Fredrickson, B.L. (1998). What good are positive emotions? *Review of General Psychology, 2*(3), 300–319. https://doi.org/10.1037/1089-2680.2.3.300

Kara, H. (2015). *Creative Research Methods in the Social Sciences – A Practical Guide*. Policy Press.

Kreek, M. de, & Bos, E. (2017). Playfully towards new relations. In S. Majoor, M. Morel, A. Straathof, W. Winden, & F. Suurenbroek (Eds.), *Lab Amsterdam - Working, Learning, Reflections* (pp. 78–88). Uitgeverij Thoth.

Muijen, H., & Brohm, R. (2018). Art Dialogue Methods – De kracht van kunst en dialoog voor het ontwikkelen van morele werkgemeenschappen. *Waardenwerk - Journal of Humanistic Studies, 73*, 33–43.

Nussbaum, M. (2010). *Not for Profit: Why Democracy Needs the Humanities*: Vol. 10999. Princeton University Press. https://doi.org/10.1016/B978-0-7506-0766-7.50004-0

Rollnick, S., Miller, W.R., & Butler, C.C. (2009). *Motiverende Gespreksvoering in de gezondheidszorg - gedragsverandering als je maar 7 minuten hebt*. Ekklesia.

Tacchi, J., Slater, D., & Hearn, G. (2003). *Ethnographic Action Research*. Unesco Publishing.

13

A/r/tography, rhizomatic storytelling, and ripple effects mapping: a combined arts-based and community mapping methodology to evaluate the impact of COVID-19 expressive arts support groups for frontliners in the Philippines

Maria Regina A. Alfonso, Adrienne M. Santos Lagmay, Joey A. Atayde, Kathleen Bautista, and M. Imelda Lukban

Introduction

The oppressive arrival of COVID-19 has had a significant socio-economic impact particularly on low- to middle-income families in the Philippines, leading to a plethora of mental health issues that exacerbate family living conditions (Malindog-Uy, 2020). Psychosocial support has been a great need.

Magis Creative Spaces, in partnership with ABJ Foundation, implemented an initiative to provide *Duyan* ('cradle' in English) groups: free online expressive arts-based psychosocial support groups for various groups of frontline workers. Focusing on the education, health care, and social welfare sectors, a total of 180 participants took part. In parallel, Magis also initiated a research project to document this initiative.

A pool of ten facilitators was arranged in pairs to create a team for each *Duyan* support group. A general sample of each session's process is as follows: (1) a moment of stillness and silence to offer prayers of healing and gratitude; (2) the introduction of facilitators and participants; (3) a grounding exercise; (4) an art activity (visual art, movement, music or a combination); (5) sharing and discussion; (6) discussion and questions; (7) group photo; (8) closing.

Co-authors Alfonso and Atayde, supervising clinicians for the project, organised all stakeholders of the initiative and reviewed key components of the programme. After each of the *Duyan* support groups were completed, all facilitators were involved in a post-*Duyan* session group process to harvest stories through drawing and storytelling.

Arts-based methodology

A combination of research processes allowed for multiple layers of data gathering. From traditional methods of data collection such as questionnaires, verbatim recordings, to arts-based and experiential methods such as a/r/tography, storytelling, and ripple effect mapping, all perspectives had an important role in documenting and evaluating the programme's impact.

Arts harvesting as data collection: merging an artistic and scientific perspective

Leavy (2014) describes how creative researchers have forged synergistic blends of art and science through a variety of artistic genres. Writing as inquiry has provided powerful examples of how to shift the dialogue about various relevant sociological issues, using lyrical form (Leavy, 2014). Narrative storytelling and visual art have become increasingly accepted, innovative approaches to bridging the growing gap between practice and research (Scott et al., 2013).

The project's artistic (poietic) and scientific perspectives came together through data collection (Stitelmann, 2020). Considering the approach of data gathering as it would be for an evaluative case study, pre- and post-session questionnaires, journal entries, and feedback forms were set up to collect qualitative and quantitative data from the *Duyan* group participants. All responses were collated in a matrix and were supported by media pertaining to the sessions: video recordings of the sessions and art created by participants during the session. Data gathered from this stage can be called primary session data.

A second dimension of data was created after the *Duyan* support groups were conducted. The research team held live virtual meetings or a/r/tography groups – harvesting sessions – to collect data from the *Duyan* facilitators and went through a process of reviewing and responding to the primary session data. Through storytelling, visual art responses, and active dialogue between the research team and the *Duyan* facilitators, new rhizomatic narratives that revolved around the primary session data were recorded in writing, audio and video, and aesthetic responses.

Figure 13.1 (entitled *Detangling*) was made in response to the viewing of a recorded session by researcher Lagmay, where the participants expressed raw emotions in response to the pandemic; the image represents the chaotic nature of their emotions outside the space, and its gradual detangling. These responses were all informed by, but independent of, the primary session data. While this next layer of data harvested during the post-*Duyan* a/r/tography group was initially considered secondary, going through the process of arts-based research led to the adoption of the perspective that data gathered

Figure 13.1: Artistic response to a/r/tography group session by researcher F. Lagmay (July 2020)

from this stage is rhizomatic: information that can evolve, be negotiated, be collaborated on, and is contextual (Cormier, 2008). This means that data was new and had no hierarchy. Instead, the information represented a lived experience, the understanding of which was essential in appropriately and deeply articulating what it meant to be (1) a participant in the support group; and (2) a facilitator in the support group.

Focus on the artistic perspective: a/r/tography, rhizomatic storytelling, and ripple effect mapping

A/r/tography as a methodology allowed the research team to merge their identities as artists, researchers, teachers, and social practitioners through aesthetic responses in art-making, writing, and storytelling. The art that emerged from these perspectives (visual, dance, music) tied together the three lenses into more data that added meaning to the research. The identities, roles, and understandings of artist/researcher/teacher were intertwined in an approach to social science research dedicated to perceiving the world artistically and educationally (Irwin, 1999).

Irwin (n.d.) defines a/r/tography as a means to asking questions through an ongoing art-making process in any type of art form, including writing in an interwoven manner to create additional and/or enhanced meanings, as seen in Figure 13.2. It is developed purposefully to include the '/', which

Figure 13.2: Written, poetic response to an a/r/tography group session by researcher J. Atayde (July 2020)

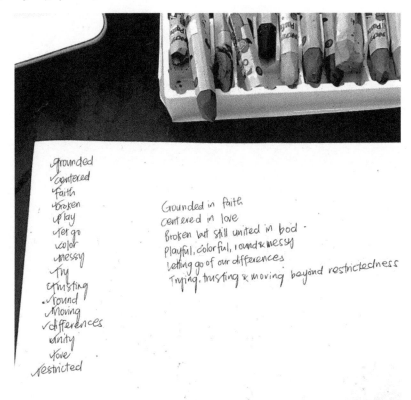

represents an equality and co-existence between the three identities. The inclusion of 'graphy' signifies a joint initiative between art and text, aligning the arts alongside the narrative.

Irwin & Springgay (2008) explain that a/r/tography is a methodology in which all three ways of understanding experiences – theoria, praxis, and poiesis – are folded together and form rhizomatic ways of experiencing the world. Being an a/r/tographer becomes social when groups of a/r/tographers come together to engage in shared inquiries, act as critical friends, articulate an evolution of research questions, and present their collective words to others (Irwin, n.d.).

Figure 13.3 reflects Lukban's impression of what happens in a virtual support group; the virtual 'bubble' provided a space for connection, communicating the message 'you are not alone'.

Complementary to a/r/tography was a process called ripple effect mapping (REM), a participatory group process aimed at measuring community outcomes in action-research; a tool that documents the results of programme efforts within complex, real-life settings (Chazdon et al., 2017). This is

Figure 13.3: Drawing response during an a/r/tography group session by researcher I. Lukban (July 2020)

relevant to community-based programmes that require documentation of outcomes. The four core elements in REM are: (1) appreciative inquiry; (2) a participatory approach; (3) interactive group interviewing and reflection; (4) radiant thinking (mind mapping) (Chazdon et al, 2017).

This method for conducting programme impact engages programme and community stakeholders to map the 'performance story' of a programme or collaboration retrospectively and visually (Mayne, 2001; Baker et al., 2011). It may also be likened to a visual rhizome, mapping an experimentation within digital and real communities (Clinton, 2003).

Organising data

Data was organised based on the main contexts of each support group: education, health care, and social welfare. All digital questionnaires, video recordings, and artwork from sessions were also collected and securely shared virtually after each group session.

An in-depth look at harvesting as a designed process

For the a/r/tographer, harvesting at the post-*Duyan* stage began with a simple frame guided by curiosity, with the intention to engage in active listening, asking questions, and responding to documentation of support groups through both verbal conversation and art-making. To prepare for harvesting sessions, the a/r/tographer would review recordings, and create aesthetic responses to these recordings.

Sharing these aesthetic responses during the post-session dialogue allowed for deeper personal reflections about the *Duyan* groups by prompting the facilitators and researchers to recall even more insights about the process. Figure 13.4, for instance, captures the observation shared by facilitators that the zoom space (with its windows) provided a cradling space, and Figure 13.5 is a visual interpretation of the moods that the researcher felt while witnessing the support group sessions with frontliners at Makati Medical Center.

The flow of harvesting sessions was guided by an outline for post-session dialogue. The objective of the dialogue was to encourage narratives from facilitators about theirs and the participants' experience of their *Duyan* sessions. The discussion was freeform, lasting one hour. Researchers had the chance to clarify events highlighted and emotions felt by the *Duyan* facilitators. Aesthetic responses strengthened the research team's understanding of what could be considered 'abstract' data, or data 'between the lines', in keeping with the idea of rhizomes. Aesthetic responses revealed new information that may not have emerged through the primary qualitative and quantitative data, turning musings into deep insight, and eventually into core research findings.

The significance of this stage of the research process is embodied by the story of one facilitator, who was COVID-19 positive during a virtual *Duyan* session. Participants were unaware of her condition, but it was a poignant experience for her. The organic flow of discussions during the a/r/tography groups created space for her to express her feelings of vulnerability; they helped her connect better with participants. She too felt cradled by the space. This new insight about the communal nature of the *Duyan* sessions developed into a core finding from the project.

Figure 13.6 was created in response to the facilitators' reflection about the power of the creative process to bring people together in the virtual space so much so that facilitators felt just as supported as the participants in the circle. Our 'harvest' – the collective aesthetic responses – was evolved into prompts to jog the emotive memory of the *Duyan* support group facilitators along with guide questions. This helped facilitators reflect on work they had done at a specific moment in time (according to traditional data), as a timeless, lived experience.

Figure 13.7 was inspired by a discussion among the researchers about the concept of *Duyan* and how the cradling effect of the *Duyan* support groups was made effective by anchor points in the form of activities, presented by the facilitators within a frame.

Figure 13.4: Artistic responses to viewing *Duyan* support group sessions independently but shared during an a/r/tography dialogue, by researchers M.R. Alfonso and K. Bautista (July 2020)

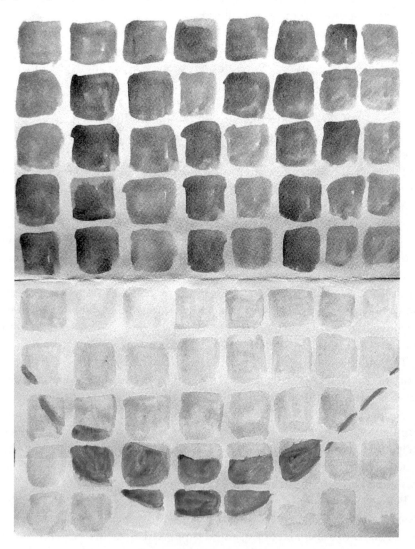

Data analysis and consolidation

To create a visual representation of the impact and reach of the *Duyan* programme, the team employed the simple mind–mapping technique from the REM method.

Figure 13.8 is an image of the *Duyan* 'performance story' (Mayne, 2001; Baker et al., 2011) or mind map based on an REM evaluation process.

Figure 13.5: Artistic responses to viewing *Duyan* support group sessions independently but shared during an a/r/tography dialogue, by researchers M.R. Alfonso and K. Bautista (July 2020)

Research findings

Findings from the *Duyan* groups revealed that there was a positive effect on participants' overall mental health, through the facilitators' embodiment of the following:

Figure 13.6: Artistic response during an a/r/tography dialogue, by researcher F. Lagmay (July 2020). Title: *Togetherness*

Figure 13.7: Artistic response during an a/r/tography dialogue, by researcher F. Lagmay (July 2020)

Figure 13.8: REM Map of the *Duyan* expressive arts group project in the time of COVID-19 (July 2020)

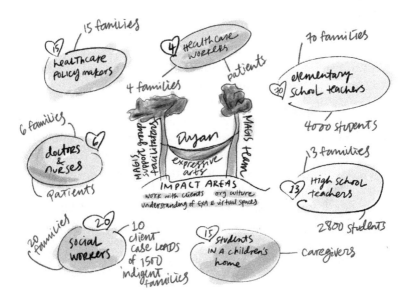

(1) *Bayanihan* – a system of mutual assistance in which the members of a community work together to accomplish a difficult task.

(2) *Pagdaramay, pakikiramdam, pakikipagkapwa* (sense of presence, connection, community) to create a calm atmosphere amidst the adjustment to a new virtual format and the use of the expressive arts therapies as the core approach to providing a safe space.

Another central theme identified in the a/r/tography group was the role of the arts in enabling the verbalisation of difficult feelings. The storytelling was enriched by the live art-making, where art pieces helped the facilitators relive their resonance with participants during their *Duyan* groups.

General themes

Creativity (Pagkamalikhain). The cradling qualities of a *Duyan*, characterised by creativity, presence, connection, and a sense of community make space for each person's inherent capacity to create and yield to art; art as a reflection of both the participants' and facilitators' human life examined and articulated, in a global climate where life has become astoundingly and devastatingly fragile.

Presence (Pagdaramay). The emotional and physical spaces also allowed participants to be present to one another. Guidelines to ensure there was this kind of respect and active listening was critical to ensuring participants managed distractions (for example, other gadgets, unnecessary distracting movements like appearing in and out of the screen). As if to mirror the metaphor, the facilitating team and even the members of the support team served as a cradle for the participants, holding the virtual space for them as they journeyed through the process of art-making and self-care. Even the participants cradled each other by attuning to one another and doing their part to create a safe and therapeutic digital space.

Connection (Pakikiramdam). At a time when people feel alone and isolated due to the pandemic, finding connections during the *Duyan* support groups was an immediate source of comfort to participants. In addition, because the *Duyan* groups included space to breathe, move, draw, write poetry, and share stories, the spirit of fun and play was alive even at a time when there were many reasons to complain and feel discouraged.

Community (Pakikipagkapwa). The safe spaces offered by the *Duyan* sessions offered an opportunity for a deepening of community among groups and colleagues that had existing relationships but were at that time either consumed by anxiety in an unusually stressful workplace (that is, the Department of Social Welfare in the Philippines in the time of COVID-19), or who were separated from each other because of the lockdown and closing of schools (that is, teachers). These existing relationships and connections within a group are valuable resources that our facilitators worked with to be able to hold space for creativity, the processing of emotions, as well as opportunities to collectively decentre from the crisis.

Dilemmas in methods

Challenges and issues

Combining a variety of methods in this arts-based process and including quantitative data created a multi-layered, multi-dimensional maze-like pathway through the research project that forced our research team to be highly flexible and patient. The issue of connectivity, the multiple processes of data collection beyond the actual *Duyan* groups, and the fluid nature of rhizomatic storytelling and art making in the post-session a/r/tography dialogues with facilitators caused the researchers to feel lost at times. Particularly for those on the team who are used to a more structured chronology of steps, adapting to the fluidity of the process was a new experience that invited a shift in understanding research and the process of harvesting data.

It is important to also mention that some members of the research team were *Duyan* facilitators or co-facilitators as well. While these members were able to switch roles throughout the project, this reality merits mention. We have not yet determined how this may have affected the integrity of the data, if at all.

On the level of implementation, a main challenge we experienced was the dependence of this research methodology on the use of an online platform. This limited our reach to only those with a stable internet connection.

Lessons learned

As a hermeneutic and postmodern practice, a/r/tography acknowledges the importance of self and collective interpretation and emphasises that these interpretations are always in a state of becoming. Particularly in the unpredictable time of the pandemic where circumstances were quickly evolving and we all were striving to adapt, this methodology allowed us to do authentic research even in the changing reality, with constantly changing variables. Because a/r/tography had the space for personal expression and response (but not interpretation), it was also helpful in defining relationships formed within the studied experiences (support group sessions), as embodied data from all persons involved. Not framing insights as interpretations allowed the integrity of the research to stay intact and veer away from unfounded reasoning.

The beauty in this methodology is that the artist, researcher, and teacher are merged into the physical body of the individual involved in the process. The body, which is certainly evolving in new ways in the time of a pandemic, plays a crucial role of the bridge to the aesthetic responses in its lived reality of COVID-19. Storytelling, writing, and drawing as art forms gave language to the experience of both the facilitators and researchers. The aesthetic responses evoked in the bodies of the researchers who created art also served as information for what was being studied (that is, the idea of the arts as a cradle). Presence and attunement, central to the *Duyan* support groups, were somatic experiences embodied in each person creating art.

The combined arts-based methodologies of a/r/tography, rhizomatic storytelling, and REM informed our process of harvesting information by presenting the possibility of different perspectives not bound by the typical standards of data collection. This combination helped to gather insight and perspectives necessary to systematically articulate frameworks and concepts that are meant to explain human experiences – an essential reference in line with our desire to make mental health more accessible to populations across all socio-economic classes.

This arts-based process was helpful in bringing a deeper structure of understanding to qualitative data and the ways in which quantitative data can fit in the telling of the story of the project. However, the process was less helpful in equipping us to report quantitative evidence, which may affect the way we are able to support claims for patterns identified.

Conclusion

Among the many stories layered into images that captured the experience of the *Duyan* support groups, a golden thread emerged reflecting that times of isolation and anxiety, such as a pandemic, have the capacity to remind us of what is essential in our human experience: we all long for the presence (*pagdaramay*) of another, connection (*pakikiramdam*), and the strength in community (*pakikipagkapawa*). But just like art has the unique capacity to surprise, the researchers were delighted at what this combined arts-based method revealed. As a parallel process to the authors' collective experiences of COVID-19, this research project brought to light an invaluable lesson critical to this time: there is an inherent capacity in all of us to cradle (*duyan*) each other, to be flexible, resilient, and creative (*pagkamalikhain*) as we live with uncertainty. Together, we are able to weave through complexities and forge ahead with hope, even in the most unpredictable of times.

References

Baker, B., Calvert, M., Emery, M., Enfield, R., & Williams, B. (2011). Mapping the impact of youth on community development: What are we learning? [PowerPoint slides]. https://connect.msu.edu/p72418074/?launcher=false&fcsContent=true&pbMode=normal

Chazdon, S., Emery, M., Hansen, D., Higgins, L., & Sero, R. (2017). *A Field Guide to Ripple Effects*. Libraries Publishing.

Clinton, D. (2003). *Theories of Media*. The University of Chicago. http://csmt.uchicago.edu/annotations/deleuzerhizome.htm

Cormier, D. (2008). Rhizomatic education: community as curriculum. *Innovate*, 4(5). www.innovateonline.info/index.php?view=article&id=550

Irwin, R.L. (1999). Listening to the shapes of collaborative artmaking. *Art Education, 52*(2), 35–40, doi:10.1080/00043125.1997.11650894

Irwin, R.L. (n.d.). *About A/r/tography.* http://artography.edcp.educ.ubc.ca/?page_id=69

Irwin, R.L., & Springgay, S. (2008). A/r/tography as practice-based research. In S. Springgay, R.L. Irwin, C. Leggo, & P. Gouzouasis (Eds.), *Being with A/r/tography*. Sense Publishers.

Leavy, P. (Ed.). (2014). *The Oxford handbook of qualitative research*. Oxford University Press. https://doi.org/10.1093/oxfordhb/9780199811755.001.0001

Malindog-Uy, A. (2020, July 19). *COVID-19 Impact on Mental Health of Filipinos. ASEAN Post.* https://theaseanpost.com/article/covid-19-impact-mental-health-filipinos

Mayne, J. (2001). Addressing attribution through contribution analysis: using performance measures sensibly. *Canadian journal of program evaluation*, *16*(1), 1–24.

Scott, S.D., Brett-MacLean, P., Archibald, M. et al. (2013). Protocol for a systematic review of the use of narrative storytelling and visual-arts-based approaches as knowledge translation tools in healthcare. *Syst Rev*, 2(19). https://doi.org/10.1186/2046-4053-2-19

Stitelmann, J. (2020). Expressive arts research colloquium: values of science and comparison with art [Class Handout]. EGS.

14

Art and artefact: displaying social work through objects

Mark Doel

Introduction

This chapter presents the origins, process, and findings of an online research project, *Social Work in 40 Objects*. The project is ongoing, and its aims are to explore the possibility of discovering meanings in social work through material objects and the stories that attach to them. The experiment is proving to be a quantitative success, with over 160 objects to date (2020) from 26 countries donated to a virtual exhibition of social work. Qualitative success is evident in the many facets of social work refracted through the objects and the wide variety of relationships to social work apparent in those who are participating.

The research methodologies that support the experiment are explored, as well as the theoretical perspectives that have deepened the analysis of the findings: these include material culture theory and museum ethnography, especially the notion of 'charged objects'. The 'snowball' method speeded and broadened the donation of objects and a 'bricolage' process helped in the playful clustering of groups of objects into themed 'collections'. The chapter explores the learning from this experiment and presents a suggested typology of objects.

Research methodology

Rationale

The wider public has direct knowledge of medicine, education, and law, but social work is experienced by only a small minority and is, consequently, poorly represented and understood (the 'bus stop challenge': try answering a hypothetical group of random strangers at a bus stop who ask you, 'What is social work?').

Medicine, education, and law can each be characterised by a single icon: a stethoscope; blackboard and chalk; the scales of justice. Social work has no iconography, least of all a defining one. It is a complex, contested discipline (the 'road sign challenge': design signage to indicate 'social work ahead' using only pictograph). In the face of this blankness, is it possible to *show* social work to this unknowing public rather than trying to explain it?

Social Work in 40 Objects was experimental in many ways, not least in the research design, though 'design' suggests a more linear approach than was the case. The methodology evolved developmentally out of these questions: Is it possible to display social work rather than articulate it? Can objects evoke stories of social work? Can these objects-with-stories help a wider audience to connect with what social work is?

Social work is considered to be 'contested', with no easy consensus about what it is. It follows that what is needed is the wide participation of people with diverse relationships to social work to muster a collection large and varied enough to be comprehensive: 40?

The project was conceived as participatory research, and – with the benefit of reflective hindsight rather than specific design – uses interpretive and hermeneutic phenomenological approaches (Koch, 1999; Lopez & Willis, 2009, p. 729), with lived experience refracted through the prism of a material object. The stories that attach to the objects give voice to social work and, in this respect, the research has strong links with narrative approaches. Broader meanings are not necessarily apparent to the individual participants but become manifest through the telling of their story and, more especially, when collections of these stories accumulate into narratives.

Methods used

The methodology brought together two contrasting ideas. The first is well developed in archaeology and museum anthropology: the finding, collecting, and display of artefacts. The second relies on advances in information technology to provide the mechanism to reach out to large numbers of potential 'donors' of objects. As Golightley and Holloway (2019, p. 558) noted: '[*Social Work in 40 Objects*] is an innovative project that combines ancient understandings of meaning and mnemonic with modern technologies that allow sharing and participation across virtual space'. Thus was born the idea of a website to collect, host, and display objects of social work – a virtual exhibition of social work.

The rudimentary plan for *40 Objects* was to establish a WordPress website, with a call for anyone with a connection to social work to propose an object (later, the term 'donate' was indicated as the notion of an exhibition developed). As well as donations, the website allowed for comments from 'visitors' to the exhibition.

Donors were requested to follow these four protocols:

• a photograph of the donated object (square, black, and white);
• a photograph of the person donating the object (square, black, and white);

- a few lines about the person's connection to social work (*not* a CV);
- a few lines/paragraphs about why they had donated this particular object/ how it connected them to social work.

The idea is similar to a collage in which hundreds of individual photographs merge into a single large portrait when viewed at a distance. So, each object is a discrete image but, when viewed as a whole, a 'picture of social work' emerges. In some ways, the four protocols in *40 Objects* mirror the requirements of the photographs in the collage: the whole can only work with the discipline of four equal sides for each individual component.

Recasting my role as researcher to that of curator, I encouraged would-be participants to shape their inchoate ideas into concrete reality. I used the snowballing technique to encourage those who had already participated to find more recruits, with the result that donors come from across the world and have multiple relationships with social work: practitioners, educators, students and service users, managers, policy makers and publishers, and from other professions. I focused the attention of would-be participants by having a goal with a deadline: a published 'catalogue', *Social Work in 42 Objects [and more]*, in which all objects donated in time would be included (Doel, 2017). The number of objects at that point was 127, and the website continues to collect.

Museum ethnography

The website had been collecting for two years when I had a chance encounter with the director of the Musée des Arts ets Métiers, Paris (Arts and Crafts). Yves Winkin introduced me to museum ethnography and, in particular, a body of French literature with the central notion of *objets chargés* (Morin, 1969), and what Winkin (2018) has conceptualised as the deaths and resurrections of objects.

The idea of a charged object is best understood through story:

> A bone fragment is found in the soil of an archaeological dig. It is carefully brushed and cleaned, identified and catalogued, then displayed in a major Exhibition, where it takes central position in a protective perspex case, an explanatory plaque carefully stencilled onto the wall. People pay to view it. In this process it has become a *charged* object.
>
> (Doel, 2019, p. 830)

The objects that acquire this charge in the *40 Objects* project are those that most powerfully bring together these three elements: object, person, and profession. Although it is the accompanying story that fuses the three elements and conveys the charge, it is the material object that makes that charge possible and gives it a home. We might be touched by a story, but we cannot touch *it,* unlike its embodiment, the object.

An example of a charged object from *40 Objects* is *Mouthpiece* (Cauvain, 2017). Cauvain re-connected with his long-estranged biological father, a man he had not known; and, just a few weeks later, tragically, his father died. Having so recently found his father, he lost him. Separation, loss, and finding were to become emerging themes (Parker, 2017). That same night, the father's flat was ransacked, and it fell to Cauvain to go and sort through his father's remaining few possessions. Among these, he found the mouthpiece to a French horn; his father had been a talented musician, composing as well as playing. The mouthpiece was all that Cauvain had 'of his father'. Happily, it is a part of his father's life that attests to his talent and joyful music-making, not to the drug abuse, abandonment, and imprisonment.

The story is a poignant one, but what makes it especially powerful is Cauvain's professional narrative, reflecting on how a social worker was central to his life in securing his legal relationship with his adoptive father. This social worker was unknown to the infant Cauvain and remains unknown to us. Cauvain, now a social worker, was then a client. Cauvain deepens our relationship with the object by offering it as a metaphor to support an impassioned plea for social work to be the *mouthpiece* for service users, to help give them voice – for social workers to be committed advocates, not deskbound bureau professionals. The more we learn about this mouthpiece, the more multi-layered we experience it to be. Indeed, recently I have pondered on the parallels between the mouthpiece as separated from its parent object, the French horn, just as Cauvain was from his biological father.

The mouthpiece is just a small piece of shaped metal, but its history, its presence, and its meanings elevate it to a charged object. No longer an insignificant piece of cold metal, *this* mouthpiece has taken pride of place in the perspex case with a side plaque and an audience.

Material culture and bricolage

We know that people make things, but how do things make people – or, in this case, make a profession? (Miller, 2010). From material culture theory comes a critical insight that is the system of things that makes us who we are and that a single object has limited meaningfulness: it is the relationship between things themselves, and between things and the human world, that brings about meanings (Baudrillard, 1968/2005). This complexity might explain why a call for a single object to 'represent' social work was unsuccessful (Scholar, 2016), whereas a participatory approach to secure a whole collection of stuff bore fruit.

Donated objects were uploaded to the website as and when they were proposed, in chronological order. This was entirely random in terms of the kinds of object donated and the themes that their stories evoked. The idea to present 127 objects in a catalogue presented a challenge of how to display them and the opportunity to re-view the collection as a whole. Playing with the idea of exhibition, I decided that the objects could be gathered into different collections, just as they might in the rooms of an exhibition space. Given the numbers involved, and with a nod to the project's title, 40 objects were highlighted in 'perspex cases' as it were, with full-text 'plaques', while the remaining 87 were presented with briefer (50-word) texts – the equivalent of the cabinets and drawers filled with additional items that visitors are encouraged to pull out for further exploration.

This playful process of arrangement and re-arrangement to achieve different meanings is sometimes referred to as 'bricolage' (Turkle, 2007; Kay, 2016). The breakthrough in my own playful bricolage happened when I stopped thinking about the objects in terms of their stories – the emergent social work themes – and fell back on their direct 'objectness'; in other words, when I was true to the material quality of the object *qua* object, rather than its symbolic or figurative nature. So, for example, one collection was named *The Fabric of Social Work,* light pun intended, and consisted of those objects whose material nature was textile – a foundling hospital token from the 1750s donated by an English researcher; a khurjini (saddle bag) by a Georgian policy maker; a lappieskombers (quilt) and a cushion by two South African students; a ball of wool by a Spanish groupworker; a kete (woven flax bag) by a social work academic in New Zealand; a hammock by an American groupworker; and a French *educateur* donated his son's school bag, made by Arts et Traditions, an indigenous cultural collective he had helped to found in Île de Réunion in the 1970s.

The collection is now four years old, so it is probably ripe for a bricolage refresh to re-shape it and attract new visitors and encourage returning ones.

Findings

The project demonstrates that the notion of objects to display meanings in social work is possible and that it crosses cultural and national boundaries (Wallendorf & Arnould, 1988; Mehta & Belk, 1991). Further work is needed to demonstrate whether an exhibition of this kind can help garner wider public support for social work and whether a material exhibition rather than a virtual one could have greater impact.

Though the objects are frequently fascinating things in themselves, they acquire further levels of meaning by contextualisation. If we saw Cauvain's *Mouthpiece* in its perspex case, we could make our own meanings out of it (Caple, 2006), but the back story – the information 'plaque' – is what seems to provoke the object's charge. Storytelling came naturally to some participants, but others' stories needed teasing out and shaping, sometimes over a period of time.

As the numbers of donated objects grew, I began to see patterns in the kind of meaning that the object was used for. This was different from the social work-related themes (loss; self-care; social justice, and so on) and different again from the collections achieved by the bricolage process already described. This further understanding of the objects led to a categorisation based on the use to which the object was put – not as an object, but in its relationship to its story. All objects fall into one or more of these categories:

- *Metaphorical (symbolic) objects* illustrate social work by making parallels between object and a facet of social work. An example of a utopian object was *Candle,* a dystopian one was *Dalek,* each object used to symbolise different characteristics of what social work means to the donor. Student social workers are especially prone to donate utopian metaphorical objects, frequently with an emphasis on the care aspects of social work.
- *Metaphysical objects* do not exist as material stuff. They are construed to illuminate what social work is or ought to be. For instance, *Real Life Library,* proposed by Dow (2017), a social work service user, reifies the lived experience of service users, playfully locating it in the equivalent of a physical library. A real-life library does not 'exist' in the material world, but it is a powerful metaphysical construction.
- *Personal objects* are drawn from an individual's own history with social work, like Cauvain's *Mouthpiece.*
- *Socio-political objects* embody the idea that the personal is the political (and, in this case, the professional is the personal is the political). Some objects were explicitly political and addressed social work's responsibility to stand shoulder to shoulder with the communities with which it works. Sokhela's *Food* is an image of a food bank in South Africa, with the plea that, 'Social work is about owning the community's problems and acting on them' (Sokhela, 2017), an explicit linkage between social work and fighting poverty and the implicit question, 'Where do you stand and what are you going to do about it?'
- *Historical objects* tell us something of social work at different stages in its development (Chambon et al., 2011). Some of these artefacts reflect powerfully on social work's current dilemmas, such as *Jane Addams' Coat* (which no longer 'exists'), speaking to the potential for hypocrisy when social workers' lives are qualitatively distant from the people with whom they work (Moldovan, 2017).
- *Practical objects* are used in direct practice. There were fewer of this kind of object than one is likely to find in technically-based professions in which objects are central to practice. The 'Talking and Listening to Children

Kitbag campaign' found that only one in five social workers used objects in their direct work with children (Ruch, 2020).

Lessons learnt

There is a strong and understandable tendency for participants to want 'their' object to reflect positively on social work. To achieve a rounded collection, I solicited objects that spoke to the 'dark side' of social work, as well. This steer was successful, for instance with Finch's (2017) *Yellow Star* reminder that social work was complicit with Nazi Germany's murderous policies. As a researcher, I would have been cautious about steering the process, but as a curator it became a responsibility.

I learned to be open-minded. My unacknowledged assumption of 'objectness' as a solid object that one could handle, something like Phung's (2017) *Chinese Bowl*, was challenged by donations that included *Trees*, a *Song*, *Eyes*, a *Real Life Library*, and *Bella*, a dog that had lived in a children's home in the 1950s. All of these 'objects' gave significant insights into social work that would not have seen light without the open call for diverse participation.

I was advised to be the gatekeeper for the website and, though I have no worries about offensive or inappropriate donations, this role helped me shape and coordinate the aesthetics of the exhibition and, on a couple of occasions, to ask donors to reflect on the degree of disclosure in their stories.

I remain hopeful for the possibility of exhibition space in a physical building, where some of the objects would indeed be displayed, with stencilled wall plaques telling the object's story, and all freely open to an enquiring general public. I am aware of the irony in a project based on the significance of the material word where all the objects are digital, *sans* what is most fundamental to an object – touch.

References

Baudrillard, J. (1968/2005). *The System of Objects*. Verso.

Caple, C. (2006). *Objects; Reluctant Witnesses to the Past*. Routledge.

Cauvain, S. (2017). Mouthpiece. In M. Doel (Ed.), *Social Work in 42 Objects (and More)*. Kirwin Maclean Publishing.

Chambon, A., Johnstone, M., & Winckler, J. (2011). The material presence of early social work: the practice of the archive. *British Journal of Social Work, 41*(4), 625–644.

Doel, M. (2017). *Social Work in 42 Objects (and More)*. Kirwin Maclean Publishing.

Doel, M. (2019). Displaying social work through objects. *British Journal of Social Work, 49*(3), 824–841.

Dow, J. (2017). Real-life library. In M. Doel (Ed.), *Social Work in 42 Objects (and More)*. Kirwin Maclean Publishing.

Finch, J. (2017). Yellow star. In M. Doel (Ed.), *Social Work in 42 Objects (and More)*. Kirwin Maclean Publishing.

Golightley, M. & Holloway, M. (2019). Editorial: Social work today – Fit and agile practice. *The British Journal of Social Work, 49*, (3), 555–558, https://doi.org/10.1093/bjsw/bcz038

Kay, L. (2016). Research as bricolage: navigating in/between the creative arts disciplines. *Music Therapy Perspectives, 34*(1), 26–32.

Koch, T. (1999). An interpretative research process: revisiting phenomenological and hermeneutical approaches. *Nurse Researcher, 6*(3), 20.

Lopez, K.A., & Willis, D.G. (2009). Descriptive versus interpretive phenomenology: their contributions to nursing knowledge. *Qualitative Health Research,* 726–735.

Mehta, R., & Belk, R.W. (1991). Artifacts, identity and transition: favourite possessions of Indians and Indian immigrants to the United States. *Journal of Consumer Research, 17*, 398–411.

Miller, D. (2010). *Stuff*. Polity Press.

Moldovan, V. (2017). Jane Addams' Coat. In M. Doel (Ed.), *Social Work in 42 Objects (and More)*. Kirwin Maclean Publishing.

Morin, V. (1969). L'objet biographique. *Communications, 13*, 131–139.

Parker, C. (Ed) (2017). *Found*. Foundling Museum: Arts Council England.

Phung, T.C. (2017). Chinese bowl. In M. Doel (Ed.), *Social Work in 42 Objects (and More)*. Kirwin Maclean Publishing.

Ruch, G. (2020). The small bag making a big difference to children's lives. www.sussex.ac.uk/broadcast/read/49555 and www.youtube.com/watch?v=hrlIDxmMYoc

Scholar, H. (2016). The neglected paraphernalia of practice? Objects and artefacts in social work identity, practice, and research. *Qualitative Social Work, 16*(5), 631–648.

Sokhela, D. (2017). Food. In M. Doel (Ed.), *Social Work in 42 Objects (and More)*. Kirwin Maclean Publishing.

Turkle, S. (2007). *Evocative Objects: Things We Think With*. MIT.

Wallendorf, M., & Arnould, E.J. (1988). My favourite things: a cross-cultural inquiry into object attachment, possessiveness, and social linkage. *Journal of Consumer Research, 14*, 531–547.

Winkin, Y. (2018). Charged objects: deaths and resurrections of artifacts in technological museums. Lecture at John Hopkins University, Baltimore.

15

Building research capacity: scaffolding the process through arts-based pedagogy

Ronald P.M.H. Lay

Research into arts-based interventions is complex as art cannot be directly translated into words. Increasingly, there has been a global incessant call for research into using the arts in a range of mental health disciplines. Ongoing debates over methodology, primarily quantitative and qualitative, persist and this just may affect one's decision to engage in research. However, research is needed for a range of reasons including providing evidence of the integrity of a discipline, asserting core competencies of practitioners, for third party and stakeholder purposes including advocacy, the formation of relevant laws, protections, and access to services, and, of course, to highlight emerging trends and contemporary best practices to effectively address a plethora of the complex needs of clients.

As such, arts-based practitioners are uniquely situated to make significant contributions to the research base given their direct engagement with the arts with individuals, families, communities, and society at large (McNiff, 2013; Thomas et al., 2020). Art is rich with metaphor and symbol, and often can be accessed and applied when answers to questions are not easily obtained nor addressed through words alone, even if the art may seem abstract at first (McNiff, 2013; Chilton et al., 2015; Boden et al., 2019; Potash, 2019; Thomas et al., 2020). Indeed, art is not the opposite of research as in the dichotomic paradigm of arts versus science, but rather art, and art making, are a type of research in and of themselves, just as research can also involve creativity and nonlinear engagement (McNiff, 2013; Kapitan, 2018).

The question is how to bridge the divide between practice and research, and arts and science, within the minds of arts-based practitioners. This chapter aims to strategically step back several paces and consider how best to encourage mental health practitioners-in-training to engage in arts-based research practices that are user-friendly, non-threatening, creative, meaningful, and aligned to their discipline. Through a purposefully scaffolded pedagogical approach, arts-based social practitioners can come to terms with their understanding of research and engage in research activity that contributes to larger contexts overall. Arts-based research strategies are gaining increasing acceptance by professional disciplines through research discourse and activity (McNiff, 2013; Boden et al., 2019; Thomas et al., 2020), and are being integrated within training programmes as part of the curriculum. The discourse is both consolidated from and informed by the underpinnings of mental health, social practice, art psychotherapy, and arts-based research. This chapter is structured into three main sections: (1) arts-based methodologies and pedagogies within higher education; (2) examples of arts-based strategies utilised in an art psychotherapy training programme in Singapore to scaffold research capacity; and (3) implications for trainees and practitioners on using arts-based research. Each of these areas is quite rich and layered on its own; however, for the purpose of this chapter, an overarching overview is provided with links to examples from within this particular context. It is these links that I hope will offer threads of similarity and relevance to a range of social practice disciplines that engage with the arts in both practice and research.

Arts-based methodologies and pedagogies: research in higher education

Working with others is rewarding, exhilarating, demanding, challenging, and even exhausting. As mental health practitioners and trainees of the discipline, we encounter complex interrelationships and experiences of attitudes, behaviour, trauma, and all things related to the human condition through relational and organisational structures and systems. All of this requires specialist competencies, resources, stamina, resilience, and problem-solving; communication typically transpires through consultation, assessment, documentation, evaluation, reports, and the like. Research into arts-based practices, or arts-based research is another intensely communicative form of dissemination and communication of the impacts of an intervention, that elevates the phenomena experienced from practice into larger spheres wherein it can be dissected, examined, and unpacked with the aim to illuminate insight, understanding, and new knowledge (McNiff, 2013; Chilton et al., 2015; Kapitan, 2018; Boden et al., 2019; Potash, 2019; Thomas et al., 2020).

Practitioners and trainees hold a wealth of information through engagement in their own practice, which is invaluable to the larger discipline and to all those they provide services to (McNiff, 2013). It becomes necessary, even essential, for practitioners and trainees to engage in research processes to expand their communication to the larger practitioner community and other audiences. Mental health practice and research both require creativity, problem-solving, ingenuity, and systematic approaches. As such, integrating art and arts–based methodologies into research, and examining art and artefacts whether created by the researcher and/or by clients within therapeutic contexts, are just some viable options available to practitioners and trainees (McNiff, 2013; Chilton et al., 2015; Kapitan, 2018; Potash, 2019; Thomas et al., 2020).

Research within mental health disciplines often requires a process of reflexivity given the interrelationships that are examined between theory and the existing research base as well as between the practice and phenomena that we are investigating. This can be daunting and, at times, confrontational. Throughout my own doctoral research journey, on the topic of experiential learning, I turned to art and art making as a way to challenge, progress, and stimulate reflexive and reflective processes (Figure 15.1).

This allowed me to sit with my ideas when I needed to contemplate the dynamics of teaching and learning, it allowed me to express the struggles and triumphs I was experiencing as I gathered and made sense of my data, it served as documented evidence of the various stages and milestones of research I had achieved, it allowed me to nonverbally and creatively work through complicated and frustrating aspects of my experience while researching, and it provided a series of outputs or artefacts that could be used for a range of other purposes such as exhibition and/or for further research. An important function for researchers creating art is that the process leads to wisdom as part of the explorative and excavating processes inherent in research (McNiff, 2013; Potash, 2019; Thomas et al., 2020).

Figure 15.1: R. Lay, 2019, *Self-Reflections and Experiential Learning: Research as a Doctor of Education Student*, digital photograph from handphone (cropped), dimensions variable

The benefits of using arts-based approaches within my own doctoral research inspired me to integrate arts-based strategies and approaches into the curriculum and pedagogies utilised within the postgraduate art therapy programme that I lead. Having this first-hand experience further led me to an informed stance while providing postgraduate thesis supervision and research mentorship to the students, alumni, and the professional mental health communities locally and abroad. The next section provides a brief account of how the practice of research was demystified by a particular postgraduate art therapy training programme in southeast Asia.

Arts-based strategies: creatively scaffolding research capacity

Experiential learning that blends theory with arts activity can enhance one's relationship to research and can even shift one's perspective on how research can be executed in ways that are creative, stimulating, enriching, and meaningful while also ensuring core skill set development as needed by the professional. There is no better way to illustrate this point than to highlight examples from practice – for this context, examples from a postgraduate art therapy training programme in Singapore. Illustrative examples and visuals created by teaching staff and students are presented throughout this section.

This training prioritises the art in art therapy and arts-based strategies were purposefully integrated into the two research modules. The intentions were: (1) to introduce arts-based methodologies into the research component of the training, which lead to the consolidation of clinical material from practice into a substantial written thesis; (2) to trace students' initial understanding of research by having them create artwork that confronted their anxiety and perceptions; (3) to develop their appreciation of complex processes during their research activity; and (4) to celebrate the completion of their training by means of a final group art exhibition that included a published exhibition catalogue in both hardcopy and online versions.

Arts-based approaches, strategies, and methodologies invoke potentially rich and complex metaphors that can add further layers of depth, associations, and meaning making to experiences. A poignant example is with a sculpture that students create at the beginning of the research module in year one (Figure 15.2). Students are invited to create a creature to represent *research* using any art materials, media, and found objects that are collected from around the classroom. On a symbolic level, this mirrors the researcher's task of looking for, collecting, and systematically organising the material. The art directive further stipulates that the creature is to be constructed in such a way as to be held in the palm of the student's hand. The point here is to encourage students to reconsider research as a doable

Figure 15.2: R. Lay, 2020, *RESEARCH as Creature*, beginner's exercise, mixed media (found objects: pencil shavings, glass container), dimensions variable

exercise and to do so within their current scope. Once completed, the student takes a photograph of the creature allowing them to figuratively reframe the initial anxiety and perspective on the seemingly insurmountable task of engaging in research. This experience generally places research in a positive light and students begin to become excited about the potential of research and of integrating the arts.

The senior research module is comprised of two distinct but complimentary components – theory and art – and are co-facilitated by an experienced

Figure 15.3: R. Lay, 2020, *Blank Greeting Card: Message to Me from My Thesis*, graduating student exercise prior to starting their thesis, pre-made greeting card, dimensions variable

practitioner and an accomplished practising artist. The two outputs of this research module are a substantial written thesis and an artwork that is exhibited as part of a group exhibition. To begin their thesis process, students are provided a blank greeting card and an envelope with the instructions to create an artwork in the form of a letter to themselves from their thesis (Figures 15.3 & 15.4).

At the end of the class session, the greeting cards are sealed and placed in a container, which is stored in the lecturer's desk for several months. The cards are returned to students at a critical point of bringing the thesis to a close and when the students seem to need encouragement the most. A majority of the students become emotional at this point and some have even forgotten about their card; this special delivery is well received and provides the essential boost to stamina to bring their thesis to completion. I am pleased to report that all students submit their signed and bound thesis on the last day of class. I am not sure if the greeting card from their thesis was responsible; however, I am convinced it played a crucial role.

Some students gravitate to art and art making, and have independently initiated arts–based strategies that have complimented their postgraduate research.

Julia Pasifull Oh for example, engaged in a weaving project in tandem with the writing of her thesis. She explains that:

Figure 15.4: R. Lay, 2020, *Message from My Thesis: Signed and Sealed*, graduating student exercise prior to starting their thesis, pre-made greeting card and found objects (string, cellophane), dimensions variable

The act of weaving captivated me and I realised that with a small wooden picture frame, a couple of wooden dowels and a strong clamp, I could take my weaving with me as I travelled and could attach it to any table in order to start work...

It is not unusual to use the metaphor of weaving for research studies (Pitcher, 2012), and on returning to Singapore I plunged into our second year of study and the major project, a 10,000 word dissertation – the weaving became my response art, a mirror of the process. The strong wooden picture frame represented the Masters in Art Therapy Course and the college framework. The warp threads, strung in a continuous tensioned line over the suspended dowels became the reams of instructions and feedback about how we should work on our dissertation, with the weft threads representing the flow of ideas, articles, books and words as I tried to settle on a topic. I started with a knotted line, then a few rows of dark threads, and took the dark colour up the sides of the weaving. Inspired by a watercolour by Cezanne I slowly built a blended curve as I tried to understand what would work in the weaving, just as I tried to understand the demands of the dissertation...

Over the 7-month placement in the hospice I sporadically worked on the weaving, which grew as my dissertation took shape... There was just enough room to fill in the final few lines and I deliberately let

Figure 15.5: J.P. Oh, 2015, *Weaving the Dissertation*, graduating student's art-based initiative paralleling her research process, weaving, dimensions variable

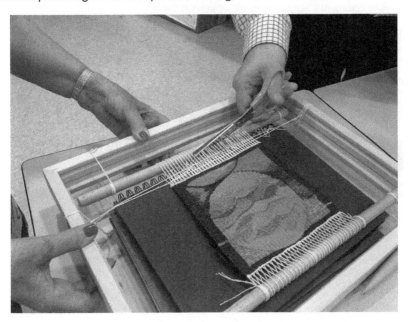

the disk intrude on the top framework. All that was left was to tie off the piece and then, as part of my final review with my course leader, to ask him to cut the warp ties (Figure 15.5).

(J.P. Oh, personal communication, September 26, 2020)

Another student utilised arts-based methodology as part of her research thesis, and this extended beyond its completion (Figure 15.6). As detailed here, Ingrid Grace Tatham contends that:

My thesis topic involved the symbolic and metaphoric use of a fish.

On completion of my thesis, I wanted to capture the experience of researching, writing, rewriting and receiving feedback from my supervisor. Creating a likeness of a fish felt like an ideal way to do this.

I drew the fish freehand onto cardboard; cut out two like pieces and holding them, stuffed crumpled pages of my final draft thesis in between, finally binding them together with masking tape to make a skeleton of my fish. After mixing a bowl of flour with water to make a paste, I tore the remaining 70 pages of my draft thesis into strips and began the very tactile and time-consuming task of dipping each page into the paste to mould the shape of my fish. It took five days to dry before I could paint it with acrylic paint and varnish.

Figure 15.6: I.G. Tatham, 2020, *The Fish*, graduating student's art-based initiative celebrating the completion of her thesis, papier mache, copy of draft thesis with supervisor comments, acrylic paint, dimensions variable

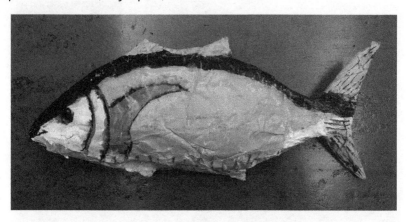

I gifted the fish to my supervisor because it represented much more than just a papier mache fish. This art piece represented not only my learning and emotion but more importantly my gratefulness for his valuable, if not always comfortable feedback, and support throughout the process.

(I.G. Tatham, personal communication, September 26, 2020)

Arts-based approaches, strategies, and methodologies offer creative ways to de-mystify research processes, while allowing educators, students, and practitioners to reframe their perspectives, scaffold skill sets, and engage in research meaningfully. Investigating and/or integrating art into research not only expands one's capacity to examine questions linked to mental health practice in ways that instigate understanding and knowledge, but that also honour the intricacies of one's lived experience (McNiff, 2013; Chilton et al., 2015; Kapitan, 2018; Thomas et al., 2020).

Implications for educators, trainees, and practitioners

If educators, students, and practitioners are making use of arts-based approaches, strategies, and methodologies as part of the research itself, special consideration must be taken into account for the art and artefacts that are created. Similar to the best practices, ethics, consent, and sensitivities utilised with research participants, data sets, and security for these, the art and artefacts must be systematically treated with respect, dignity, and ethics. For example, consent to use the artwork, the descriptions, and all other related data within the research must be obtained, and this also extends to the parameters of confidentiality, ownership of the artwork, and the storage of artwork and related material. It is the attention to these additional dimensions that further adds credence and credibility to arts-based approaches, strategies, and methodologies.

The art media, materials, art, and artwork do not necessarily need to be complicated and can include what is readily available and/or easily expressed. For example, Figure 15.1 is a photograph taken from a mobile phone, and Figure 15.2 used found objects within a space, the postgraduate art therapy classroom. On other occasions, depending on the interests and skill level of the student, the artist, the participant, and/or the researcher the materials, the metaphors, the pragmatics of the artmaking, and the artwork itself may be more time-consuming and advanced (Figures 15.5 and 15.6). Just like any other methodology or therapeutic intervention, it is up to the researcher to delve deeper into the traditions, underpinnings, and practices of art, art making, art media, and materials as well as any related cultural aspects of these to effectively apply arts-based approaches, strategies, and methodologies to either research or practice.

Arts-based approaches, strategies, and methodologies in contemporary research acknowledge the complexities of the human condition, the human experience, and the myriad cultural and lived contexts of those to whom we provide services (McNiff, 2013, 2019). This is achieved by allowing multiple perspectives, lenses, and frameworks from which to uncover insight, understanding, and new knowledge. Arts-based methodologies advocate engagement with the arts, promote reflection, acknowledge that the lived experiences are difficult to put into words, and support new ways of looking at phenomena (McNiff, 2013, 2019; Chilton et al., 2015; Boden et al., 2019; Potash, 2019; Thomas et al., 2020). Expanding traditional research conventions to include and embrace arts-based methodologies appropriately adheres to the underlying essence of research in sophisticated and functional ways. The human condition and experience are complex and it is only befitting that additional methodologies are accessed in the attempt to make sense of these.

Acknowledgements

Conceptualisation of experience into text requires inspiration and for this I express my gratitude to the teaching team and postgraduate students at LASALLE College of the Arts, Singapore, and in particular, to Julia Pasifull Oh and Ingrid Grace Tatham, MA, AThR for granting me their permission to include their artwork and descriptions in this chapter.

References

Boden, Z., Larkin, M., & Iyer, M. (2019). Picturing ourselves in the world: drawings, interpretative phenomenological analysis and the relational mapping interview. *Qualitative Research in Psychology, 16*(2), 218–236. https://doi.org/10.1080/14780887.2018.1540679

Chilton, G., Gerber, N., & Scotti, V. (2015). Towards and aesthetic intersubjective paradigm for arts based research: an art therapy perspective. *UNESCO Observatory Multi-Disciplinary Journal of the Arts, 5*(1), 1–27.

Kapitan, L. (2018). *Introduction to Art Therapy Research* (2nd ed.). Routledge.

McNiff, S. (2013). Opportunities and challenges in art-based research. In S. McNiff (Ed.), *Art as Research: Opportunities and Challenges* (pp. 3–9). University of Chicago Press.

McNiff, S. (2019). Reflections on what 'art' does in art therapy practice and research. *Art Therapy: Journal of the American Art Therapy Association, 36*(3), 162–165. https://doi.org/10.1080/07421656.2019.1649547

Pitcher, R. (2012, July 31). http://thesiswhisperer.com/2012/07/31/writing-a-thesis-is-like-weaving-on-a-loom/

Potash, J. (2019). Arts-based research in art therapy. In D.J. Betts & S.P. Deaver (Eds.), *Art Therapy Research: A Practical Guide* (pp. 119–146). Routledge.

Thomas, R., Morrison, T., Saunders, S., Pfaff, M., Gifford, W., Boulanger, J., Hammond, B., & Hammond, C. (2020). Situating our selves: using mixed media to convey experiences of psychosocial cancer research. *Arts & Health: An International Journal for Research, Policy and Practice, 12*(2), 116–138. https://doi.org/10.1080/17533015.2018.1494453

16

Art as a way of improving participatory action research: an experience with youngsters with an intellectual disability and their families

Carlota García Román, Linda Ducca Cisneros, David González Casas, and Andrés Arias Astray

This chapter describes the use of different artistic expression strategies in a participatory action research process. The protagonists of this project are young people with intellectual disabilities and their families in the context of a socio-occupational training programme at the university.

The main objective of the research is to explore themes around the overprotection–autonomy continuum from the participants' perspectives. A set of artistic techniques from different disciplines (visual art, performing art, and music) were used as a means to discuss and define the terms and their implications. Critically, this was in a participatory manner. At the beginning, the young people and their parents worked separately and independently following the same research steps and performing similar activities. The process and the methodology created opportunities to bridge the gap and increase mutual understanding that would not be possible through the daily interactions of normal life.

Concrete examples are presented that highlight the benefits and difficulties of introducing activities not commonly found in a university environment. The analysis also includes a critical reflection about the possible use of art techniques in participatory action research projects with people with intellectual disabilities.

Introduction

Throughout history, people with intellectual disabilities have faced many socio-cultural barriers that have placed them in a position of inferiority in relation to the rest of society (Corrigan, 2014). The most common life plan for human beings is to achieve an adequate standard of living, have good relationships, have the freedom to make decisions based on personal convictions, and participate actively in family and community life. These aims are often unattainable dreams for people with disabilities (Abbott & McConkey, 2006). Despite the unquestionable progress in the conceptualisation and social recognition of the group (Roth et al., 2019), its social position and role clearly limit the possibility of living a full life. This fact is connected to access to education. People with disabilities experience great difficulties in finding supportive and inclusive spaces to eliminate the stigmas that promote exclusion (Madaus, 2011).

This research is part of the Univerdi programme, a University of Jaén certificate,[1] managed and run by university lecturers. Its main objective is the social and professional training of people with intellectual disabilities.

The staff responsible for the programme asked the authors, who are specialised in group work research and intervention, to intervene in what appeared to be a case of 'bullying' among the participants. Our group always reframes the requests it receives, trying to depathologise them and look for determinants and ecological solutions and actions in the participants' community. Therefore, the first idea was to create positive support network and respect dynamics to alleviate the circumstances described. In the first session carried out with the participants, it was detected that the problem could not be described as bullying. The origin of the problems and the barriers to group development were serious overprotection by the families. The participants were demanding more freedom due to the empowerment process within the course and the families were having trouble responding to those needs.

Overprotection based on the stigma associated with disability is based on disjunctive normality and abnormality (Davis, 1995; Foucault, 2012), in which people with disabilities are treated in ways close to infantilisation in the different settings in which they interact with the family. This limits their possibilities for social and personal development. Some cross-cutting questions were raised in relation to the programme that were crucial for the welfare of the participants. What is the purpose of training people with disabilities in social and employment matters if basic aspects such as autonomy are not covered? Can we understand a full life without promoting the right to participation, self-esteem, and a sense of belonging?

The authors reflected upon these questions first, since people with intellectual disabilities are often excluded from most decisions about their personal and social lives and, of course, also from research that addresses aspects of their lives (Johnson & Walmsley, 2003). They questioned their position of power with respect to the protagonists in the study and their scientific practice, since one of the main premises of the study was to work *with* people with disabilities and not *for* them. As a result of this, an emancipatory and participatory model was adopted (Cocks & Cockram, 1995; Truman et al., 2000), in which the main objective of the research is to fight against inequalities with the people who are suffering as a result of them.

Participatory action research

As noted above, the researchers were dealing with an incapacitating social system that oppresses and subdues groups that do not conform to the prevailing cultural canons. In this context, it was important to talk about the liminal groups and spaces in which people with intellectual disabilities are 'integrated', objectified, and constructed as abnormal according to the expropriation of citizenship and dignity (Almeida, 2009). Considering this, there is a need to create mechanisms that eliminate, or at least try to counteract, these social synergies that promote and maintain the exclusion of the group. The aim is to facilitate the participation of people with intellectual disabilities in the issues that affect their lives. In this context, participatory action research (PAR) is a tool to give greater power to the group of people with an intellectual disability, that is, to build knowledge from the bottom up (Fals Borda, 1993) and to make minority wisdom scientific.

The debate on the need to emancipate people with disabilities and to ensure that they have control over their own lives should not be dominated by the exogenous view of external observers in the name of 'science', nor even by the view of specialists working in the field of disability. Emancipation must involve participatory action by people with disabilities, participatory action that identifies their demands, desires and knowledge, and that can generate spaces for horizontal empowerment (Colmenares, 2011). In addition, we need to rethink disability itself. Although it is true that nowadays social constructionist positions are mainstream in the specialised literature on disability, it is also true that the attitudes of citizens and the daily practices of protection and educational organisations continue to support outdated and iatrogenic models of care for people with intellectual disabilities. In this sense, micro- discriminations and unnecessary over-protection are especially relevant due to their capacity to cause dependence where independence should be promoted (Gallagher, 2002). Constant criticism and reflection about one's own intervention and research practices are necessary. The principles of reflexivity in its design, along with symmetry in its development, become fundamental. Reflexivity is understood as constant vigilance about the consequences of plans, projects and their development. Symmetry refers to the distribution of decision-making power in actions and interventions. PAR fully incorporates these two principles.

Participatory action research with people with disabilities from the social work perspective

Social rights, understood as static entities that guarantee a dignified life, are not enough to ensure autonomy and personal development (Aguilar, 2013). Social workers must help ensure that resources are available to meet the needs of people with intellectual disabilities, while promoting processes that maximise their personal autonomy. People with learning difficulties must be the main protagonists and the professionals must be by their side, not to teach them, but to accompany them and as a source of support (McConnell et al., 1997; Adams, 2008).

The global definition of social work (IFSW, 2014) and all the ethical codes and practice standards of the profession (for example, IASWG, 2015) refer to the importance of the principle of autonomy. When working with any group, and therefore also when working with people with intellectual disabilities, the principle of symmetry and adopting a horizontal position in relation to the exercising of power is imperative if professionals are to be loyal to the principles of social work. The needs and values of the subjects must be prioritised, in addition to promoting their social and personal emancipation (de Lorenzo, 2007).

Based on the above, we understand that PAR with people with intellectual disabilities from the social work perspective must pivot around the capacity of the subjects to make their own decisions. Therefore, practices should be aimed at:

• understanding the real needs of the people with disabilities themselves;
• recognising the right to their own development based on their values and beliefs;
• providing resources to promote a process of self-reflection and personal growth and responsibility.

The use of art in research with people with disabilities

The use of art in participatory action research methods is considered relatively new in the social sciences and social work, but is becoming more popular and widely implemented (Wiles et al., 2011; Sinding et al., 2014). However, art has been used as a working technique in groups and research since the beginning of the profession (Coad 2007; Kelly & Doherty 2017). Mannay (2017) states that leaving aside the 'novelty' of the methodology, it is important to reflect upon its implementation and consider the vast existing knowledge about the use of art for research purposes.

The use of art in this participatory action research is mainly for epistemological reasons. If the objective is to define concepts affecting the participants' lives from their point of view, we need to find different participation methods, considering their capabilities and limitations.

The environment can play a very important role in allowing and encouraging participation by people with disabilities (Abbott & McConkey, 2006; Seale et al., 2015) and that is the main criteria for designing and selecting the research methodology in this project.

In this epistemological study the authors, together with the participants, asked many questions while searching for the most suitable methodology. Will activities provide the environment that allows for participation? Can we use the same techniques for parents and their children? Is it possible to allow people with different cognitive abilities to express themselves? Will these techniques allow the participants to express their opinions? Will the activities be useful for discussion? Will the researchers be able to obtain valid information?

After a thorough exploration of participatory methodologies (Knowles & Cole, 2008; Leavy, 2017), the researchers decided that art could be a good solution. In the first place, art allows different manners of expression that help to overcome the classical object–subject of study division, so important in PAR (Fals Borda, 1999). By facilitating spaces and opportunities for active participation, the authors try to dissipate this tension. Art is not considered in its aesthetic sphere but in the communicative one, enabling real participation.

The position, role and status of researchers and participants (parents and young people) are clear: they work in partnership, defined as 'collaborations in which people with and without disabilities who work together have both shared and distinct purposes which are given similar attention and make contributions that are equally valued' (Bigby et al., 2014, p. 8). Art helps to identify these different stakeholder purposes, because it is not limited to closed answers and instead opens an array of issues that might not have been considered beforehand (Coad 2007; Leavy, 2017).

The use of art techniques is generally associated with emancipatory research (Finley, 2008; Osei-Kofi, 2013; Swartz & Nyamnjoh, 2018), allowing interactions between the members, researchers, and the environment, full participation and engagement in the activities presented, and the promotion of critical thinking. The more the participants can reflect upon their position in society, the more they will be aware of the difficulties they face and the possible ways to overcome them.

In addition to the personal improvements that can be achieved, this research should also aim for social transformation and changes in the social environment. The use of art in research leads to the general wellbeing of the participants, enhancing self-esteem, and promoting empowerment processes. Art permits not only the display of knowledge about their experiences but also the collective acquisition of knowledge about the structures that prevent them from exercising their rights (Kapitan et al., 2011).

Art techniques were chosen on the basis of the evidence. They have already been implemented satisfactorily in other projects on which the researchers based the design of this research (Coad, 2007; Jurkowski, 2008; Foster-Fishman et al., 2010; Kapitan et al., 2011; Hamel, 2015; Calsamiglia Madurga & Cubells Serra, 2016; Erel et al., 2017).

The research techniques were designed to be inclusive, but not to specifically address people with intellectual disabilities. The idea is that knowledge construction is achieved through relationships and interactions between the participants. So, the main objective of these techniques is to build trust and a positive relationship between university researchers and the participants and to create opportunities for the participants to display their competences. (Mannay, 2017). Most of the activities used to promote reflection and knowledge were not specifically designed for people with a disability, but instead were based on different research projects with different participants and contexts.

Art is generally used in combination with other research strategies, such as discussion or groupwork activities (Coad 2007; Leavy, 2017). In our case, this resulted in methodological innovation and the inclusion of all participants. By introducing different forms of communication, such as discussion, writing, drawing, theatre, photography, and songs, all the participants could give their opinion somehow.

The study

The Univerdi programme lasted for two academic years and took place at the University of Jaén. The protagonists in this study were the 20 students on the Univerdi programme and their parents. The students were aged between 17 and 29 and had been diagnosed with a minor or moderate intellectual disability.

Design

The theoretical basis discussed above formed the foundation for the first meeting of the university researchers, held to design the proposal. From the beginning, it was important to focus on the engagement of the participants, especially the students. They were the ones who had to decide the research objectives and topics. This was decided for underlying epistemological reasons, and because they are the experts on their own lives. This is irrespective of whether it was aimed at promoting empowerment or critical thinking.

A kick-off meeting was then held with the participants in which their experiences and concerns were identified. At that stage a self-diagnosis was initiated in which the participants presented their ideas, values, and needs in relation to the overprotection–autonomy continuum.

As researchers, it was essential to carry out a self-reflective process highlighting any limitations, issues, and obligations to be acquired. This self-reflection was the driving force behind establishing the dynamics and objectives to be achieved during the intervention process (Zuñíga et al, 2016).

Finally, the resources needed for the project and the involvement of the participants were evaluated to ensure the viability of the PAR. In the first phase the sessions were recorded[2] and during both phases a diary was kept by the authors.

As a result, the following main objectives were agreed:

- to explore the overprotection–care continuum;
- to define the most important issues related to the overprotection–care continuum;
- to promote autonomy and self-determination;
- to generate reflective processes and critical thinking among the participants and their families;
- to encourage actions that promote change in the community.

Research never takes place in an ideal environment. It has to be adapted to the circumstances and available resources, sacrificing spontaneity and autonomy in the research process. In other words, the authors would have liked a less managed way of allowing and promoting participation.

It is important to consider that the timing of the research was constrained by the academic calendar of the university and the course itself. Thus, to achieve the objectives, some decisions had to be made.

- *The structure of the sessions.* It was important for the sessions to have a clear structure. At the beginning, there was a group summary of the previous session. After that, a technique was introduced in small groups or individually. Next, the groups shared their findings with the whole group and a conclusion was reached.
- *Groupwork.* As the participants had different cognitive abilities, the formation of the groups could not be left to the participants in the activities. Groups had to be formed so that they would work properly. On many occasions, when groups did not function as expected, the whole group reflected on that fact. The authors triggered the discussion through some group activities.
- *The group of participants and the group of their families worked separately and simultaneously in different rooms doing the same activities.* Findings from the two groups were then shared. The researchers were the conveyors of the ideas. It was a great responsibility to try to convey the needs and opinions accurately and this was done with the permission of the participants. All needs and opinions resulting from the group discussion were conveyed, rather than conveying those of the individuals. We could see that in each session, the young people gained a better understanding of the behaviour of their parents. At the same time, parents were surprised about some topics that worried their children, such as sexuality and the freedom to make their own choices.

Table 16.1: Summary of the research process

Stage	Duration	Objectives	Techniques
1.1 Pre-research	Three sessions Jan–Feb 2018	Define topics that need to be explored further	– Group discussions – Art-related (theatre, painting, music)
1.2 Exploratory Research	Five sessions Feb–June 2018	Explore the topics in a collaborative manner (students and parents)	– Group discussions – Art-related (theatre, painting, music)
1.3 Evaluation	One session June 2008	Evaluate the research process and decide whether to continue	Workshop with families. Collage
2.1 Research	Nine sessions Oct–Nov 2018	Investigate a chosen topic further	– Photovoice – Research techniques (interviews, information search)
2.2 Communication of partial results	Two sessions Dec 2018	Communicate the results	– Presentations to parents and Univerdi teachers
2.3 Evaluation	One session Dec 2008	Evaluate the whole process	– An interactive game

Figure 16.1: Drawings made by participants during the pre-research stage indicating their future life plans

Figure 16.2: Drawings made by participants during the pre-research stage indicating their future life plans

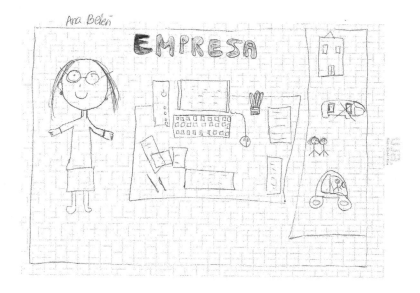

- *Power dynamics*. This topic is a crucial element for reflection and consideration in any PAR, especially with vulnerable groups as participants (Bradbury-Jones et al., 2018)). There were some issues to be decided and questions to be considered: What degree of power could be given to the students within the time constraints while ensuring that results were obtained? To what extent were the students prepared to give their opinions without much guidance? Was it possible to balance the findings to place more importance on the students' perspectives rather than just those of the parents? Thus, even though the authors were aware of the managed nature of the activities proposed, they tried to give opportunities for free expression to the students and value their views.

The research process

In the following section, a short summary of the sessions will be given to describe the research process in detail, with special attention being paid to the artistic techniques. This is summarised in Table 16.1.

Stage 1

The first stage comprised nine 90-minute sessions involving two separate but simultaneous groups (parents and students). Through art techniques that allowed discussion, the main issues and needs were defined and explored separately by the young people and their families.

Pre-research

During this sub-stage, the main objective was to establish the basis for future research: present and start to explore the main issues, promote groupwork, and propose the research.

Session 1. In ten years… Objective: to explore the idea of quality of life. During the first session (it was the second time that the authors had met the students and the first parent meeting) a group presentation was of key importance.

Drawing was the technique chosen to explore the quality of life concept. Students had to draw how they imagined their lives would be in ten years. Parents had to draw how they imagined their children´s lives would be in ten years. This allowed all participants to give an opinion independently of their ability for oral expression.

Some other topics were also explored, such as the right to have a life plan, the real possibilities the environment had to offer and the barriers they might face.

Session 2: Building bridges. Objective: to promote groupwork and mutual support. This activity (Cohen, 2015) consists in the creation of a group sculpture and a reflection about the degree of participation and teamwork. Material (scissors, paper clips, cello tape, and cardboard) was assigned to each person in the group and they were told to build a bridge for a toy car. The activity provided a concrete way to discuss an abstract topic: how people collaborate in a group and the different contributions each person can make according to their abilities.

Session 3: Research project proposal and group discussion. This session was for students only. They watched a Prezi presentation on the steps for researching the overprotection–autonomy continuum: creating groups; defining the concept; discussion, creation of material and debate; and sharing results. They gave their opinions in groups and talked about the definition of overprotection. They all shared examples of overprotection and autonomy.

Exploratory Research Sessions 4 and 5. During these sessions, the objective was to explore and define the topics that the students highlighted as the most important for research. A bottom–up approach was followed. They had to give real examples of overprotection they had experienced. Using a theatre technique of sharing stories (Boal, 2002), they all had the opportunity to express themselves. Each person had to think about a real situation, then share it with a partner and between them they had to choose the one that was the most common situation. Then they had to join up with another pair and, in the larger group, decide which was the most common situation. Through this procedure, it was ensured that the stories were relevant to most of the participants. They represented a few in a short theatre improvisation that led to discussion.

In the end, five topics were selected by the students:

• freedom to spend more time with friends – independence;
• trust between participants and their parents;
• independent living;
• sexuality;
• freedom of choice (for example, clothes).

Session 6 (students only). In this session, the main objective was to promote critical thinking and reflection about the social conditioning of their development. A very short documentary was shown to promote discussion (Fundacion Prevent, 2014). Watching documentaries can trigger discussion and it is very good material for research (Mannay, 2017).

In this activity, students had to think about an alternative ending for the documentary and note this down in the groups. The results were shared, discussed, and linked to the previously chosen topics.

Session 7: problem solving and discussion (part 1). This session took place in two different groups (parents and students separately). Each group had to choose a topic from session 5 and portray a situation, trying to offer a solution. The main results were written down by the authors.

Session 8: problem solving and discussion (part 2). In this joint session the two groups interacted. The main objective was for each of the two groups, parents and students, to understand the needs and concerns of the other group. Because of the power reasons mentioned above, and to allow freedom of expression, the authors made sure that the students were not in the same group as their own parents.

The activity from session 7 was repeated but students and parents had to choose a problem and reach a joint solution. They had to present the results in a creative manner of their choice: writing a story, roleplay, collage, singing a song, and so on.

Evaluation Session 9. In the PAR process it is essential that participants are involved in the evaluation (Alberich Nistal, 2008). Parents and students were separated for the evaluation, but the results were shared with the whole group.

The evaluation was anonymous and consisted in creating a collage of words and concepts related to: concepts learned, feelings about the research process, lessons learned that were put into practice, possible improvements to the research, and whether they would like the research to continue in the following school year.

Stage 2: more in-depth research

Several changes were introduced at this stage in response to the evaluation process. This phase was only led by the students since they determined that they should be the ones to conduct research. Moreover, the intention was for the sessions to not be so well structured since autonomy was promoted and encouraged.

The topics explored in the first phase were identified and the Photovoice technique was chosen as the research tool (Jurkowski, 2008). Photovoice is a methodology that uses photography as a tool to express the problems or needs that minorities face each day in order to promote critical thinking and social change (Lopez et al., 2005).

During the first eight sessions, the students were divided into groups. Each group had to choose a topic and conduct research using photography and related information. They could also use other techniques to report the results in the last two sessions.

To improve group dynamics, each session consisted in an activity to promote broad participation and allow time to work on the research project. Artistic activities were used in combination with discussions and information searches. The group work activities have been omitted from this section to place more emphasis on the research process. However, they were crucial in running the groupwork.

Session 1 and 2: planning. These first two sessions were used to repeat and recap the research topics, create the groups, and set the specific research timings and features. There was a summary of the previous findings and the new features of the research were discussed. In groups, they had to organise themselves and choose an aspect they wanted to explore more.

These two sessions were a great challenge because of the students' conceptualisation limitations. It was important and a challenge for the authors to play the process facilitator role, trying to guide the research process without interfering with the student's objectives.

Session 3. The objective of this session was to narrow down the topic they wanted to research and to define the techniques they wanted to use.

Two questions were asked in order to guide the activity:

- Why did you choose the topic?
- What difficulties and opportunities might you find?

They had to create a poster with magazine clippings and coloured paper. The poster acted as a concrete object to look at, so that they could remember the topic and work on it.

Session 4. After a theatre group activity to promote cooperation, the Photovoice technique was introduced. They had to think about what pictures they would take, take pictures during the week, and present them in the following session. They asked other students questions about their ideas.

Sessions 5–9. Students worked in groups during these sessions, presenting pictures and looking for information. Finally, most groups decided to present the findings in a formal manner, through a PowerPoint presentation. Despite the authors promoting a more creative and easier way to show the results of their work, the students insisted that it was a university activity and that was the way they wanted to give the presentation.

They also insisted on looking for information online and talking to their family members and people in the community.

At the beginning, the instructions were vague but the authors realised that the guidance had to be stronger. Thus, questions were formulated for the students to answer in relation to the pictures they had taken and the information they were using to explain them.

- What is the main issue? (research subject)
- What is the current position in relation to the topic? Why do you think the issue is important for society? What solutions are you proposing or imagining?

Session 10: final presentation (part 1). Each group had to make a formal presentation of the Photovoice/research process to the rest of the group. Each person had a chart to fill out to give feedback on the other students' presentations.

Session 11: final presentation (part 2). Students had to present their project to the Univerdi teachers and parents who were given the same chart to provide feedback.

The results of the research were satisfactory and moving for the students, parents and teachers.

Evaluation

A game was created to remind everyone of the most important concepts learned about groupwork and research. In each section they had to solve some problems using the knowledge acquired during the course. They also had to give opinions about the research and training process. At the end, they had to open a present that contained a mirror to demonstrate that they were the most important and valuable aspect of the research process.

Conclusion

People with disabilities experience impediments when giving opinions and reacting to the limitations created by the social structure. PAR appears to be a way to promote inclusive research. However, it is important to be critical about all research methodologies and keep in mind that inclusive research is not the panacea for achieving inclusion and listening to people's voices. Moreover, not everyone with a disability and not all their parents are willing to participate actively and it is important to respect that (Bigby et al., 2014).

The study has some limitations that were mostly related to time constraints, the diversity of the group, and the students' lack of prior PAR experience. On some occasions it was hard to decide to what degree the research process should be providing help and instructions. The authors tried to be aware of the limitations and decided that it was better to increase the amount of guidance rather than do nothing at all. During the daily analysis of the sessions, the aim was to make the best decision to promote empowerment.

As Seale et al. (2015) report, participatory research has its problems, but we need to examine the outcomes and benefits to progress in participatory methods.

Art proved to be an effective research tool and opened up an array of possibilities for expressing and understanding the issues affecting students' lives.

The whole process was very highly rated by students, teachers, and parents. It was also positively valued by the researchers themselves. The research process allowed the students and their families to talk and discuss issues that were taboo, such as sexuality and independent living. Moreover, the reflection allowed participants to be aware of and understand the similarities and differences in the difficulties they face. Overprotection was recognised as a common situation for all of them, which allowed them to see it as a social problem rather than an individual one. They were able to express their opinions freely in formal and informal ways.

During the whole process the authors received reports about improvements in autonomy and responsibility for some students. In the same way, many parents encouraged autonomy on a more frequent basis.

The whole process was a satisfying and life-changing experience, especially for the authors, who changed their initial opinions and prejudices about the possibilities of implementing PAR with people with disabilities.

Notes

[1]   This project is financed by the ONCE Foundation.

[2]   It was impossible to record the second phase due to one of the students refusing to be filmed. Their wish was of course respected and there was no further pressure exerted to convince them.

References

Abbott, S., & McConkey, R. (2006). The barriers to social inclusion as perceived by people with intellectual disabilities. *Journal of Intellectual Disabilities, 10*(3), 275–287.

Adams, R. (2008). *Empowerment, Participation and Social Work*. Macmillan International Higher Education.

Aguilar, M. (2013). *Trabajo Social: Concepto y metodología*. Paraninfo.

Alberich Nistal T. (2008). IAP, mapas y redes sociales: Desde la investigación a la intervención social. *Revista de Trabajo Social Portularia, 8*(1), 131–151.

Almeida, M. E. (2009). *Exclusión y discapacidad: entre la redistribución y el reconocimiento*. Noveduc.

Bigby, C., Frawley, P., & Ramcharan, P. (2014). Conceptualizing inclusive research with people with intellectual disability. *Journal of Applied Research in Intellectual Disabilities, 27*(1), 3–12.

Boal, A. (2002) *Games for Actors and Non-Actors*. 2nd. ed. Routledge.

Bradbury-Jones, C., Isham, L., & Taylor J. (2018) The complexities and contradictions in participatory research with vulnerable children and young people: a qualitative systematic review. *Soc Sci Med, 215*, 80–91.

Calsamiglia Madurga, A., & Cubells Serra, J. (2016). El potencial del teatro foro como herramienta de investigación. *Athenea Digital.Revista De Pensamiento e Investigación Social, 16*(1), 189–209.

Coad, J. (2007). Using art-based techniques in engaging children and young people in health care consultations and/or research. *Journal of Research in Nursing, 12*(5), 487–497.

Cocks, E. & Cockram, J. (1995). The participatory research paradigm and intellectual disability. *Mental Handicap Research, 8*(1), 25–37.

Cohen, C.S (2015). *Bridge Building for Effective Teamwork*. cohen5@adelphi.edu for additional information.

Colmenares, A. (2011). Investigación-acción participativa: una metodología integradora del conocimiento y la acción. *Voces y Silencios: Revista Latinoamericana de Educación, 3*(1), 102–115.

Corrigan, P.W. (2014). *The Stigma of Disease and Disability: Understanding Causes and Overcoming Injustices*. American Psychological Association.

Davis, L.J. (1995). *Enforcing Normalcy: Disability, Deafness, and the Body*. Verso.

de Lorenzo, R. (2007). *Discapacidad, sistemas de protección y Trabajo Social*. Alianza.

Erel, U., Reynolds, T., & Kaptani, E. (2017). Participatory theatre for transformative social research. *Qualitative Research, 17*(3), 302–312.

Fals Borda, O. (1993). La investigación participativa y la intervención social. *Documentación social, 92*, 9–22.

Fals Borda, O. (1999). Orígenes universales y retos actuales de la IAP. *Análisis Político, 38*, 73–90.

Finley, S. (2008). 6 arts-based research. In J. G. Knowles, & A. L. Cole, *Handbook of the arts in qualitative research: Perspectives, methodologies, examples, and issues* (pp. 72-82). Sage, https://www.doi.org/10.4135/9781452226545.n6

Foster-Fishman, P., Law, K., Lichty, L., & Aoun, C. (2010). Youth ReACT for social change: A method for youth participatory action research. *American Journal of Community Psychology, 46*(1–2), 67–83.

Foucault, M. (2012). *El poder, una bestia magnífica. Sobre el poder la prisión y la vida.* Siglo XXI.

Fundación Prevent (2014). *Lo incorrecto. Una nueva mirada hacia la discapacidad.* www.youtube.com/watch?v=SBLiBLb23ZA

Gallagher, E. (2002). Fundamentals of theory and practice revisited: adult clients with mild 'intellectual disability': rethinking our assumptions. *Australian and New Zealand Journal of Family Therapy, 23*(4), 202–210.

Hamel, S. (2015). Translation between academic research, community and practice: a forum theatre process. *Canadian Journal of Action Research, 16*(3), 27–41.

International Association for Social Work with Groups (2015). *Standards for Social Work Practice with Groups.* www.iaswg.org/assets/2015_IASWG_STANDARDS_FOR_SOCIAL_WORK_PRACTICE_WITH_GROUPS.pdf

International Federation of Social Workers (2014). *Global Definition of Social Work.* www.ifsw.org/what-is-social-work/global-definition-of-social-work/

Johnson, K., & Walmsley, J. (2003). *Inclusive Research with People with Learning Disabilities: Past, Present and Futures.* Jessica Kingsley Publishers.

Jurkowski, J. (2008). Photovoice as participatory action research tool for engaging people with intellectual disabilities in research and program development. *Intellectual and Developmental Disabilities, 46*(1), 1–11.

Kapitan, L., Litell, M., & Torres, A. (2011). Creative art therapy in a community's participatory research and social transformation. *Art Therapy, 28*(2), 64–73.

Kelly, B., & Doherty, L. (2017). A historical overview of art and music-based activities in social work with groups: nondeliberative practice and engaging young people's strengths. *Social Work with Groups, 40*(3), 187–201.

Knowles, J.G., & Cole, A.L. (2008). *Handbook of the Arts in Qualitative Research: Perspectives, Methodologies, Examples, and Issues.* Sage.

Leavy, P. (2017). *Research design: Quantitative, Qualitative, Mixed Methods, Arts-Based, and Community-Based Participatory Research Approaches.* Guilford Publications.

Lopez, E., Eng, E., Robinson, N., & Wang, C. (2005) Photovoice as a community-based participatory research method. In *Methods in Community-Based Participatory Research for Health* (pp. 326–348). Jossey-Bass.

Madaus, J. (2011). The history of disability services in higher education. *New Directions for Higher Education, 154*(1), 5–15.

Mannay, D. (2017). *Métodos visuales, narrativos y creativos en investigación cualitativa.* Narcea Ediciones.

McConnell, D., Llewellyn, G., & Bye, R. (1997). Providing services for parents with intellectual disability: Parent needs and service constraints. *Journal of Intellectual & Developmental Disability, 22*(1), 5–17. doi:10.1080/13668259700033251

Osei-Kofi, N. (2013). The emancipatory potential of arts-based research for social justice. *Equity & Excellence in Education, 46*(1), 135–149.

Roth, E.A., Sarawgi, S.N., & Fodstad, J.C. (2019). History of intellectual disabilities. In J.L. Matson (Ed.), *Handbook of Intellectual Disabilities* (pp. 3–16). Springer. doi:10.1007/978-3-030-20843-1

Seale, J., Nind, M., Tilley, L., & Chapman, R. (2015). Negotiating a third space for participatory research with people with learning disabilities: an examination of boundaries and spatial practices. *Innovation: The European Journal of Social Science Research, 28*(4), 483–497.

Sinding, C., Warren, R., & Paton, C. (2014). Social work and the arts: images at the intersection. *Qualitative Social Work, 13*(2), 187–202.

Swartz, S., & Nyamnjoh, A. (2018). Research as freedom: using a continuum of interactive, participatory and emancipatory methods for addressing youth marginality. *HTS Theological Studies, 74*(3), 1–11.

Truman, C., Mertens, D., & Humphries, B. (2000). *Research and Inequality*. University College London.

Wiles, R., Crow, G., & Pain, H. (2011). Innovation in qualitative research methods: a narrative review. *Qualitative Research, 11*(5), 587–604.

Zuñíga, C., Jarquín, M., Martínez-Andrades, E., & Rivas, J. (2016). Investigación acción participativa: Un enfoque de generación del conocimiento. *Revista Iberoamericana de Bioeconomía y Cambio Climático, 2*(1).

Epilogue

Ephrat Huss and Eltje Bos

What did we learn from this book? To summarise, in the first section, arts were used with different populations, including the elderly, cognitively challenged, single mothers, homeless youth, women with addictions, women with refugee status, and the experience of shifting gender identity within these contexts. We saw examples of multiple art methods, both free and directed: These included music recording, directive group art activities, fine art, poetry, photography, and theatre. These were used to capture the phenomenological experience of research participants. This enabled all of us to understand the different groups' experiences, coping strategies, and evaluation of the settings in which they live.

The second part of this book showed how arts-based research can be used with marginalised children not as projective for psychological diagnosis, but as a way for the children to teach researchers how they cope and what they need. This section included examples of using fine art images as a trigger for a narrative, Photovoice, and shared art activities.

Both the above sections used arts to situate phenomenological experience of service users within specific contexts, and to capture how they experience those contexts. This goes beyond understanding the other, to using their self-defined experience as a basis for interventions and for setting policy.

The final third section of the book used arts-based research methods within community contexts. It focused on methods that create a space for communication within the community about the community, and that help reach a unified community narrative. These methods were used as a participatory and evaluative research methodology. The variety of arts methodologies demonstrated in the book included the use of crafts, painting murals, creative place making, photography, mapping techniques, play-back theatre, 'rhizomatic storytelling', and 'ripple effects' arts.

The introduction to this book claimed that arts-based research is relevant to social work research specifically. We hope that the chapters have demonstrated this relevance. Many chapters showed how arts-based research helped to excavate and bring forth to be heard, the silenced experiences of marginalised groups, such as the elderly, refugee children, homeless youth, single mothers, and those with physical and cognitive disabilities. Most chapters also situated personal experience within specific social contexts. For example, undergoing loss and gender transitions within the context of poverty and cultural transition, the experience of children of their care home, and the experience of being a refugee child, and meeting another social context through photography. They focused on ways of coping and meaning-making within a specific cultural construct, such as homelessness, post-disaster, and cultural transition. Many chapters focused on research participants (children, youth, and old people) as active copers and meaning-makers in their own lives. Additional chapters described how arts were used to co-produce knowledge with service users and also with social-practitioners, for example, by showing how arts can help to excavate and communicate practice knowledge of social workers, explore issues of social work identity in a bottom-up way, and enable service users to describe their experience of care services in indirect ways that protect them. Additionally, chapters showed how existing power systems were disrupted by amplifying marginalised voices and by questioning social definitions by using art in a shared reality context, such as single motherhood, refugee status, and others. Finally, some chapters demonstrated how the artworks created during the research, such as murals, music-making, and community theatre, served as ways to disseminate findings back to the community rather than encapsulating it within a research context.

We hope that these multiple and varied examples described in the book have helped to clarify the rational for using arts-based research in social work. We have seen how arts is not an encapsulated entity, rather can be used as a projective tool in different cultural contexts, an expressive process, a way to create special community events and places, a way to intensify or to shift didactic and political messages. This means that in terms of research, we saw how the projects described in the different chapters utilised arts as a method, subject, or end product of the research. These chapters have provided examples for multiple methods, including music, directive arts activities, fine arts, theatre, photography, objects, crafts, and creative place-making to name a few. Some chapters used arts to embody a research process, others focused on an art product as the subject of the research, or on research participants' reactions to the arts product. We hope that through the examples in this book the concept of social arts as having multiple roles and discourses in different cultures and social contexts (and as being different from fine art or psychological art) has been clarified. We think that the inclusion of arts-based research in social work as described in these chapters helps to map out how to connect to the arts and humanities as a 'third pillar' of social work.

In sum, we hope that our theory of the connection between arts-based research and social work research has been convincing. We also hope that it has clarified, demystified, and broken down the general concept into specific doable methods, directives, and examples.

Index

Page numbers in *italic* type refer to figures and photographs; those in **bold** type refer to tables.